THE PRACTICE OF STORY

THE PRACTICE OF STORY
Suffering
and the Possibilities of Redemption

Mindy Makant

BAYLOR UNIVERSITY PRESS

Cover Design and Artwork by Hannah Feldmeier

Library of Congress Cataloging-in-Publication Data

Makant, Mindy, 1969–
The practice of story : suffering and the possibilities of redemption / Mindy Makant.
248 pages cm
Includes bibliographical references and index.
ISBN 978-1-4813-0070-4 (hardback : alk. paper)
1. Redemption—Christianity. 2. Suffering—Religious aspects—Christianity. 3. Storytelling—Religious aspects—Christianity.
I. Title.
BT775.M255 2015
234'.3—dc23
                                        2014048048

Printed in the United States of America on acid-free paper with a minimum of 30 percent post-consumer waste recycled content.

CONTENTS

ACKNOWLEDGMENTS

The seed for this book was planted nearly fifteen years ago in a series of conversations I had with Dan Bell. I thank him for continuing the conversation and goading me into turning my doubts and struggles into a book.

I remain ever grateful to Stanley Hauerwas, Greg Jones, and Sam Wells. They each read and commented on early drafts of this book. All three are incredibly gracious, and each, in his own way, continues to shape me as a theologian and a person. Their voices no doubt echo throughout this project; I only hope these echoes do justice to their wisdom, grace, and friendship.

I would also like to thank Rebekah Eklund, Heather Vacek, and Celia Wolff, each of whom also read and commented on early drafts of various chapters and whose friendship (and provisions of chocolate, coffee, sticker charts, clappy people, and hospitality) sustained me through the initial writing of this book and continues to bring me joy.

I am grateful for my students at Lenoir-Rhyne University. Parts of this book have been the foundation for seminar courses I have taught in which I have learned at least as much from my students as they have learned from me. And I would like to thank my colleagues, especially David Ratke, Jonathan Schwiebert, Michael Deckard, Devon Fisher, and Jennifer Heller. Their collegiality and friendship make me a better professor and scholar; they make coming to work a pleasure.

Of course, I am grateful to the editorial staff at Baylor University Press, especially Carey Newman. Carey has given more energy to the development of this project than I could have ever expected. His care and attention have made this a better book and me a better writer.

And last, but hardly least, I owe my family everything. Their love and support mean more to me than words can express. They made this project manageable as they increasingly took on more laundry, cleaning, shopping, and cooking duties. They did this with grace and with love, always encouraging me to keep writing. My children—Hannah and Jordan—have grown up during the writing of this book. I am proud of the young adults they have become and honored to discover that we have become friends along the way. And I offer my most profound thanks to my husband, Russell, whose steadfast love and companionship has sustained me (often literally, as he has become an incredible cook during my hiatus from the kitchen that book writing demanded) for more than a quarter of a century. I am glad we have chosen to travel this road together; it is to Russell that I dedicate this book.

Introduction

THE SUFFERING SELF

S tories matter. The stories that we tell not only illustrate who we are; they give shape to our very being. That this is so should not be surprising to Christians. After all, Israel not only knew who she was because of a story; she was who she was because of that a story. Israel's very being is storied into existence. Likewise the church is the church, the body of Christ, exactly to the extent that it takes part in God's story, that it embodies the narrative of our Lord. The church is because of the story it remembers, tells, and—in the remembering and telling—embodies. The church, in other words, is storied into being.

Individuals are likewise storied into being. That is, who we are, and the core of our being, exists in and through our stories: those we tell, those that are told to and about us, and—most importantly—those we embody for good or for ill. Of course, not all stories are created equal: war, genocide, political torture,

school shootings, child abuse, rape. Each and every day, stories
of atrocious suffering are being written on the bodies and souls
of those all around us.[1] In some stories suffering is little more
than a temporary complication, a glitch, in the plot of an otherwise harmonious narrative. Some stories, however, are horribly
deformed, morphed into extended nightmares of violence and
fear and torment.

That we are storied into being, that our very selves are constituted by stories, is experienced as a gift to those embedded in
primarily happy stories, in stories with fairy-tale endings. But
that we are storied beings is experienced as an acute threat to
those trapped in nightmarish narratives of profound suffering.
However, at the heart of the Christian faith is the hope that we
are not abandoned by God to fate; we are not stuck with, and
eternally defined by, our stories of suffering. We are, instead,
promised and given stories of redemption. For those whose lives
end abruptly as a result of violence, redemption is now coterminous with salvation. But untold thousands, perhaps even mil-
lions, of people around the world (a disproportionate number
of whom are women and children) suffer from violence daily
with little hope of an end. For the sake of those who exist in
the overlap, the tension between stories of experiential suffering
and promised redemption and an exploration of what this promise means in concrete situations of suffering is crucial.

Redemption is a collision of narratives. These two stories, the
story of suffering and the story of salvation, often—and, perhaps
to some extent, always—appear to wrestle for primacy within
the lives of individuals and communities. The story of redemption occurs at the point where the story of individual suffering
and the story of the body of Christ intersect; it is where suffering
meets salvation. Redemption is the new narrative we are invited
to receive even in the midst of the narrative of nightmarish suffering. And in the reception of our story of redemption, we find

ourselves, and even our stories of profound suffering, being redeemed. The difference between the story of suffering and the story of redemption is not—as depicted in *The Life of Pi*—a question of which story you prefer.[2] It is, instead, a question of which story is ultimately true. Theology rightly understood is, first and foremost, an exercise in learning to tell the truth and to narrate all of life truthfully.[3] Narrating life truthfully requires learning to see that it is the story of redemption—not the story of suffering—that defines God's people both collectively and individually. And this is true no matter how profound the suffering.

To equate redemption with ultimate salvation, and thus to imagine redemption as only possible after death, is to give in to a hopelessness and despair that run contrary to the promise of the gospel—we *are being* saved. That is what redemption means. However, if redemption is not merely something to be longed for in the next life, questions about the relationship between suffering, the memory of suffering, and the experience of redemption loom large. The temptation to imagine that the redemption of suffering, if it is indeed possible at all, necessarily means forgetting the suffering is understandable. However, logically, and more importantly theologically, this is simply incoherent.

Human identity is inherently temporal. We do not merely exist temporally, but we experience our existence in and through the passage of time in such a way that our identity is bound to our temporality. The experience of profound suffering, as a temporal experience, has a formative impact on identity. *All* of our experiences shape our identity; our experiences form the stories that make up our very being. The story of suffering does so in a myriad of complex and troubling ways.[4] The promise of the gospel, however, is that God is actively at work in the world making all things new, even stories of suffering. This necessarily means that suffering *can* be redeemed—that there is no thing, no suffering, no memory of suffering that can ultimately overpower the redemptive work of Jesus. And the redemptive work of Jesus is evident now, if only in occasional glimmers, in even the most profound situations of suffering. Redemption is a temporal reality, experienced *in* time and taking place through time.[5] That it is evident does not, however, necessarily mean it is immediately visible. Redemption is a particular type of revealed knowledge that is best seen by one who has been trained to see.[6] The community of the church has been gifted with particular concrete practices which shape the imagination of disciples such that they can see, and are therefore called to bear witness to, this redemption. Secular therapeutic practices help individuals learn to cope with the memory of suffering; by contrast, ecclesial practices train the imaginations of both communities and individuals to see suffering's redemption.

Remembering the past through the lens of an imagination shaped by the promise of the future actually allows suffering to be re-remembered as Christians learn to view and imagine the past from a different perspective. It is such a way of remembering that turns the memories of the past into a witness for the future. Such an understanding must take seriously the *reality* of memory and yet not envision memory as an ultimately defining power because it takes more seriously the ultimate reality of redemption.[7] It is in the remembering of the past that it is possible to witness the redemptive hand of God—transforming memory from a burden of the past into a gift of grace and the promise of a future over which the painful memories of the past have no power. The remembering of suffering is transformed into remembering redemption.

Remembering redemption rather than forgetting suffering is compelling both theologically and pastorally. Because memory is an integral part of human identity, any account of redemption must include the redemption of the most horrendous of memories. Put quite simply, if memory is not redeemed, the individual is not redeemed. An account of redemption that omits the worst of memories is an account of a god whose power is severely limited. It is only the promise of redemption as an eschatological reality—and the recognition of that redemption now, even if only in fleeting glances—that is able adequately to address the damage of suffering.

Eschatologically all memory is doxology.[8] Penultimately, the memory of profound suffering, like any other memory, can be re-remembered anticipatorily through the lens of the knowledge that the world is moving from resurrection to Parousia. And this knowledge—which always comes as revelation—means that suffering must not be forgotten in order to be redeemed, but that it must be remembered doxologically in light of the promises of God.[9] Remembering the redemption of suffering writes a new story and invites us to participate now in the narrative of the promised new creation as restored and re-storied selves.

1

THE LOGIC OF SUFFERING

Suffering is a surd; logically speaking, suffering simply should not be. And yet it is. Suffering makes no sense and yet demands answers. Suffering seems to undermine all that is good and right and salutary in the universe. Suffering seeks accountability; it yearns for justice. Both the experience and the awareness of suffering raise acute existential and theological questions. Questions of the cause of suffering—of its origins and more significantly of its ends—are quintessential questions that strike at the core of what it means to be human.[1] Suffering cries out for answer to two primal questions. The first is the question of how. If God is good, if God's creation is good, and if humans are created in God's image, suffering simply should not be. And yet it clearly is. The second question, given that suffering *does* indeed happen, is that of *why*. The presumption is that since suffering is, it must be allowed by God. And insofar as it is allowed by God it must serve, or be made to serve, a greater purpose.

Much like a desire for a cure is at the core of medical research, at their root, the questions of the how and why of suffering attempt to render suffering intelligible in the hopes that by understanding its causes, suffering itself may be avoided, even eliminated. So the study of suffering approaches it as if it were a virus or a cancer, attempting to first establish a genealogy of suffering's cause(s).

Attempts to determine causation are hardly a modern—or postmodern—phenomenon. Aristotle offers what is perhaps the most nuanced taxonomy of causation.[2] He suggests four categories of causation: material, efficient, final, and formal. For a piece of lead crystal stemware, the material cause is the lead crystal. The efficient cause is the manufacturer; it is the "mover" or "maker" of the thing itself. The formal cause is an idea; it is the form of the material, in this case that of a piece of stemware. Formal cause is perhaps the most difficult to understand precisely because it is an abstract idea or the origin of an idea. And final cause is the telos of the stemware; it is intended to be used for wine and to add a distinctive touch of elegance to a table setting. The lead crystal stemware shares certain qualities with a lead crystal vase; they have the same material cause and perhaps the same efficient cause. Likewise the lead crystal stemware may share certain qualities with a red Solo cup; both participate to some degree in the same final cause and perhaps to some extent in the same formal cause, the very idea of cupness. No single cause is sufficient; it is the combination of the four causes that explains the ontological particularity of the lead crystal piece of stemware.[3]

Aristotle's schematic of causes can be made to address the existential questions suffering generates by making clear the role of material causes in making suffering possible. A lead crystal piece of stemware, unlike a red Solo cup, is made from a fragile material that is easily broken. Analogously, osteoporosis makes an elderly person's broken hip possible because it leaches calcium from bones, making them deteriorate over time. The suffering in the aftermath of Hurricane Katrina was made possible to some extent by the material realities of a city constructed below sea level as well as by the myriad social and economic realities that trapped those least able to escape in areas of greatest risk. In this sense the material cause—part of the how—of suffering is vulnerability. That is, vulnerability is the material condition that makes suffering possible.[4]

However, vulnerability alone fails to offer a sufficient explanation of the how of suffering. Many pieces of crystal stemware are never broken. Many vulnerable elderly people suffer from osteoporosis and yet never break a hip. Likewise many vulnerable people live in relatively unsafe conditions along low-lying coastal areas, and yet their homes are never destroyed by a hurricane. Material conditions alone cannot explain suffering. The second part of the how question is what Aristotle refers to as the efficient cause; it is *what* happens, in conjunction with the necessary material preconditions, that causes suffering. The waiter drops the stemware. The elderly person with osteoporosis trips and falls. The town built below sea level is subjected to a direct hit by a Category 5 hurricane.

An explanation of how suffering occurs is to be found at the intersection of the material and efficient causes. Neither is sufficient for suffering on its own; both have to be in place for suffering to occur. The distinction between material and efficient cause is heuristic rather than empirical; such a division makes conversation about the causes of suffering easier, but it has no impact on the actual experience of suffering. In the experience of the one suffering, the material and the efficient causes are nearly indistinguishable. And more importantly, the *why* behind the material and efficient causes remains unclear. In a good creation, vulnerability, falls, and hurricanes are hardly logically necessary, and they may even appear to be logically incoherent. The experience of suffering calls into question — or at least *seems* to call into question — the goodness of creation, even the goodness of God. The questions of suffering thus demand a theological response, a response that requires more explicitly theological language, the language of sin and finitude.

Questions of sin and evil often lurk just beneath the surface of the problem of suffering.[5] Though it is not always possible to draw a direct line from sin to suffering, the two exist in relationship to one another. A doctrine of sin, while not answering all questions about suffering, helps to clarify the complex relationship. Unlike the doctrine of the Trinity or of the incarnation, however, the church has never agreed upon a single understanding, or doctrine, of sin.[6] Christians spend a fair amount of time and energy talking about sin, but what is meant *by* sin is not always clear.

In theological conversation, sin is often cast as a noun or as a group of nouns. That is, sin is understood to be a thing, something nameable and therefore classifiable. Or perhaps it is more often thought to be a variety of things — a constellation of habits, personality traits, attitudes, and so forth. There have been, through the ages, a variety of taxonomies of sin. A basic distinction is often drawn between venial and mortal sins.[7] Closely related to this is the listing of the so-called seven deadly sins.[8] This classification of sins is a way of identifying and ordering sins — often in a hierarchical manner — the primary purpose of which is to aid in the avoidance of sin. Such classification finds its roots in the Scriptures. In the Levitical code, sin is broadly classified in terms of appropriate punishment. Some sins are worthy of punishment by death; other, lesser, sins are punishable by other, lesser, means. Following the law insured that punishment for sin is meted out in a way appropriate to the category of sin; it is a juridical response to sin. Similarly, in the Gospels, even Jesus suggests a distinction between sins that are forgivable and those that are not: "Therefore I tell you, people will be forgiven for every sin and blasphemy, but blasphemy against the Spirit will not be forgiven" (Matt 12:31; parallel in Mark 3:29).

In his Letter to the Galatians, Paul identifies a variety of sins as the works of the flesh in contradistinction to the works of the Spirit: "Now the works of the flesh are obvious: fornication, impurity, licentiousness, idolatry, sorcery, enmities, strife, jealousy, anger, quarrels, dissensions, factions, envy, drunkenness, carousing, and things like these. . . . By contrast, the fruit of the Spirit is love, joy, peace, patience, kindness, generosity, faithfulness, gentleness, and self-control" (Gal 5:19-23). In distinguishing between the works of the flesh and the works of the Spirit, Paul does not intend to provide a comprehensive catalogue of sin, but this passage does illustrate that in Paul's thinking, and in the thinking of the early church, sin often functioned as a noun and was conceived of and organized in taxonomical format. It also demonstrates that this categorization of sins served a pedagogical purpose. Something that can be identified, named, and classified can therefore be understood, taught, and learned.[9]

Another common way of conceiving of sin is in terms of human behavior. Sin is often understood to be a human action that is contrary to God's intentions or commandments and therefore stands in contradiction to created human nature. Sin is deviant human behavior. Moreover it is deviant human behavior that is knowingly and willfully chosen. Clearly this is related to sin as noun, particularly as a perversion of the will. In addition to being the *thing*, the perversion, sin is also the evil humans *do*. This understanding of sin can also be found in Scripture. Sin enters the world by way of human action, which is in violation of a directly stated mandate of God, "You shall not eat of the fruit of the tree that is in the middle of the garden, nor shall you touch it, or you shall die" (Gen 3:3). From the moment of creation God lays ground rules for how humans are to relate properly to God, and sin is when humans knowingly, willingly, violate these rules, thereby damaging this relationship with God and bringing upon themselves divine judgment.

Precisely because sin is understood to be a willful act of disobedience it warrants divine punishment.[10] Such an understanding of sin does not necessarily explain *all* suffering as punishment for sin, but it certainly suggests such a causal link. In fact, in the book of Exodus, immediately after the giving of the Ten Commandments to Israel, Moses tells Israel that God gives the law so that Israel will not sin. The law is necessary for the identification of sin primarily so that sin can be avoided and so that, when sin is committed, it can be atoned for. This understanding of sin as willful disobedience to God's command, and therefore a culpable and punishable act, is not restricted to the Old Testament. In Luke's Gospel, chapter 15, the so-called prodigal son speaks of having sinned against heaven and of therefore being unworthy of his status as son (15:21). Not only is the son's sin clearly a violation of a divine command (the command to honor one's mother and father), but there also appears to be, at least in the son's mind, a clear connection between his sin and his subsequent suffering.[11]

Similarly, in John 8 when the woman caught in adultery is brought to Jesus and he declares, "Let anyone among you who is without sin be the first to throw a stone at her" (8:7), it is arguable that Jesus is thinking of sin as a verb, that he is saying that only the one who has never *sinned* stands in a position to judge one who has. However, even if Jesus' use of "the sinless one" in participle form is not necessarily referring to sin as action, even if his intention carries more of an adjectival force, his imperative addressed to the woman, "do not sin again" (8:11), clearly understands sin to be something that one chooses to do or not to do; otherwise the command not to do it makes little sense.[12] Similarly, in John 9 when Jesus is questioned as to why a man was born blind (was it because of the man's sin or that of his parents?), the implication seems clear that in the question of who sinned the disciples have in mind the commission of particular wrong acts that brought about divine punishment in the form of blindness.[13]

Evil is then sometimes understood to be sin magnified — it is one person doing an awful lot of sinful things or a really large group sinning collectively. The suffering of sin as a verb can be the result of sin in one's own life or in the lives of others. A young college student has too much to drink and drives himself home. He is subsequently severely injured in a one-car accident when he runs off the road and crashes headfirst into a tree. Or he destroys the lives of a young family as he runs head-on into their minivan as they are returning home late one evening. Greed can cause suffering in one's own life when it is the root cause for a life spent in pursuit of more material goods at the expense of relationship with one's family. Or greed may result in suffering when those who have plenty pursue more at the expense of those who are in need. The potential of sin to cause suffering appears nearly limitless. And the Doppler effect of sin results in suffering that is rarely self-contained but instead radiates outward.

This individualistic account of sin minimizes the pervasive power of sin and evil and fails to take into account the greater scriptural witness of sin as both uncreated (and therefore unnatural) and invasive power.[14] While clearly it is true that sin is both verb and noun, sin is also a modifier, a descriptor, both of the fallen created world and of all human actions in this world. In other words, sin is not only morally wrong human acts, but it is also the manner in which morally good human acts are done.[15] Sin has an adverbial quality in two aspects: the intention behind the act and the nature of the relationships between subject and object.[16]

Sin is also rightly understood to be a descriptor of the state of the world, the fallen creation, of which humans are merely one small part. Sin, in other words, is an adjective that describes the condition in which all human existence and interactions take place.[17] Sin rightly understood is all of the above. It is, of course, a wrong human act. But sin is also a state, a condition of the fallen world, and a power that continues to bind all of creation. Suffering is an all-too-often consequence and symptom of sin, even when a particular experience of suffering cannot be traced to a particular instance of sin.

In addition to the experienced realities of sin, suffering is also sometimes a result of human frailty and finitude. To speak of finitude as a material cause of suffering is to describe the ways in which human beings suffer due not to any fault of their own or of others—*not* as a consequence of sin—but to the fact that finitude is often experienced (whether rightly or wrongly remains an open question) as an obstruction, as a reminder that they are creatures and not the Creator.[18] Finitude has to do with vulnerability of both body and soul; thus, the suffering of finitude would include the suffering of illness as well as the heartbreak of fragility in human relationships. Extraordinarily difficult and painful things sometimes just happen—a parent develops Alzheimer's disease, a child is born with cystic fibrosis, or important intimate relationships are irrevocably destroyed—and human beings suffer in body, spirit, and mind.

Finitude is also both the material and the efficient cause of the suffering that results from human clumsiness. Sometimes it is literal clumsiness that leads to suffering—a hiking trip leads to suffering after a tumble off a cliff, or a diving accident leads to paralysis after water depth is misjudged. And sometimes the clumsiness is metaphorical—suffering occurs as a result of careless words spoken, as well as of unintentional, nonviolent acts, which cause pain or grief for others. The reality of lived experience as embodied creatures in a fallen world means that, at times, the fragility of human existence will be experienced more poignantly than others. At such times fragility is experienced as a type of suffering.[19]

The boundary between sin and finitude is far from absolute; in fact, this boundary is quite permeable. Finitude cannot be decisively separated from sin as much of what is experienced as finitude is evidence not of natural finitude but of fallen finitude. Though the suffering of sin is the result of created finitude, it is not a part of God's created intention for the world but the result of the fall.[20] And though contemporary discourse frequently includes references to "natural" disasters, the tragic suffering that results from hurricanes, tsunamis, tornadoes, or forest fires cannot rightly be deemed "natural" precisely because it is not a part of the created intention of God.[21] Rather, natural disasters evidence the ways in which the fall has ruptured, and continues to rupture, the relationship between God and *all* of creation as well as amongst creation, not merely between God and humanity. And yet the suffering that results from weather-related disasters cannot be isolated from human sinfulness as it is no coincidence that those who are most vulnerable in society—the poor, the elderly, the young—often suffer most acutely, both in terms of frequency and severity, ostensibly as a result of "natural" occurrences because they lack the resources to protect themselves.

However, identifying the material conditions necessary for suffering and determining the efficient causes of suffering (whether that of fallenness or of finitude) does nothing to explicate (or, more importantly, to ameliorate) suffering. "How" does

not answer "why." Why requires a return to Aristotle's taxonomical vocabulary as why seeks to categorize suffering by both
a formal and a final cause. The discovery of a formal and final
cause would be satisfactory exactly to the extent that the suffering can be seen to serve an ultimate purpose, to participate in
some way in the working out of God's will. If suffering can be
understood to be teleological — to have an end, a purpose, toward
which it tends, an end that has been ordained (or redeemed) by
God — it would be rendered bearable. A teleological account, as
an account predicated upon an understanding of both the sovereignty and the providence of God, of the why of suffering necessarily merges Aristotle's categories of final (toward what end,
for what purpose) and formal (conforming to a particular idea
and therefore to the will of the originator of the idea) cause.

One way of seeking to render suffering teleological is to
understand suffering to be evidence of special election, a theological rendering of "Only the good die young." The suffering of
special election is any suffering "for doing good" (1 Pet 3:17).
The story of the suffering of special election is overwhelmingly
found in accounts of the church's martyrs, beginning with the
stoning of Stephen in Acts 7.[22] Suffering of this nature is understood to be an expected part of faithful discipleship and may
be considered a badge of honor.[23] To the extent that suffering
is earned through a sacrifice of self for the sake of the gospel of
Jesus Christ, this pain-as-privilege is often spoken of as being
redemptive. The church has a clear tradition that speaks of suffering as redemptive, a tradition with the distinct potential to
be deeply problematic on a theological level.[24] Recognizing that
it is *not* the suffering but Jesus who is redemptive is theologically crucial. Martyrdom has a rather complex history within
the Christian tradition.[25] Martyrdom, rightly understood, does
not *seek* suffering for suffering's sake. Rather, martyrs accept,
even embrace, suffering rather than reject God. As such, their

suffering is the embracing of the positive good, which is God. Were it possible to both embrace the positive good of God *and* avoid suffering the violence of martyrdom, this would, of course, be preferable.

Rather than seeing suffering itself as a sign of election, an alternative way of seeking meaning in suffering is to envision the *survival* of suffering as a sign of special election, a notion that is often reduced to nothing more than good fortune or luck. A focus on the survival of suffering can often seek to minimize or even deny the severity of suffering by suggesting that precisely because the suffering could have been worse it must not have been that bad.[26] However, the recognition that things could have been worse may also be a legitimate recognition of the sheer horror of what could have happened, of the (more) severe trauma that was narrowly escaped—the diving accident that leaves a young man paralyzed, but still alive, or the swimmer attacked by a shark or an alligator who loses *only* an arm or a leg—and is an honest response of thanksgiving. And, at other times, a focus on the surviving of suffering may be an earnest appreciation, even a sense of awe, at the inner resources of those who have suffered. Understanding the survival of suffering as a sign of God's grace, a form of special election, demonstrates a commitment to make something meaningful out of an otherwise meaningless experience.

The sense of good fortune often blurs together with the notion of special election such that suffering is experienced as vocational—both in the sense of being called to suffer (as the martyrs) and in the sense of suffering making possible a special vocation that would otherwise remain elusive (the image of the wounded healer). In his Letter to the Philippians, Paul outlines the suffering of his imprisonment, suffering that he counts as a privilege (1:29) because it is for the sake of Christ. But he also proclaims that it is his suffering that allowed his proclamation of the gospel. The good fortune of his suffering, in other words, is that through it the word of God is spread in a way it otherwise would not have been.

Another common way to understand suffering is to see it as character building. Suffering as character building is not unrelated to understanding suffering as fortune, the key difference being that of intent. If suffering is seen as a matter of good fortune, the development of character is, at best, incidental to the suffering and often in spite of it. A teleological notion of suffering as character building implies that the improvement in character is precisely the point of the suffering. Suffering may be perceived to have been orchestrated by God for the express purpose of building up an individual or a community, and the suffering may, then, be experienced as a form both of purgation and of testing. This is the suffering that St. Paul describes as both productive of hope and evidence of the activity of the Holy Spirit (Rom 5:1-5).

Suffering that is character building is presumed to have a pedagogical intent. God either allows or orchestrates suffering in order to teach a particular, necessary, albeit perhaps painful, lesson. This lesson can be positive (dependence, trust, or faith), or it can be purgative, weeding out a negative trait (greed, gluttony, or lust), but the point is the same: the suffering is instructive; it is for the good of the one who suffers. In telling the Corinthian church of his sufferings in Asia, Paul suggests that God allowed (or designed) his sufferings—sufferings that were severe enough that Paul experienced them as a death sentence—"so that we would rely not on ourselves but on God who raises the dead" (2 Cor 1:9).

A final impulse toward rendering suffering teleological is to see it as a matter of just deserts. This is the suffering that is understood to result from the sufferer's own sinful actions; in a sense this suffering is self-imposed, contingent upon the actions of the sufferer, even if suffering is not the intended outcome. And though suffering may or may not theologically be understood as divine retribution, suffering is often considered under the broader theological category of justice. And as such, suffering is sometimes understood to be a pedagogical form of punitive discipline.[27]

Any attempt to develop a taxonomy of suffering for the sake of understanding its cause and to render it meaningful is a form of theodicy.[28] The project of theodicy is doomed to fail. The problem with any theodical response to suffering, with any attempt to rationalize suffering through categorizing its causes, is that, though each response has some scriptural warrant, in trying to make sense of suffering these responses often fail to attend to the fuller message of Scripture.[29] Suffering's great horror is that no sense can be made of it. Suffering is utterly inexplicable. Though a material and efficient cause may be identifiable, and though a final cause may be discernible (that is, though some purpose, even a positive one, may be found for—or imposed upon—the suffering), this neither lessens nor explains the suffering; it merely describes the circumstances under which the indescribable occurred. But description of context is not explanation. To say that a particular individual violently assaults another because of political or social pressure, mental illness, distorted notions of power, or even demonic possession does not rightly locate suffering in a larger narrative that makes sense of the resultant suffering itself. A theologically tenable formal cause of suffering cannot be found. Suffering does not conform to any precept of God. It is not a divine idea. And, in the end, in the face of suffering, attempts at explanation are necessarily reduced to the deeply problematic binary of either blaming God or mounting an argument to exculpate God.[30]

Profound Suffering

Profound suffering is suffering in extremis. Whereas less severe suffering may be mollified by any one of the explanations considered above, experiences of profound suffering are experiences of suffering that cannot be attributed to any action on the part of the one suffering—neither in the positive sense of evoking suffering due to one's faithfulness nor in the negative sense of bringing about punishment for sin. And profound suffering is experience of suffering, often unspeakably horrific suffering, that can be attributed neither merely to finitude nor to the inevitable peccadillos of ordinary fallenness. Profound suffering is the suffering of oppression and violence, the suffering of hatred and abuse. These situations can be neither explained nor justified as pedagogical, character forming, or redemptive. And to regard them as a necessary dimension of finitude, or to attribute them to the inscrutable will of God, is, at best, a distortion and, at worst, a perversion of the gospel. Though related to the suffering of fallenness, these situations of suffering exceed the rational depth any account of sin can possibly offer. Profound suffering refuses mollification. Profound suffering is so intense, so total, that the sufferer cannot be pacified with any theodicy because the sufferer has experienced suffering as complete and total abandonment by God.

Profound suffering affects every dimension of the life of the one who has suffered: physical, social, and personal. Profound suffering destructively permeates every aspect of an individual's identity. The suffering in only one arena of life can be made bearable by wholeness in the others. Physical or psychological suffering can be made tolerable by the support of a loving community. This suggests that pain is, to some extent, culturally and socially constituted. Thus, some physical pain can be given a personal and social meaning that ameliorates suffering—for instance, the pain of childbirth or preparing for extreme athletic events. Though empirically painful, these experiences are also normatively mingled with anticipation and joy, whereas the pain of profound suffering delivers only horror and helplessness.

And even social suffering can be endurable for one who is well in body and soul. That social suffering can be rendered tolerable is evidenced by those who have been ostracized for various reasons by society, or by those who have chosen to live reclusive lives, and yet have done so sound in body and mind. But for one who suffers physical and psychological distress in the absence of community, the suffering becomes overwhelmingly acute — profound. In profound suffering no dimension of one's life or being remains impervious to suffering's effects.

The totality of profound suffering is not, however, solely defined by its inclusion of all dimensions of human experience. Profound suffering is also characterized by a purposeful perversion of power. Profound suffering is the result of the deliberate, perhaps even systematic, exploitation of vulnerability by one in a position of greater power and privilege.[31] Power is also physical, social, and personal. And in situations of profound suffering, all three dimensions of power are used as a weapon against the vulnerable.[32] Profound suffering is thus experienced as overwhelmingly total, an assault against the body, mind, and soul. Profound suffering affects every dimension of one's identity. Profound suffering creates a sense of utter helplessness to ameliorate the suffering. And this powerlessness makes profound suffering complete and absolute. Precisely because of its totality, profound suffering can be said not to form identity but rather to de-form it.

One way to make the totality of profound suffering clear is to distinguish between immediate suffering, which might aptly be called *injury*, and the *damage* of suffering, which perdures in the heart and soul sometimes long after the initial injury to the body has healed. The key to differentiating between injury and suffering is context. An *injury* is the harm done to the body of a human person without consideration of the manner in which the harm was done. An injury is, in a sense, merely a pathological concern. A broken arm is a broken arm and needs only to be set properly.

Suffering, however, requires a narrative; it takes into account the damage done by the circumstances in which the arm is broken.[33] An arm that is broken as a result of participating in a favorite sport is quite a different thing than an arm that is broken in an attempt to protect a child from the flying debris of a tornado. And an arm that is broken in a car accident is quite different altogether from an arm broken in the midst of a violent assault. Though the injury remains essentially the same and requires the same medical treatment, the concomitant suffering will vary drastically, from essentially no lasting damage to the extreme damage associated with traumatic injury. It is the narrative in which suffering is embedded that defines the event of suffering itself.

A way to illustrate this distinction further is in terms of the remedy for the suffering.[34] The nature of an injury—whether physical, psychological, or social—is such that it is often something that may be cured; when the injury is remedied the injured person is restored to a previous healthy state. A broken arm once it has been set will, in time, show little evidence of having ever been broken. No residual damage remains. The broken bone will, assuming it is set correctly and in a timely fashion, be as good as new; it will be, functionally speaking, as if the injury never happened. Suffering, on the other hand, may well leave a wound that defies cure. The injuries resulting from a weather-related disaster, car accident, or violent assault will ordinarily merely require the healing of medical treatment. Whereas an injury allows for a cure in which a previous state can be restored, healing cannot simply restore a previous state because of the extensive nature, the total devastation, of suffering. Suffering changes the being, the very core of the identity, of the sufferer. Because of the all-encompassing nature of the woundedness of profound suffering, suffering cannot be undone. The previous, unsuffered state of being never can be again.

Due in large part to an increasing social awareness of post-traumatic stress disorder (PTSD) over the past decade, discussions of trauma have become more common not merely in the therapeutic realm but in popular literature and theological conversation as well.[35] "Trauma," as used in the field of psychiatry, has a specific meaning and is not necessarily coterminous with suffering. Trauma is defined by the *Diagnostic and Statistical Manual of Mental Disorders IV (DSM)* as "experiencing or witnessing an event that involved actual or threatened death or serious physical injury to oneself or others and to which the traumatized person reacted with intense fear, horror, or helplessness."[36] Trauma, in other words, is determined by an individual's emotive response to an event rather than by the event itself.

Prior to 1998, trauma was defined by the American Psychiatric Association as "an overwhelming event that was *outside the range of usual human experience*."[37] In other words, it was the abnormal nature of the event itself that largely determined whether or not something could be considered trauma. The current language has been changed primarily in recognition that much of what has been considered trauma (and has required the ongoing psychiatric care determinative of trauma) is empirically within the range of ordinary human experience for a statistically significant portion of the population.[38] However, in speaking of profound suffering, the definition "outside the range of usual human experience" is both heuristically helpful and theologically significant because, regardless of the statistical normalcy of the experience of traumatic suffering, to speak of the suffering of violence and trauma as normal is to fail to recognize its alien theological and ontological nature and is a denial of the intended goodness of God's creation.[39]

Examples of trauma per the *DSM* definition include, but are not limited to, war, torture, physical assault, sexual assault, child abuse, and kidnapping. A theological notion of suffering cannot be limited by a technical understanding of trauma; however, the psychiatric understanding of trauma and the theological category of profound suffering overlap in many ways. Profound suffering, as a theological rather than purely psychiatric event, is defined as suffering that is so utterly overwhelming and total as to damage one's identity and call into question the very possibility of redemption. Profound suffering, in other words, raises the very acute question of whether or not one has been abandoned by God. A theological discussion of profound suffering honors the insights of psychiatry—particularly in regard to the damage of trauma to identity—while recognizing that profound suffering creates an epistemological crisis in terms of ontology and soteriology, a crisis psychiatry is ill-equipped to address. A theological understanding of the profound suffering of trauma suggests the following definition:

> [I]ntense and enduring pain of a physical, psychic, or social nature, resulting from the intentional violent actions of another human being(s), the memory of which is disorienting or disintegrating of personal identity, destructive of social bonds, and crippling of the individual's capacity to imagine a future unbounded by the past.[40]

Though all three elements (physical, psychic, and social) must be present for suffering to be profound, extreme suffering in any one aspect will necessarily lead to suffering in the others such that what may initially be a situation of lesser suffering can, in time, become profound. Theologically nothing hinges on trying to draw a fence around what is or is not profound suffering, and obsessive concern with determining what qualifies suffering as severe enough to be considered profound too easily leads to a contest of comparative suffering—something that is counterproductive on every level imaginable. Though it seems foolish to suggest that gradations of suffering do not exist (some suffering *is* qualitatively more pernicious than other suffering), a perceived hierarchy of suffering does nothing to help one learn to see God's redemptive activity in the midst of suffering and can instead become quite a distraction.

The key question is less one of determining what is and is not suffering, and more of recognizing the damage done by suffering and its impact on the experience of redemption in this lifetime.

The exclusive focus on the intentional harm of physical violence is in no way intended to diminish the experiential suffering of less overt forms of violence. It is, rather, to suggest that the suffering of acute physical pain is inherently incapacitating in a way that emotional pain may or may not be, as well as to suggest that where physical violence exists, suffering is definitionally physical, psychic and social.[41] It is possible for suffering to be psychic or social without being physical, but physical suffering, particularly when it is willfully inflicted by another, necessarily will be both psychic and social.[42] And, though the categories of sexual and physical violence cannot merely be collapsed, not much is at stake in attempting to disentangle sexual and physical violence. Whereas physical violence may or may not involve overtones of sexual violence, sexual violence is always inherently a form of physical violence, regardless of the severity of physical injury sustained. Sexual violence is an exploitation of the vulnerability of one person by another person in a position of greater power—whether that power is exclusively physical or not.

Profound suffering does not occur in a vacuum. Situations of acute, profound suffering are often the foreground of situations of insidious chronic suffering. Profound suffering cannot be extracted from the concrete social and political situations that give rise to it. The routine use of rape as a weapon of war is possible because of the political and cultural environments in which misogyny is perceived to be normative, in which women continue to be viewed as inherently subordinate to men, and in which sexual assault results in condemnation of the victim rather than of the perpetrator. Child abuse and domestic violence continue to abound only to the extent that the wider social and cultural world in which families are located tolerate violence against women and children. Political torture proliferates in a political and social world in which fear of the other becomes so pervasive that the perceived need for the protection of self and nation easily becomes justification for a violence that knows no bounds.

Situations of profound suffering are often surrounded by a shroud of shame and secrecy.[43] Stigmatizing the victimization of any particular act of violence increases the depth of suffering of those so victimized. In addition to a climate of secrecy, any environment in which the insidious violence of racism, sexism, poverty, drug abuse, and/or alcohol abuse is rampant easily becomes a crucible for profound suffering.[44] An acute facet of the hopelessness of suffering is that the environment that created the conditions of suffering is, itself, an inescapable part of one's identity, reinforcing the totality of profound suffering. Precisely because of the totality of suffering in every dimension of one's life, the suffering manifests itself in ways that damage every dimension of human identity: past, present, and future.

Because the most intractable situations of suffering (those that are so total, so complete, as to seem beyond hope) are the ones that most challenge the possibility of redemption, it is crucial to focus theological attention on the most horrendous situations of prolonged and severe physical violence — situations of child abuse, domestic violence, and state-sponsored torture—any given incidence of which may be the acute foreground of a background of chronic suffering of varying degrees of intensity. This is not to deny the potentially devastating effects of a single occurrence of physical violence. And, of course, many similarities exist between the damage done by the suffering of recurrent, long-term violence and by single attacks of violence. The difference is primarily one of degree: what happens once—as profoundly horrific and traumatic as it is, for instance, in a single instance of rape—may be a regular occurrence for those in situations of ongoing violence.

Suffering has its own internal logic—a logic that, while reflecting contemporary theological and cultural presumptions, and therefore to some extent externally conditioned, is not solely determined by these presuppositions, but takes on a life of its own. The logic of suffering is pernicious, and the power of this logic of suffering is a de-formative power; it is a power that is always parasitic on the good. The logic of suffering tacitly assumes that the past defines the future—that history, including biography, is and ought to be determinative of present and future reality. Moreover, the logic of suffering suggests that the sufferer is rightly defined by the suffering, that a moral calculus exists in suffering (an element of proportionality to suffering), and that the suffering one experiences is, in fact, one's due. This type of fallacious logic frequently entails a category error. That is, profound suffering is accepted under the guise of redemptive or pedagogical suffering. Or it is accepted as a necessary, albeit unfortunate, aspect of God's inscrutable will. Thus, redemption is presumed to be ruled out by the very logic of suffering itself.

The logic of suffering binds and destroys. The logic of suffering leads to despair and to death. The Christian story of God's redemptive and creative love working in the world both refutes and subverts suffering's specious logic. The theological problem with profound suffering is not with the pain that it causes, though the pain may be immeasurable and needs to be addressed both pastorally and medically. The theological problem with profound suffering is not even the many and various ways in which suffering may cause the one who suffers to question or to doubt the goodness, even the presence, of God, though this is, of course, a serious pastoral concern. The theological problem with profound suffering is found in the very logic of suffering itself, in the parasitic nature of suffering, the ways suffering damages the soul, the way suffering diminishes those created in the image of God and deforms the imagination—both of those who suffer and of those helpless to stop the suffering—such that blindness and paralysis often result from suffering. The primary theological problem with suffering is that suffering develops, sustains, and nurtures an inability to see the redemptive hand of God active in the world and consequently renders those who suffer unable to respond to God's promises in faith.

The message of the gospel is *not* that the innocent suffering of human violence makes sense—after all, nothing about the crucifixion of the Lord of heaven and earth is sensible. Rather the message of the gospel, of the incarnation, is that God refuses to abandon those who suffer in and to their suffering. Profound suffering cannot be explained. No answer—no explanation—exists that can make sense of it, can make it "OK." Nor will the de-forming effects of profound suffering simply go away of their own accord. And, though good can come from secular therapeutic practices, profound suffering cannot be cured. Because of the insidious nature of profound suffering, suffering, once undergone, has a way of constituting the identity. Profound suffering can never be unsuffered. No magic cure exists to "fix" one who has suffered.

All suffering — even the most profound suffering — can, how-ever, be redeemed.[45] God's response to the suffering inflicted by human cruelty is not to deny the profundity of its effects, nor is it to make sense of suffering, to infuse it with meaning. Rather, God's response to suffering is resurrection. God's response to suffering is redemption; it is new life.

2

THE REALITY OF REDEMPTION

To say that the world is not as it ought to be is, perhaps, a tautology.[1] The reality of suffering is evidence of a world gone awry, a world that has veered so far off its intended course as, at times, to seem helplessly lost. Suffering is not God's intention for creation. Suffering has *never* been God's intention for creation. Suffering is, simply put, not the way it is supposed to be. It is as if all of creation has been cast in the wrong play, with the wrong script. The script God would have us enact is a narrative of peace and justice and love, not a script of violence and sin and suffering. God's plans are "for your welfare and not for harm, to give you a future with hope" (Jer 29:11).[2] Redemption is the word for this future with hope.[3] Redemption is God's creative intention for all of creation.[4] Redemption is the re-narration — the *new* narrative — of a world whose story has been derailed but has more importantly been set back "on track." Redemption is both the new story, the story God always intended for the world to embody, and the embodied experience of that story.

Redemption is not, however, a return to a prelapsarian past. Rather, redemption is the new thing of which Isaiah speaks.[5] Redemption is *how* God is at work in the world. Redemption is dependent not upon human ability to imagine (or will) it to be so and not upon a chink in the armor of suffering (as if God needs to find suffering's Achilles' heel) but upon the character and nature and power of God. Redemption depends upon the hope that God is faithful, that the same God who delivered Israel from slavery in Egypt and who raised Jesus from the dead is indeed bringing new life out of suffering.[6] As an intention and act of God, redemption is not dependent upon human experience or knowledge or sight; redemption is happening whether we see it or not.[7] That redemption can be witnessed and experienced is pure grace, but the deeper reality of redemption is not dependent upon experiential knowledge. Redemption cannot be reduced to a possibility, to chance, to something some (limited number of) people may be lucky enough to experience. Nor can redemption be reduced to a private, individual (and therefore contingent) experience (past, present, *or* future), but redemption is realized, actualized, in the particular, concrete event of Jesus Christ.[8] Redemption is an actual ongoing (not static!) reality. Redemption cannot rightly be understood to be a stagnant or passive state of being, something that we might hope to receive (or achieve) someday. Redemption cannot be merely a future hope reserved either for the chosen few or for the few who chose rightly. Redemption is a cosmic, new narrative, a new story in and through which God is remaking all of creation.

Suffering, however, seems to call the veracity of such a story into question; suffering poses acute existential and theological questions about the possibility of redemption.[9] Profound suffering is often experienced as so total, so overwhelmingly destructive of selfhood, as to defy the possibility of redemption. Suffering's narrative is experienced as too powerful to be overcome. Suffering is experienced as irredeemable. However, the question of whether or not profound suffering can be redeemed is misguided (theologically, not existentially) insofar as it rests on the theological presupposition that suffering is prior to any redemptive activity of God and suggests the possibility that God is limited by the depths of human sin and evil. Such a question assumes that redemption is nothing more than God's response to suffering and calls into question God's ability to offer an adequate response. But, redemption is more than merely a response to a question or a solution to a problem. Redemption is not a divine form of moral calculus devised as an afterthought to counter the effects of the fall. Redemption is *the* theological reality of God's intention for creation, a reality that suffering interrupts, often rather abruptly. Suffering can be experienced as an obstacle to redemption, an obstacle that may well render redemption absolutely inconceivable. But—and this is a critical, theological "but"—suffering does not and cannot negate the reality of redemption.[10] Redemption both precedes suffering in an ontological sense and will also ultimately outlast suffering in a temporal sense. Simply stated, redemption is what God *has done* and *is* doing, not merely a promise of what God will do. Redemption is God's prior commitment to God's creation; it is God's way with creation.

Despite redemption's theological primacy and ultimacy, suffering is often experienced as a disruptive contingency, one with the perceived potential power to obscure the reality of redemption. Suffering is not the cause of redemption; it cannot and does not bring about redemption. Redemption is God's intention. Suffering disrupts—but does not thwart—that intention. While suffering *seems* to call this primacy and ultimacy into question to the extent that the existential realities of suffering diminish human identity, the Christian conviction is that redemption has the last word. God triumphs over the powers of death and all who would use death or the threat of death as a power in and through the resurrection.

Redemption is God's way of being with and in the world. Two of the most prevalent metaphors or images of redemption — both in Scripture and in theological conversation — are liberation from a (past) state of bondage and promised reception of the (future) gift of new life.[11] Though both are important and helpful theological metaphors, seeing these two images as a temporal binary is fraught with theological dangers. Chief among these is the temptation to presume that liberation addresses a *past* state of sin and suffering while the gift of new life remains an elusive promise for the *future*. The redemption of profound suffering can be relegated neither to the past nor to the future; redemption occurs in the overlap of time — in the convergence of past, present, and future. The redemption of profound suffering is a present, an actual (but not a static), state of new life liberated from bondage to the past.

No matter how right the theological claim, the fact that redemption is happening is far from self-evident. The gap between the realization of redemption and the experience of suffering is potentially overwhelming. This gap is hardly a modern (or postmodern) phenomenon. A profound tension exists — in the writings of the New Testament, in the history of theological reflection, and in the lived experiences of Christians — between the "now" and the "not yet" of redemption.[12] Having been baptized into the life, death, and resurrection of Jesus Christ, and having received the gift of the Holy Spirit, Christians rightly speak of salvation, of redemption, as an event that has already happened.[13] However, Christians continue — as does the rest of creation — to live in a world that is experienced as anything but redeemed.[14] This tension of an inaugurated but not fully realized eschatology is one of proleptic anticipation.[15] The audacious Christian claim is that an event that occurred in the past (the resurrection) and will be completed in the future (the Parousia) governs the present.[16]

That the present is governed by both the past and the promised future acts of God to bring about redemption necessarily means that redemption is happening *now*.[17] God is actively sustaining and redeeming all of creation at this very moment.[18] This reality has (at least) two important theological implications. The first is that creation does not have to wait for some end time for redemption. The present cannot merely be ignored in hopeful expectation of a better future. The second is the logical flip side of the first: creation has not yet been redeemed. Sin and suffering still abound.

This claim results in an experiential tension that neither can, nor ought to, be resolved on this temporal side of Jesus' return. Navigating this tension requires avoiding both the Scylla of escapism and the Charybdis of fatalism. An overly futurist eschatology—one that downplays the reality of Christ's resurrection—is one in which redemption is too easily sentimentalized or perhaps altogether abandoned.[19] On the other hand, an overly realized eschatology—the claim that the event of Christ's resurrection has procured redemption and now must merely be lived into—is one in which no space exists for honest and faithful mourning of the experiences of sin and suffering.[20] The church necessarily lives always in this time between the times, expectantly awaiting the fulfillment of the promise that has already been realized *in* the act of the promising because the one making the promise is God.[21] In the meantime, the time between the times, the redemption of sin and suffering remains promised and initiated, but only realized in part. All theological conversation about redemption must recognize both this tension and the poignancy such tension entails.

The recognition of redemption as an actual state of new life is the heart of a theology of redemption. A theology of redemption trusts that God is, indeed, redeeming all things, making all things new.[22] *And that this redemption is happening now.* Because redemption is *how* God loves the world, nothing — "neither death, nor life, nor angels, nor rulers, nor things present, nor things to come, nor powers, nor height, nor depth, nor anything else in all creation" (Rom 8:38-39), including the most profound situations of suffering — remains beyond God's redemptive reach.[23] It is the entire world — not merely the individual Christian — that God is redeeming. Redemption extends to every aspect of creation. Redemption as a reality, in and through the event of Jesus, necessitates the concomitant, and often overlooked, recognition of the sheer enormity of the scope of redemption.

No element of creation is left untouched, no matter how marred by sin and violence. Insofar as redemption is cosmic in scope, it includes situations of even the most horrendous suffering without being particular to or contingent upon suffering. Because redemption is cosmic, it has very particular implications. Redemption always entails participation in something greater than any particular situation of suffering. Redemption *is* experienced. It is embodied — this is the claim, after all, of the incarnation.[24] In Christ, God assumes humanity in all of its vulnerability to suffering for the sake of its redemption. This embodied redemption is itself embodied in particular communities and in very particular individual situations and lives.

In the eighth chapter of the Letter to the Romans, Paul speaks of the whole creation both being in bondage to sin and decay and longing for redemption.[25] Paul seems to equate the longing for redemption of creation with the longing for redemption experienced individually. Paul's writings reflect the reality that things are amiss in the world—in all of creation, not merely within the moral world of human activity. And further, Paul's writing witnesses to his understanding that the gospel is the announcement of God's intention and of God's action, of setting things right. Though Paul certainly recognizes the poignancy, the fatality, of human sin, he also suggests that the overwhelming damage of the fall is of a cosmic rather than merely individual scale.[26] The scope of the fall is much greater than any account of individual sin can possibly recognize. The tragedy of human existence is not that we sin but that we are enslaved to the powers of the present evil age. That we sin is merely the human symptom of a vast cosmic problem.

Paul speaks of this divine intervention in apocalyptic terms. But to describe what he means by apocalypse, Paul uses the verb *erchomai*, "to come on the scene."[27] In Greek, *erchomai* does not conjure up images of an unveiling of something that has been present but hidden all along, but instead suggests an image of an alien-type invasion.[28] In other words, the apocalypse of Christ is not a sudden revealing of a Jesus who has been present but hiding all along. The apocalypse of Christ is a cataclysmic cosmic invasion of divine power that dramatically alters the state not only of humanity but of the entire cosmos. The apocalypse of Christ changes everything. Nothing, including suffering, remains untouched. Redemption, then, can neither be merely a return to a prelapsarian Edenic state nor be reduced to exclusively individual terms. The apocalypse of Christ means something radically different from anything the world had known or could possibly imagine.[29] Paul shows that this apocalypse is nothing short of God bringing into existence a new creation. The new creation of redemption is *not* instantaneous; new creation is not an instance of spontaneous combustion.[30] Suffering is not redeemed by virtue of a latent but inherent characteristic of suffering, as if suffering itself was inherently seminal to redemption, nor is it as if a light were switched on, automatically dispelling the shroud of sin and suffering. Rather, redemption is something that God *is doing* through what God has done in Christ and as an extension of God's very being. Thus, we are now in the position of watching and waiting for the completion of the invasion begun and revealed in Christ.

The consequences of the cosmic condition of sin reverberate through human communities. Humans are inherently relational creatures. Because human personhood is predicated upon relationship, sin damages the very relationships upon which our being depends. The condition of fallen humanity disorders our relationships such that the manner in which humans interact with one another is inherently deficient. This deficiency in relationality manifests itself both in the direct violence of profound suffering and in the more subtle forms of violence that tragically disorder the human social world: sexism, prejudice, greed, to name but a few. That humans relate to one another violently is not merely a symptom of sin but a manifestation of sin itself.[31]

Theological discourse about individual redemption is often subsumed in conversation about the doctrine of justification as articulated by (or at least attributed to) Martin Luther.[32] Luther understands the human condition to be one of bondage to "sin, death, and the devil." Drawing on Augustine he describes the bondage of the human condition as being *incurvatus in se*, "because of the viciousness of original sin."[33] Insofar as sin is not merely a sinful act but a "propensity toward evil," which results in many sinful acts causing harm and rupturing relations, redemption necessarily entails individual forgiveness of sin.[34]

Redemption cannot be exclusively understood in terms of forgiveness exactly to the extent that suffering cannot be understood exclusively in terms of sin. Even when suffering is the result of sin, it is often *not* the sin of the one who suffers.

Thus redemption of the suffering itself and of the memory and experiences of the one who suffered certainly cannot be a matter of the sufferer being forgiven. Nor can it be understood to be the sufferer offering forgiveness to the one who has sinned.[35] The Gospel of Luke in particular, however, narrates the story of a Jesus who has come to bring redemption primarily to those most marginalized in society.[36] And though forgiveness is a part of this redemption, forgiveness is not all Jesus offers. Rather, Jesus seeks to radically alter the narrative of the marginalized, to bring them new life in a tangible, this-worldly manner.[37]

The claim that redemption is occurring simultaneously at three levels has the potential to mislead as it may appear to imply that there are separate spheres of existence called cosmic, social, and personal.[38] Whereas the theological reality is precisely the opposite, the cosmic, the social, and the individual cannot be separated into discrete spheres. They are distinct modes of existence—the individual cannot merely be subsumed into the social or communal. But they are inseparable, inextricably intertwined with one another and experienced simultaneously. No individual exists apart from community. Similarly, no communities exist apart from the larger creation. The experience of redemption is one of interconnectivity—individual redemption does not exist outside of the community. Likewise, redemption of the cosmos necessarily involves the redemption of very particular individual persons and situations.[39]

The claim that redemption is happening does not, of course, explain *what* redemption is, what it means experientially and existentially. The redemption of disparate individual communities, persons, and situations makes it clear that redemption as an objective reality does not mean that redemption looks the same to all people at all times and in all places. The claim of redemption's objectivity in the event of Jesus does not, and cannot, render it abstract; redemption is not a universal blanket laid

over all of the suffering of the world, covering over their particularities. Instead, the objective reality of redemption means that
particular instances of suffering are always redeemed *in* their
particularity. Thus, though redemption is always participation
in the on-going salvation story of God, what it looks like, how
it is experienced, is unique to the particularities of the individual situations crying out for redemption.[40] Redemption must be
context specific; it must be seen in its particularity because the
situations in need of redemption vary so greatly. The redemption necessary when one has sinned grievously against another
differs drastically from the redemption necessary when one has
been sinned against, and both of these differ radically from situations in which one has suffered the effects of severe storms,
tragic accident, or serious illness. Therefore rather than being
defined, redemption can only rightly be described. Redemption,
like suffering, requires narration.

In considering the redemption of situations of profound suffering (situations where one has suffered at the hands of a violent other), questions of redemption can be particularly acute
because the damage of profound suffering penetrates to the
very core of a person's identity. The injuries to the body are
often much easier to treat and heal than the damage done to the
heart and soul of one who has suffered violence. Redemption
necessarily involves a healing of the soul. Soul healing cannot
simply be equated with psychological well-being but involves
an awareness of God's healing presence with and in one's life.
Redemptive healing is movement toward a state of shalom. It
entails much more than merely "getting over" the suffering of
the past so that one can "move on." The redemption of profound
suffering is the wholeness, the moreness, of shalom, of the recognition of God's presence in one's life. The redemption of the
person shattered by violence—and particularly of the shattered-
ness that perdures long after the wounds have healed, or even

when physical wounds defy healing—can be counterintuitive; the very notion can seem impossible or absurd, even. However, the witness of Scripture is that the redemption of profound suffering is not a mere possibility but instead an ever-occurring reality.

The Sermon on the Mount is arguably intended not as an ethical imperative but instead as primarily descriptive.[41] Jesus, in other words, is saying, "When you see these things—those who mourn being comforted or when you see mercy or peacemaking . . . , then you know you are in the presence of the kingdom of God." And where and when the kingdom of God is at hand, redemption will be also. Analogously, though no definitive checklist for determining where and when a shattered life is redeemed—where new life begins—can be devised, the new life of redemption can be described. Redemption can be reduced neither to a checklist nor to a series of therapeutic stages or steps. Redemption cannot be proven. It can, however, be witnessed to and described.[42]

The Practice of Redemption

That redemption is an ontological reality does not make it self-evident. Redemption is apprehended through description, through learning to see rightly what God has done, is doing, and promises yet to do.[43] Even in the aftermath of profound suffering. Learning to describe, to narrate, redemption in all of its particularity is the necessary prerequisite to learning to see redemption.[44]

Narration is the act of telling a coherent story. Narration cannot simply consist of the stringing together of random, disconnected events, but is instead the arrangement of events in such a way that they tell a story that both has and offers meaning. As such, the ability to tell the story of one's life in a more or less coherent narrative is integral to personal identity.[45] Narration gives meaning to the story of one's life by placing the individual experiences and memories of a life into the context of a larger whole.[46] This placement within creates meaning. Narrative continuity is necessarily a constitutive element of identity whether the identity is individual or communal.

Redemption is itself an identity claim. Redemption offers a re-narration of a life story, even a life story soiled by profound suffering. This re-narration is one in which the story of suffering remains recognizable—the identity of the sufferer is not obliterated—and yet it also overrides the identity claims of the previous story(ies) of suffering. Not only is redemption the story of the Christ event that transforms one state (sin and suffering) into another (salvation), redemption entails the weaving of individual human narratives with the narrative of God's continued activity in the world.[47] Narrating redemption includes the ability—perhaps necessarily in a retrospective fashion—to narrate the suffering of the past while simultaneously locating this narration in the larger story of God's redemptive activity—even if in a way that remains to some extent tentative and anticipatory.

Narratives—whether of suffering or of redemption—are embodied. Human beings do not merely *have* bodies but rather *are* bodies.[48] Incorporation includes an at-homeness with one's body, a state of being comfortable in one's own skin, even a recognition of the created goodness of the body. This embodiment is not limited, however, to the boundaries of one's own skin. Individual narratives are not embodied independently. Individual, communal, and cosmic narratives are inextricably interwoven. An independent human being with an identity unformed by relationship with others is nothing more than a fanciful chimera. Individual identity is always a complex admixture of the unique ways in which any given person interacts with the various social groups of which he or she is a part. Redemptive incorporation, then, involves the incorporation of the individual body into the body of a people whose story is being re-narrated through participation in the story of Jesus. This incorporation into the body of Christ subverts the ruptured community of sin and suffering. The vulnerability of the body is both the formal and the efficient cause of human suffering, and yet through incorporation God makes the body both the material and the final cause of redemption.

Redemption is not merely the embodying of a narrative. It is the embodying of a particular narrative with a particular trajectory and telos. This trajectory can be described in terms of vocation.[49] Vocation is necessarily other-directed. Whereas narration necessarily concerns itself with one's own story, one's own suffering, and is the beginning of the healing of a past of suffering, and whereas incorporation entails the joining of one's own life to that of others in a way that includes reciprocity, though that can, without a sense of vocation, remain inward focused, vocation focuses one on the ways in which one's own past experiences of suffering and one's ability to re-narrate that suffering within the new body in which one has been incorporated offer the opportunity for using the pain and suffering of the past in a positive and constructive—even a redemptive—manner.[50]

Though by no means absolute, each of these dimensions of redemption contains an element of temporality. This temporality, however, is less one of tense and more one of orientation. Narration tends to address (to face, in a sense) the past; incorporation, the present; and vocation, the future.[51] Vocation is a calling; it entails both a trajectory and a telos for one's life. In the same way that narration attempts to make sense of the past, and incorporation anchors the body securely in the present, vocation attempts to find meaning for the future, a meaning that is directly connected to both the narration of the past and the incorporation of the present. Vocation, as a dimension of redemption, is the surprisingly wonderful ways in which God's work in the world can take past elements of one's narrative—elements that may have been forgotten or may have been so horrible as to make one wish they were forgotten—and use these very elements in the creation of a calling, of a way of making something beautiful.[52]

Though these dimensions of redemption are neither necessarily hierarchical nor reducible to consecutive stages that must be followed in order, they are interrelated, and in an important sense, they build upon one another. The dimension of vocation presupposes the dimension of both narration and incorporation. A future trajectory, the ability to find ways to incorporate the past into a future that is life giving, builds upon the redemptive narration of the past and incorporation of the present. And yet because these are not stages or phases to be passed through—but as the ongoing works of God are dynamic—any movement in one dimension has a ripple effect through the other dimensions.

Even in situations of seemingly intractable, profound suffering (and perhaps especially in such situations), *that* redemption is happening does not make redemption self-evident. The ability to recognize redemption requires a certain vision—eyes to see—a vision that can be developed in and through participation in the practices of the church.[53] The church's reliance on particular, embodied practices to narrate the story of salvation suggests that not all language, not all narration, is discursive. The experience of redemption—like the experience of suffering—is often language defying. The church enacts and embodies the language of redemption in and through its practices, simultaneously mediating and providing a new narration of the experience of salvation.[54] The narrative of the church is what it does. The narrative of the church does what it is. And insofar as those who have experienced profound suffering are also brought into the experiential narration of the church, their story, too, becomes transformed by the church's narration. In providing a narration of redemption—even if it remains a predominantly nondiscursive narrative—the practices of the church enable experiences of profound suffering to be re-narrated as experiences of redemption.

That the ability to see redemption is aided by learned imaginative habits suggests an epistemology of redemption. This redemptive knowledge, however, is not a knowledge that procures salvation but instead a transformational knowledge that makes possible the recognition of redemption. The experiential knowledge of redemption is found in the "dialectic of memory and of hope."[55] The narration of redemption neither forgets nor denies the past; instead, it remembers and re-narrates the past—including the suffering of the past—in tension with the promised eschatological hope of the future, well aware of the seemingly intractable tension between the two. This knowledge is inherently apocalyptic; it is revealed, made visible, within the context of the confession of Jesus' lordship within the missional assembly of the church whose identity is transformed—turned upside down—by Jesus.[56]

Redemption, the transformation of a world turned upside down, is the new creation of which St. Paul speaks. The new creation of redemption is neither a return to an (imagined) prelapsarian state in which sin and suffering do not exist nor the destruction of all that has been tainted by sin and suffering. Moreover, the promised new creation is not a renewal of, or an improvement upon, the present creation. If it were, this would suggest an inert utopian potential within the present creation merely awaiting an impersonal spark. Rather, new creation is possible only in and through the transcendent power of God made manifest in the person of Christ Jesus. This transformed new creation is solely dependent upon the power of God's imaginative act of redemption. This necessarily refuses to brook the suggestion that any particular ecclesial practice, or constellation of practices, guarantees redemption. This is not an instrumentalization of ecclesial practices—the practices are not a means to an end (the redemption of suffering) but an inherent part of the end of worship.[57] That they make visible God's healing and redeeming presence in the world is a gift of grace that cannot be fabricated but only received and made known.[58] Rather, this is to suggest that God works in and through the practices of the church,[59] shaping the imagination of the body of Christ in such a way that glimpses of the redemption that God is always already about may become visible.[60] In the face of situations of profound suffering, ecclesial practices—as a constellation of practices—are both proclamatory and performative.[61] That is, they first of all proclaim the truth of the mystery of God's redemptive activity in the world—that suffering does not, in the end, provide the definitive narration. And, in so doing, in ways that remain always a mystery, the gift of ecclesial practices is that they make manifest the very redemption to which they continue to bear witness.

3

NARRATION
The Remembering Self

Washington, Adams, Jefferson, Madison, Monroe . . . "We hold these truths to be self-evident . . ." Hydrogen, Helium, Lithium, Beryllium, Boron, Carbon . . . "Please Excuse My Dear Aunt Sally." HOMES: Huron, Ontario, Michigan, Erie, and Superior. "Four score and seven years ago . . ." Mercury, Venus, Earth, Mars, Jupiter, Saturn, Uranus, Neptune, (Pluto). "Every Good Boy Does Fine." Kingdom, Phylum, Class, Order, Family, Genus, Species.

Memory is often thought of in terms of simple recall—the ability to remember discrete bits of information. Those who are able to recall telephone numbers, multiplication facts, and the answers to all manner of trivia questions in an immediate and ostensibly automatic manner are credited with having a "good" memory. This understanding of memory envisions the brain as a set of storage bins, each of which contains unrelated, distinct bits (or bytes) of information. A *good* memory, then, is presumed to be the ability to identify and open the right container at the right time so that the contents, which remain preserved and untouched—and therefore unchanged—while in storage, can be accessed as needed.[1]

Memory is also often thought of as the ability to call to mind experiences of the past (Do you remember the time we went hiking and saw that momma bear and her cubs?) or as the ability to perform some task—the ability to remember how to ride a bicycle or execute an Eskimo roll even though these tasks may not have been performed in years, or even decades, because the necessary techniques have been properly stored in the memory. And there are also less conscious or cognitive ways of remembering—the way in which certain sounds, shades of color, slants of light, or scents conjure up emotive responses that seem to have little relation to the present, and that point to a memory just beyond the threshold of cognitive recognition.

Identity and Memory

Identity and memory are corelative realities. The self cannot exist independent of memory as memory is a constitutive part of what it means to *be* a self.[2] And, as a corollary to this, memory cannot exist apart from the existential reality of both individual and corporate identity.[3] Thus, conceptualizing how suffering affects individual identity necessitates first considering precisely what is meant by "memory," which is a considerably more complex reality than popular linguistic practice may imply.

In order to distinguish between different modes of memory, neuropsychologists have created taxonomies of memory. Though there are a variety of technical distinctions, generally speaking these taxonomies include the categories of long-term memory, short-term memory, and working memory.[4] Within each of these categories, memory can be further divided. For example, the recall of information involved in the memory of phone numbers or internet account passwords is often referred to as semantic memory. Such memory is essentially unrelated to personal experience as it has to do with the ability to accumulate facts without regard for how the information is accumulated. Episodic memory, on the other hand, is less concerned with raw data but is the ability to remember significant events from explicit personal experiences. Whereas semantic memory is necessary to function as an independent adult in a culture increasingly reliant upon numbers and codes and in which a broad range of disparate knowledge is assumed, episodic memory is necessary for the development of interpersonal relationships as the memory of shared experiences is an important element of human bonding. In other words, both episodic memory and semantic memory are crucial for the development of personal identity: episodic memory provides a sense of selfhood whose being extends in time and space, while the functional identity of one who lacks semantic memory would be significantly diminished.

While retaining the language of semantic and episodic memory, neuropsychologists also speak more broadly (and perhaps more helpfully) of explicit and implicit memories. Explicit memory is, by its very nature, narratival. Such memories include the recall of facts as well as the memory of particular events. Thus, semantic memory and episodic memory are both facets of explicit memory. Implicit memories, on the other hand, are non-narratival and include motor skills (learning to eat with a fork or ride a bike) as well as operant-conditioned (coming to a complete stop at a red light) and emotive (startling in response to sudden noises) responses to stimuli.[5] Implicit memories, though not memories that can be consciously recalled, directly impact behavior in wide-ranging but particular, predictable—and yet often unrecognized—ways. So, whereas explicit memory plays a larger role in conscious identity, implicit memory impacts identity in subtle ways, which generally remain unrecognized.[6] The interplay of explicit and implicit memory, specifically the interplay of explicit episodic memory and the implicit memory of emotion, forms the psychological core of identity.

The suggestion that the self occurs at the intersection of explicit memory of what is most often thought of as recall and the implicit memory of emotion begs the question of why recall alone is an insufficient descriptor for memory. Memory is, of course, the ability to recall facts or events, perhaps especially the events that seem most formative. But memory understood as nothing more than the rote recall of seemingly disconnected facts is not a sufficient understanding of memory precisely because such a notion is an insufficient basis for any paradigm of individual identity—of an identifiable sense of selfhood—in relationship with others.[7] Memory, and its two inseparable component forms (explicit and implicit), is not the accumulation of disjointed facts but instead is what provides the narrative continuity necessary for selfhood to exist.

Recognizing the significance of the narratability of memory is crucial to understanding the relationship between memory and suffering. Narratival memory is the story we are able to tell of ourselves.[8] The unity of narratival memory provides life with a sense of coherence. In short, narrative makes memories make sense by providing a context, embedding them in the midst of something larger than any individual, or individual's, memory. That I vividly remember being a young child watching a rushing veil of cascading water from just inches behind it only makes sense within the narrative of a hiking trip that is set within the larger narrative of the preservation of national forests. Narrative memory makes sense of who we were in the past and therefore of how we became who we are today. Narrative makes the journey from point A to point B—how Cinderella married Prince Charming or how a little shepherd boy became a king—make sense. The self is thus, in a literal sense, "what the past is doing now."[9] And the way in which the story of the self is known and reinforced is memory.

That memory is a primary source of personal identity—that the self is "what the past is doing now"—necessitates recognizing memory as more complex than mere recall. Knowledge of the multiplication tables or the capitals of all fifty states—though not an insignificant factor in the creation of personal identity—cannot provide an adequate account of who one is or how one becomes who one is. Only when such facts can be located in the memory through the narrative of how such information was acquired, do they become a part of narratival memory. Narrative gives shape to the biographical contingencies of a given self. And narrative incorporates seemingly insignificant singular memories into the crucial building blocks of individual identity. Narratival memory is a helpful way to think of memory in relation to identity formation to the extent that, unlike recall of seemingly unrelated and trivial facts, narratival memory locates memories in a coherent story. Stories, no matter how seemingly circuitous or tortuous, lead somewhere.[10] Similarly, narratival memory has a goal, a telos, toward which it tends. Stories of individual and family memories, as well as stories of the collective memory of entire nations and people (for instance, stories of George Washington's fabled inability to tell a lie or of Rosa Parks' refusal to give up her bus seat), form the psyche of those who participate in the sharing. Such stories are constructive of individual identity precisely to the extent that they connect individuals to the larger narratives that constitute corporate life.

The formation of identity is contingent upon memory and upon the ways in which individual narratives interact with the potentially endless combination of formative narratives. Who human beings are is always in large part determined not only by these narratives but by the people whose lives intersect ours within, and tangential to, these narratives, as well as by the narratival memory of these significant others. My story cannot be merely *mine* but is complexly communal. Another way to say this is that there is no self outside of narratively inscribed relationship with others; humans are socially and narratively constituted, and, though there are heuristic distinctions between the social and the narratival, the one cannot be isolated from the other. Individual character, selfhood, is dependent upon our memories of our experiences within these broader narratives, but the very notion of memories—how experiences are perceived and therefore encoded in the memory—are contingent upon any number of factors particular to these narratives. And, of course, individuals are not merely passive recipients of identity formation at the whim of others' narratives but actively involved in the processes of shaping and forming the identities of the others with whom they interact. Similarly, individuals are not merely passive experiencers of memory. A level of reciprocity always exists between selves and memories. Each individual actively responds to, and consequently shapes, memories while being ever shaped by those very memories.

A Theological Account of Memory

Memory expresses itself primarily in the form of narrative, and these narratives are constitutive of human identity.[11] But a narrative is not an ethereal, untethered concept. Rather, a narrative, by definition and on account of its inherent temporality, requires a telos.[12] In order for time to be ordered so that it can be remembered and attended to, it needs a goal toward which it tends.[13] Without this goal the narrative of memory is open ended in such a way as potentially, perhaps even inevitably, to render the story meaningless. A theological account of memory situates the narrative of individual memory within the larger temporal and narratival framework of God's memory. God is both the foundation and the telos of the narrative of memory. Rather than allowing the narrative to be restricted to *my* story of *my* life and *my* suffering, a theological account of memory incorporates the small narratives of particular lives into the grand narrative of God's continued presence in the world. A theological rendering of memory both requires and allows hope for the future.

However, to suggest that memory is largely a matter of narrative does not, de facto, locate memory within the larger framework of God's narrative. Such right location is analogous to the abductive work of the observant sleuth in a mystery novel.[14] The key to the satisfactory conclusion of a mystery novel is the explanation the detective is able to offer at the end of the story that not only solves the crime but makes sense of the many clues and missteps along the way. This explanation provides a second narrative. The primary narrative is the story that is evident to everyone—a murder, a theft, a weapon—but the second narrative is the one that cannot be told until the end, until all the missing parts are accounted for: Colonel Mustard in the billiard room with a candlestick. This story makes all the seemingly disparate facts make sense. This second narrative is not merely an alternative narrative; rather, it is, in the end, the narrative that matters—the ultimately determinative narrative—as it is the one that rightly locates the disjointed elements of the primary narrative.

A theological account of memory is one in which the act of remembering is analogous to the impatient reader of detective fiction who sneaks a peek at the final few pages. The memory of the past can be viewed through the lens of what the storyteller already knows about the rest of the story. The theological account of the past is necessarily selective. The details of the past are attended to in a way that is significantly re-ordered and re-prioritized by an understanding of the more comprehensive (if less immediately apparent) narrative. The import of the narrative is found not in a verbatim re-creation of the primary narrative—removing pristine memories from the storage bin of the past, as if such were possible—but in the production of a second narrative that makes sense of the past in light of the already revealed future. The objective of a theological account of memory is *not* necessarily to make sure that not a single jot or tittle is out of place but to make the story make sense in view of a bigger picture.

This claim necessarily raises the question of truth.[15] In terms of memory, "truth" is often understood to be the purview of the historian; truth is thought to be directly related to a presumed objective historicity, to a commitment to describing events as fully as possible, in chronological order, and in something of a direct correspondence manner such that events that happen only once are told only once, and events of a repeated nature are told in a repeated fashion. A one-to-one correspondence between the event itself and the telling is presumed. And the storyteller attempts neither to compress nor to expand time in the telling. The second narrative, on the other hand, is akin to a literary narrative that arranges the order of the telling of events and highlights particular aspects of the story, compressing and expanding time as needed, in order to emphasize that which is most significant for the point the writer is making, in order to make clear the relationship between events and the story's telos.[16] Such narrative has an element of discernment, of moral judgment—not all events are judged to be of equal narrative import. A narrative is not an attempt at conveying a Sergeant Joe Friday "just the facts, ma'am" story but instead focused on conveying the greater truth behind the individual events that constitute the narrative. The point of a theological account of memory is that what is true is what rightly locates the past within the narrative of God's redemptive activity.[17] The details are not insignificant, but they are not privileged either. The rendering of past events that constitutes the second narrative, that which makes sense of all of the seemingly senseless elements of the past, is also true. The details and the narrative are different dimensions of the *truth* of memory.

Insofar as the detective participates in the story in real time, not merely reflectively, the detective is an integral part of the detective novel in the way that, by virtue of temporality, a historian simply cannot be.[18] Of course this means that historians have the advantage of a future vantage point because they are, by definition, chronologically outside of the events. The Christian account of memory, however, is told from within the story, with a perspective much like that of the detective, and yet also with the knowledge of the end of the story, granting a perspective similar to that of the historian. There is a complex interplay between the memories and the telling of the story such that telling the story is, itself, a part of the story as is the storyteller.[19] Consequently not only does the story itself (the memory) shape the identity of the storyteller; the storyteller shapes the story, *and* the storyteller is shaped by the act of telling the story. Not only does the knowledge of the end of the story affect the telling of the story; the telling of the story impacts the story itself because the telling of the story is an integral part of the story. In this sense a theological account of memory is bound by the knowledge of what God has done, is doing, and promises yet to do while simultaneously remaining open to the continued presence and movement of God within that story.[20]

Suffering and Memory

Profound suffering, as defined in chapter 1, refers to intense and enduring pain of a physical, psychic, or social nature, resulting from the violent actions of another human being(s), the memory of which is disorienting or disintegrating of personal identity, destructive of social bonds, and crippling of the individual's capacity to imagine a future unbounded by the suffering of the past. Profound suffering is perhaps the greatest threat to a coherent narrative of memory because such suffering is generally experienced as an unintelligible disruption to what is, or would be, an otherwise coherent narrative. And this is perhaps most poignantly so in the case of theological memory. The narrative of profound suffering is experienced as antithetical to the narrative of a loving and healing God. Profound suffering calls into question the very possibility of a narrative in which the past and, more to the point, the memory of the past can be experienced and remembered as redeemed.

If suffering itself is particular and largely depends upon perception, the *memory* of suffering is even more so, and any discussion of memory necessarily requires asking questions of reliability. This raises the question of reliability of memory, particularly of memories of perceived intense suffering from times past, perhaps long past. Insofar as memories are generally conceived in predominantly cognitive terms, a matter of rationality, and suffering is largely a matter of emotive response to that event, conventional wisdom would seem to suggest that any increase in emotional content would necessarily result in a correlative decrease in reliability of factual recall. The more terrifying or infuriating an event, the more the experience of that event is presumed to be distorted in and by the memory. It is not that the (presumptively rational) memory itself cannot be trusted but that the (presumptively irrational) emotion cannot be trusted.

However counterintuitive it may be, research in the field of neuroscience consistently suggests that intense emotions actually increase the likelihood that an event will not only be stored in the memory but be stored accurately. Strong emotions—most acutely fear and anger—are stored vividly in the memory because the events that trigger such emotions are intuitively presumed to be relevant for safety and survival in future situations.[21] Because emotions impact the perception of an experience, strong emotions—particularly feelings of intense fear, horror, or helplessness—increase the brain's propensity to store an event in memory, indelibly etching the experience in the psyche.

A second contributing factor to the reliability of the memory of suffering is temporality. The longer the duration of suffering, the more embedded the suffering is in the memory and psyche. The catch-22 of suffering that extends over a long period of time is that events that are commonplace tend to be rendered generic. Though quotidian events over an extended period of time are remembered, they are not remembered in their particularity. Long-term torture victims, for example, will acutely remember being tortured, but they may struggle to separate one incident of torture from another. The routine nature of the suffering greatly increases the likelihood both that the suffering will be remembered and also that the particular instances of suffering will blend together in such a way that distinguishing one day's violence from another becomes nearly impossible. The more commonplace—that is, frequently repeated—an event is, the more the distinct incidents blur together and become conflated into one seemingly interminable memory. Due to the heightened emotional response to a particular situation of suffering, the ability to clearly distinguish one episode from another may be lost when repeatedly faced with situations that evoke an intense emotional response such that for a particular episode to stand out requires an even greater level of intensity or horror.[22]

The damage done by suffering perdures in the memory and the soul often long after the actual event(s) have passed and any physical injuries may have healed. The greatest challenge suffering presents to the memory is one of incorporation into a coherent life story. Suffering, by virtue of its own internal logic, is to some extent unnarratable; it refuses to become a part of a coherent narrative. And it is precisely this inability of the individual to make narrative sense of suffering that poses the greatest challenge to the memory of suffering.

As an experience of utter overwhelming, suffering is inherently unnarratable. To borrow language from St. Paul, the experience of suffering is often too deep for words. Regardless of how accurately the events of suffering can be narrated, the nature—the intensity and the horror—of the suffering itself remains, at best, only partially expressed. The experience of pain, particularly physical pain, has the ability to reduce the sufferer to a pre-linguistic state in which guttural cries and sounds are all one is capable of producing.[23] Physical pain undoes years of cognitive and linguistic development. One of the constitutive elements of suffering is that it renders the sufferer powerless—or exposes the reality of the powerlessness—of the one who suffers.[24] In the midst of profound suffering—as well as in its aftermath—no words can describe the experience of suffering accurately, to invite another into the suffering. Lacking adequate vocabulary, the victim of suffering is at a loss for words.

This loss of language connected to suffering needs to be understood as much as a loss of agency as a loss of vocabulary. If the sufferer could alleviate suffering, she would; to suffer is to be at the mercy of suffering. Because suffering involves a loss of agency, and language production requires agency, profound suffering renders one mute. It is not merely the case that one cannot express suffering because words fail to convey adequately the depth of suffering (regardless of how true this is) but rather that the power of speech is a casualty of lost agency.[25] The production of language requires an agent, an acting, choosing subject, one who can both pick the right words to say *and* give voice to them. Suffering, however, renders the sufferer an optionless object of someone (in the case of violence) or something (in the case of illness or natural disaster) else's agency.[26]

In addition to a loss of language, profound suffering distorts the perception of time.[27] One way chronological experience is distorted by suffering is through recurring, invasive memories, or flashbacks, of past traumatic events. However, suffering distorts time even when the distortion is not evidenced by invasive memories. Profound suffering itself results in a perceived loss of past and future. In the midst of suffering, time is rendered moot.[28] Lost is any sense of time before the suffering began, as well as any hope that a time free of suffering will ever occur in the future. Time is frozen *in* the moment of most intense pain, and in that moment there are no others.[29] Pain demands one's complete and total attention. This is most immediately and notably true of physical pain, but the same can be said of intense psychic pain. In the midst of suffering, time is lost, both in the sense that the time of the suffering itself is lost and in that the sense of time in the midst, and perhaps aftermath, of suffering is destroyed.

Narratives, of course, require both language and sequence. This combination of loss of language and loss of temporality renders suffering unnarratable. Narrative memory is an attempt to make sense of life, to see the chain of seemingly disjointed, discreet events as forming a coherent whole, which confers a sense of identity. Narrative memory assumes a story, and profound suffering refuses to be a story. Because the nature of suffering is such that there is no past, no present, and no future, there is a loss of the temporal ordering necessary for narration. With no sense of a time before suffering, and no sense of a future without suffering, time has no forward motion and seems to spiral back on itself such that the suffering person is constantly reawakening to the suffering of the past as a perpetual state of present.[30]

Despite this unnarratable nature of suffering, the memory of suffering continues to play a formative role in the identity of the sufferer. Memory is a form of epistemology; it is a way of knowing. Moreover, memory—including the memory of past suffering—cannot be un-known. However, rather than being a knowing that is simple recall of facts, the memory of suffering is a knowing that exceeds sheer cognition. Here the distinction between explicit and implicit memory is critical. Explicit memory includes the ability to recall facts as well as the ability to narrate events (e.g., the events of one's life). Explicit memory and its impact are more obvious because they are readily available to the conscious mind. Implicit memory, however, is arguably even more powerful of a formative force precisely because it is largely unrecognized, and yet it continues to modify behavior. Because suffering becomes an integral part of memory, and memory is itself a type of knowing, the knowledge of suffering renders the sufferer acutely aware of the vulnerability of suffering; and this awareness—whether available to the conscious mind or not—impacts interactions both with one's own memory and with others. Insofar as knowledge creates a biochemical change, memory (and therefore the memory of suffering) is encoded in the DNA, almost literally, such that present behavior is always being to some extent modified both by past experience and by the interpretation of that experience.[31]

The behavior modification of implicit memory largely functions through the development of habit. Habit is a primary form of non-narratival memory. An easy way to recognize the mnemonic nature of habit is to think of simple tasks such as making a sandwich or riding a bike. For a young child, learning to do such tasks requires intense concentration. Skills, both physical and cognitive, must be learned and remembered before they can be mastered. Once the skill is mastered it can become habit, a sort of second nature. Spreading peanut butter ceases to require any seeming cognitive engagement. The fact that it no longer needs to be recalled, however, hardly means it is forgotten. Rather than requiring conscious effort, a particular memory becomes an integral part of one's identity. The child is now an independent sandwich maker. The same can be said of all sorts of activities—perhaps this is most evident in the playing of sports or musical instruments. This means some distinction must be made between memory and cognition. In such activities clearly memory is at play, especially early on, but the more proficient one becomes, the less cognition is involved in performing what are really extremely complex, sophisticated tasks.

The same can be said of habits of being and relating; being and relating are dependent upon memory. The memory of suffering is, itself, dependent upon mnemonic habits. Two primary habits of memory result from the implicit memory of suffering, each of which entails the prolongation of the loss of agency experienced in the event of suffering itself and is, in its own way, a perversion or distortion of memory. The first is that of over-identification with suffering, and the second is that of denial or repression of suffering.

Overidentification of suffering can take two forms. One is to identify with suffering such that one comes to see oneself as a sufferer by definition. This is the self-identification with the memory of suffering that results in an embodiment of the shame of one's suffering.[32] The flipside of overidentification with suffering is a glorification of victimization. Suffering becomes a badge of honor worn to garner sympathy or respect. The resulting identification of oneself as vulnerable victim often leads to habitual self-protective behaviors such as avoidance of public places or particular groups of people. The identification of oneself as sufferer—whether as an embodiment of shame or as an object of sympathy—entails, among other things, a passive resignation to what may be perceived as inevitable, as fate.

Similarly the denial or repression of the memory of suffering can take two forms. The first is an explicit denial of the suffering. This denial can be conscious or subconscious. It is a refusal to acknowledge, perhaps even to one's self, that one has suffered greatly, that one has been, in fact, a victim of an intensely painful experience. The second form this can take is to acknowledge the event of suffering while denying its emotive power or impact on one's life. It is a stoic insistence that things were not as bad as they may have seemed, a way of claiming a level of invulnerability against the power of the suffering undergone. Rather than self-protective behaviors, the refusal to acknowledge one's vulnerability to suffering often manifests itself in self-destructive behaviors, including excessive drug and alcohol use as well as repeatedly (perhaps intentionally) placing oneself in patently dangerous situations, greatly increasing the likelihood of repeat trauma.

Whether one responds to the memory of suffering by over-identifying with it or by denying it, and whether this overidentification or denial of the memory of suffering is conscious or unconscious, though perhaps interesting, is not the point. The salient point is that the non-narratival memory of suffering is deeply embedded in the memory and psyche and therefore continues to play a formative role in habits of being and relating, whether recognized or not. This is so even, and perhaps especially, when suffering is found to be unnarratable.

Therapeutic Healing of Memory?

The healing of trauma, and specifically of the memory of profound suffering, is popularly approached from a therapeutic perspective in which the primary objective is for the sufferer to regain an ability to function normally according to criteria based on presuffering function.[33] There is a sense in which healing is considered in terms of undoing the damage of suffering, of returning to a (perhaps fictive and idealized) presuffering state of relative innocence (including at the very least a freedom from the fear of suffering) and happiness. Though the means of getting from a state of intense suffering to a state of being over this suffering may vary (from talk therapy to drug therapy to institutionalization), the process of healing is generally broken down into a very similar set of steps or stages.[34]

The first criterion is that of establishing safety, a physical removal from—and treatment for any subsequent injuries as a result of—the situation responsible for the suffering. However, as a consequence of the residual memory of danger, a memory that may well have the force of habit, the need to establish safety goes well beyond the physical requirement that one is no longer in harm's way. Emotional and spiritual safety is also a vital need. This first phase of healing requires a place and a time of sanctuary, of respite from the suffering in which the habits of hypervigilance instilled by the experience of suffering can be unlearned. Additionally, because of the perceptual nature of suffering, its healing requires not only an objectively safe environment (a violent spouse is no longer living under the same roof and sleeping in the same bed); the perception of safety is as important as the reality of safety. Lacking the perception of safety, healing is rendered partial at best.

The very nature of the memory of profound suffering makes this a much more complex criterion than it may appear to be on the surface. The perception of safety proves to be notoriously elusive. Because suffering is linked to memory as a way of knowing, one who remembers profound suffering cannot be unaware of the reality of suffering. If, by definition, what it means to suffer profoundly is to be helpless to prevent the suffering, then suffering cannot be reduced to a preventable occurrence in which taking certain steps offers a guarantee of future safety. If nothing could be done to prevent or end suffering in the past, then it is impossible *not* to remain acutely aware of vulnerability to the same or similar suffering in the future.[35] And insofar as it is possible to develop a sense of mastery, albeit illusory, over the environment such that there is a sense of security that no such future suffering is possible (or at least that it is highly improbable), questions are raised as to whether or not the previous suffering may have been prevented or halted, resulting in a cycle of guilt and shame.[36]

The second phase or stage of a therapeutic notion of the healing of suffering is coming to terms with memories. This means being able to tell the story of suffering in such a way that gradually, with subsequent retellings, the story loses power over one's life.[37] Because suffering is often experienced as if one were an object of another's agency rather than an agent in one's own right, being able to narrate the suffering—often many times—restores some degree of agency. Ultimately the goal of telling the story is to be able to recall and narrate it in a way that is, though not necessarily detached, clearly free from the fear, anger, or sadness correlative to the suffering.

Underwriting the advocacy of therapeutic retelling of stories of suffering are two common yet seemingly contradictory rationalizations. However, they have the same goal—to tell the story in order to rob the story of its power. The first, most common, rationale for telling the story of suffering is that in telling it one can come to forget it. The theory is that recovery initially requires many tellings of the story but that in time the story will lose its potency and therefore no longer need to be told. Given sufficient time, it may even recede entirely from one's conscious memory.[38]

In addition to forgetting, in cases where suffering is the direct result of another person's action, particularly when the action was of an intentionally malicious nature, the goal of such retellings is not merely to forget but to forget in order to make room for forgiveness. This admonition to forgive and forget is not limited to Christians or even to religious persons more broadly; secular therapists and contemporary cultural wisdom often urges those who have suffered to forgive. Such forgiveness, however, may be a purely functional, therapeutic forgiveness in which the reasons for forgiving, and therefore forgetting, are solely concerned with feeling better.[39] Forgiveness—predicated upon forgetting—becomes an instrumentalized way of progressing through the stages of grief toward recovery, voiding it of its theological and moral content.

The second rationale for telling the story of suffering is exactly the opposite. Rather than telling the story to forget, the sufferer is urged to tell the story in order to remember. Remembering is generally urged on the presumption that there is a relationship between remembering and preventing similar suffering from happening in the future.[40] This is understood to be the evolutionary reason that memories that are embedded in conjunction with strong emotions tend to last. Remembering those things that have hurt or threatened us in the past makes us more prone to avoid similar settings, situations, or people in the future, increasing the statistical odds of longevity. However, this again raises the critique of prevention—by its very nature suffering is something outside of our control and beyond what might have been reasonably anticipated and therefore cannot be avoided in the future by sheer force of careful planning, regardless of the accuracy of memory.

No matter how justifiable the rationale for or against remembering, the question of whether to remember or forget is often moot. While it is undoubtedly possible to increase the chances of remembering something deliberately, the converse of this is simply not true. Forgetting is rarely, if ever, an act of the conscious will. Repressed memories, insofar as they do occur, are not a matter of the will but instead a sign of the incomprehensibility and profundity of suffering.[41] Memory more broadly, and particularly the memory of suffering, is not something over which one necessarily exercises control. The question is less one of whether or not suffering ought to be remembered and rather more of what to do with the memories—those often profoundly disturbing explicit and implicit memories that continue to shape identity, whether recognized or not.

The goal of therapeutic healing is cast in terms of a recovery of control. It is to become (again presumptively) the captain of one's own unconquerable soul and the master of one's own fate—wounded maybe, but unafraid.[42] The theological problem with such a goal is that ultimately to be the captain of one's soul is not freedom and healing but both an illusion and a form of bondage. In the case of extreme suffering, being the captain of one's soul is to be the captive of a wounded and suffering memory. For most therapeutic models, the end goal is acceptance—the acceptance of suffering as fact of the past such that it is possible to move on, confidently facing the future despite the suffering. The telos of such healing is hardly one of redemption. It is an increased level of tolerance for the memory of past suffering.

The difficulties with each of these stages begs the question of whether healing the memory of suffering is actually possible from a therapeutic perspective—or, if those who suffer are left to do the best they can with little expectation of anything like wholeness. Instead of healing it seems that the best one who has suffered profoundly can hope for is a life that moves on as if the suffering had never occurred. The schizophrenic necessity of living as if the very suffering that has left an indelible mark on the soul never occurred does not, however, sound like healing. Therapeutic healing is more a matter of making do than making new.

Narration: The Transformation of Memory

For those who have experienced profound suffering, the beautiful new creation of God's redemption begins with the seemingly irredeemable memories of this suffering being transformed. This transformation requires both lament and repentance. Lament and repentance exist in a tension that both is made possible by and makes possible a right relationship with God—a relationship characterized both by boldness andby obedience.[43] This right relationship with God—particularly in relation to the specific haunting memories of past suffering—is the beginning of the transformation of memory.

Lament

Lament is an expression of pain, grief, anguish. Lament gives voice—even in the inchoate form of prelinguistic moans and cries—to what is experienced as inexpressible suffering. Lament can express either inconsolable weeping (Rachel, for example) or a railing in anger (some of the imprecatory psalms). Or both. While most frequently associated with unjust suffering, lament can also be an expression of deep sorrow for sin committed. Lament can express the sorrow and anguish over the haunting memories of powerlessness in the face of suffering, as well as for complicity in sin and participation in systems of sin. Lament is an appropriate response to the very grammar of sin, which creates the conditions in which suffering flourishes. Lament refuses to accept the often well-intended platitudes that everything will be fine, that suffering will, in the end, prove to be a meaningful part of God's plan for life. It is, in other words, a refusal of theodicy. Lament is a refusal to be reconciled to the suffering of sin, which continues to rupture the creation God declares good and promises to restore. As such, lament is acutely aware of the not-yetness of God's kingdom.

Though by no means the only form of lament, the lament psalms are the paradigmatic form of lament. One of the most notable aspects of these psalms is that they begin with a personal address to God; they are intended to be the beginning of a dialogue with God, and, as such, they anticipate a response from God.[44] Lament, not unlike the cries of a young child, assumes a hearer who has the power, the authority, and—most importantly—the will to *do* something about suffering. Lament is an honest opening of the self to God; it is both a refusal of false comfort and a plea for help.[45] It acknowledges deep disappointment, even despair, with God's apparent tolerance of suffering. Lament is perhaps the most faithful act possible in situations of profound suffering, as to lament is to name with poignant honesty the pain and desolation of suffering before God in expectation that God not only should care about such suffering but should be moved to act.

Because profound suffering often renders the sufferer mute, without a language to give voice to the experience of the inexpressible pain of suffering, those who have suffered often need to be given the tools to cry out in lament. The scriptural tradition of lament provides not only a form but also a vocabulary for expressing what is experienced as inexpressible. As such, the lament tradition offers a vehicle for the expression of pain and even fury to those left voiceless in their suffering. Lament, particularly the lament psalms, can provide words to express the rage and the sorrow and the sheer terror of suffering when suffering has been experienced as an utter overwhelming. Yet, lament is far from formulaic; lament allows those who suffer a way to voice the particularity of their suffering in such a way that draws God into their suffering such that it is no longer borne alone but shared by God.[46]

Lament—though a cry of helplessness, of powerlessness—
in the face of profound suffering is not a passive resignation to
suffering. It is, in fact, an active resistance against the evil of
suffering. The act of lament is an act of proper boldness. Lament
is a calling to account for suffering. It is the recognition of the
dissonance between what is and what ought to be. Lament is
the language—even as a language composed more of cries and
sighs than of words—"of the painful incongruity between lived
experience and the promises of God."[47] When those who have
suffered—and, in and through memory, continue to suffer—
recognize their own accommodation with suffering and cry out
against this state of being, such is a moral judgment upon the
suffering and is a first step in a reclamation of agency, assertion
of selfhood. The boldness of lament is in the presumption that
suffering is not just or right and that one is in the right to com-
plain against it, even to demand its cessation.

Insofar as lament, as addressed to God, is not a wallowing
in self-pity over the experience of powerlessness but an insistence, even a defiant insistence, of self-worth, it is a reclamation
of agency, a refusal of the powerlessness of suffering. Lament
has a destabilizing effect on the status quo of suffering. It does
not undo the suffering of the past or even the memory of the suffering. It does, however, challenge suffering's claim to primacy
and ultimacy. This reclamation of the agency of lament is a step
in the direction of redemption. It is an active stance toward the
grief, the anger, and the fear of suffering; lament is a stance that
makes possible the first steps toward claiming the story of suffering as merely one part of one's own story.[48]

That lament is a personal address to God does not make
lament exclusively, or even primarily, a private act. Liturgical
expressions of lament both instruct a community in the ways of
lament and provide a structure through which lament is shared
by the community so as not to become the burden of a single

individual.[49] The liturgy of the church plays a crucial role in the teaching of lament. Though the anguished cries of lament are a natural, human response to inexplicable suffering, the channeling of lament toward God in expectation of a response is a practice to be taught and a habit to be internalized. Liturgical practices of lament provide a framework for expressing the pain, grief, fear, anger, and even rage that accompany experiences of sin and suffering. The liturgical practice of lament situates the suffering in a communal context, which forms a "safe container for the chaos" of the emotions of suffering.[50] The practice of praying the Psalter, including the psalms of lament and even the imprecatory psalms, is one way the liturgy can form a people capable of lamenting.[51] Learning to pray the Psalter can form a people able to engage God rightly and honestly through the entire range of human emotions, even (and perhaps especially) those emotions experienced as dangerously unholy and unworthy of bringing before God.[52]

In addition to teaching those who suffer how to lament well, the liturgy teaches those who are not suffering to recognize the suffering of the marginalized and of the powerless. Lament is a vehicle for the doing of justice in the world by the refusal to accept injustice as normative.[53] If the voices of those who suffer are successfully silenced—and if such a silencing is unchallenged and uninterrupted—then the witness of the church that the powers of death and all who rely on death or the implicit threat of death for power have been overcome in and through the resurrection of Jesus is rendered suspect. The role of the church in solidarity with the marginalized voices is not only providing space for lament but actively seeking out those who need help finding the voice to lament.[54] Learning to lament boldly with those who suffer, learning to become poor in spirit with those who mourn, can be a means of grace not only for those who suffer but for those in positions of relative power and privilege as well.[55]

Repentance

Lament does not stand alone in the face of profound suffering. The faithful human posture—even in the midst of horrific suffering—before God also includes repentance. This is emphatically *not* a matter of blaming of victims either for complicity in their victimization or for their vulnerability to victimization. It is, instead, a suggestion that repentance is as much a mode of remembering as is lament. Lament remembers in a way that looks at the damage of the past as being at odds with the promises of God, whereas repentance remembers the past by looking forward, reorienting the memory toward God's promises. Lament and repentance are postures *toward*—lament the proper posture toward suffering and sin, and repentance the proper posture toward God. Lament and repentance are mutually interdependent, complementary modes of response to suffering.

It is not the case that lament is exclusively appropriate to suffering and repentance to sin. Rather, both lament and repentance are an appropriate response to both sin and suffering. Lament is, in a sense, the proper boldness before God, the sorrow that demands redress. Repentance is the proper obedience, the realigning of the human will with God's. Both lament and repentance are communal practices to be learned in and through participation in ecclesial communities. The ecclesial practices of lament and repentance do not, themselves, redeem such memories. Rather, lament and repentance are tools by which the Holy Spirit works in and through the church to develop the imagination necessary to see the work of redemption that is always already in progress.

Conventional wisdom considers repentance as primarily, if not exclusively, the appropriate response to complicity in sin—whether through intentional acts of commission or through unwitting participation in larger structures of sin. However, repentance is also an appropriate response to the memory of suffering. Repentance in situations of the suffering of violence is *not* a question of relative guilt or innocence but first and foremost a renunciation of the logic of suffering. In situations of violence, even and perhaps especially when one is victim of violence, repentance means denying the logic of the myth of redemptive violence, refusing to succumb either to victimization or to revenge. It is a refusal to grant suffering primacy in determining identity. Likewise, this renunciation is a refusal to grant the status of ultimacy to the powers of sin and death upon which suffering depends. Repentance is a way of remembering the past in which one is continually reoriented—and consequently by which one reorients the memory of suffering—both by and toward Christ.

To say this is necessarily to say that repentance is NOT primarily sorrow for wrongdoing. Repentance is not merely feeling sad for the commission of sins or for the implicit (or explicit) participation in structures of sin.[56] That is not to suggest that the commission of sin will not cause sorrow, as it certainly both can and should. Nor is it to suggest that in repentance there can be no sorrow, as, again, there both can and should. But repentance, the rethinking of the narrative of one's life in light of Jesus, entails a change—both a turning from and a turning toward—and insofar as sorrow turns, its turn is inward and unproductive.[57] But this does not negate that a part of repentance is the realignment not merely of thought and act but of desire and emotion as well.

Likewise, repentance is NOT penance as it is commonly practiced. Repentance can be reduced neither to contrition over nor to punishment for wrongdoing. In fact, repentance understood merely as punishment for sin runs the risk of actually avoiding repentance.[58] When repentance is seen as a way of "making up" for sins, the logic too easily follows that, once atoned for, sin is over and done with and can be forgotten. Again, there is no cause for change, leading to a cycle of sin and punishment, albeit a self-inflicted punishment. So, though an element of contrition over and acceptance of consequences for past sin may be involved in repentance, the obedience of repentance is not, itself, contrition or remorse, or the act of "making up" for a particular sinful act.

Repentance understood as renunciation and as reorientation focuses the energy of the memory toward God. It may seem counterintuitive, morally misguided even, to speak of repentance in regard to the memory of unjust, unprovoked suffering. However, the call to repentance is not exclusively for the overstepping of bounds, for the commission of acts of violence or injury, but it is also for accommodation to a loss of selfhood—even when this loss is neither consciously nor willfully chosen, in fact even when it is passionately fought against.[59] Repentance for a diminished self is necessary in order to restore the harmony and communion intended by God for all creation with God—there is a direct correlation between the extent to which individuals are diminished and the extent to which all reciprocal relationships are likewise diminished. This diminishment of relationship may, in fact, be a significant part of the lament of suffering, but it is also something for which active repentance, as an active turning toward the light of Christ, is appropriate.

Remembering suffering as an act of repentance requires recognition of one's own role in suffering. And this is the case for both victims and perpetrators.[60] This is not to blame victims for their suffering but to suggest that the experience of suffering—even overwhelming profound suffering—does not, in fact, negate human moral agency. It is the suggestion that in the aftermath of situations of profound suffering there is a needed renunciation of the suffering—a denouncement of all that allows for and perpetuates systems of power and vulnerability that make such suffering possible—including tacit acquiescence to suffering and to the way suffering has been internalized and remembered. It is a recognition that profound suffering is dehumanizing for both perpetrator and victim. To repent of suffering is to remember suffering in the light of the story of Jesus; it is to remember suffering as something that is being redeemed. Such a way of remembering is nothing short of a radical conversion.[61] This conversion frees us from the memories of past suffering *not* by causing us to forget past suffering but by inviting us to re-member the suffering of the past in a more truth-filled light.

Remembering as an Agent

Lament and repentance are both acts that require intentional agents; neither happens passively. Whereas suffering, particularly the suffering of violence, renders subjects as objects, lament and repentance are necessarily deliberate acts of moral subjects. Through the boldness of lament and through the obedience of repentance, the memory of past suffering can be claimed, owned, in such a way as to restore the agency of the sufferer. A theological notion of agency, however, cannot be constrained by the modern desire to separate the individual from the historical contingencies of biography, nor can it ascribe deterministic power to biography. Likewise, agency cannot merely be understood to be coterminous with power (a conjoining that definitionally renders those who suffer as nonagents). Rather than being a prepossessed power or inalienable right, agency is discovered in the ability to own one's past, including both the acts committed and the experiences undergone.[62] Agency, then, is a choice (in fact, it is a moral choice) that can be made *in spite of* situations in which one is powerless to act.

Insofar as the memory of suffering is a memory of having been a passive victim of violence, a truthful remembering of the past made possible by the reclamation of agency found in lament and repentance is transformative, redemptive, because its power lies in the story of suffering having been retold neither to defuse nor diminish its power, but to relocate it in the context of God's story of new life.

This understanding of agency as taking ownership of one's past, in all of its messiness, even in the midst of overwhelming suffering, does not undo the memory of past suffering. Nor does the act of claiming the suffering of the past as one's own condone that past; insofar as the claiming of the past suffering hinges on lament and repentance, a condoning of suffering is precluded. However, if it is correct that the greatest and most damaging power of the memory of suffering is its power and propensity to leave one unable to narrate the past, and that this loss of voice coupled with the memory of suffering as having been a stripping of agency, the reclamation of agency that comes from finding a voice and telling a truthful story—a story that remembers and laments the agony of suffering while repenting and renouncing the logic that makes such suffering seem inevitable, and enables one then to claim one's life as one's own—is a glimmer of the redemption yet to come.

Redemption is the process by which God takes the damaged bits of the past—whether past sin or past suffering—and creates something new and beautiful with, rather than despite, these bits. Such memories are redeemed, neither in being forgotten nor in being "gotten over," but in the weaving of a new, larger narrative that neither denies the horribleness of the past nor grants it ultimacy. This second narrative, a narrative of agential memory, begins to imagine ways in which this memory, even the memory of profound suffering, may fit into a story that is much larger than the experience of suffering itself.

To do this is not to deny the horror of haunting memories, but through practices of lament and repentance it is to begin to imagine ways in which God may use past experiences to shape a more beautiful story. Such a way of remembering, rather than denying the horror of past suffering, recognizes that the memories of suffering are neither ultimate nor defining. The agential memory of the second narrative means that the truthful story told through the practices of lament and repentance do not stop there but offer the promise of a future that is greater than the past could have imagined. Through practices of lament and repentance, memories of past suffering may come to be remembered in such a way that the suffering of the past can indeed be claimed as one's own in a way that is open to God's continued redeeming and transformative work in the present and in the future because it is enabled to envision, to imagine, God's hand redeeming and transforming the past.

4

EMBODIMENT
The Experiencing Self

The word "community" is often used interchangeably with "neighborhood" and connotes a degree of physical proximity. Thus it can mean the people with whom we have daily interactions by virtue of our living arrangements. The term is not, however, limited to geography but also routinely employed to imply a similarity of interests or commitments. For instance, the notion of community is frequently invoked in speaking of the "gay community" or the "African American community." In this case, community suggests not a connection based on daily interaction but a connection of an ontological nature. Appeals to "community" as a cultural nostrum—a panacea for all the perceived losses of modernity—are commonplace. These calls for community, however, increasingly refer to groups of people with some perceived but superficial commonality, whether it be geographical or sociopolitical.

This reduces community to something that—though in some vague sense definitive of identity (not, perhaps, unlike the way a common penchant for chocolate chip cookies might be) has little or nothing to do with relationship and therefore has little impact on the actual formation of the character by which identity is necessarily constituted. Sometimes this call for community is a symptom of the individualism of benevolent humanism that seeks not real engagement with others but the path of least resistance. Such sweeping and varying uses of "community," however, unfortunately render the term void of its intended content—that a community is a group of people united in meaningful *communion* with one another—and consequently fail to recognize the crucial character of community in the formation of identity.

Equally problematic is a competing concomitant cultural understanding of individual identity as the unseen essence hidden deep inside an individual, independent of any community. It is the bifurcated notion that the "real me" is the latent core underneath the trappings of social expectations, roles, and familial and political allegiances, and that the people in my neighborhood (or other social groups) are of little, if any, significance—in fact, are perhaps instead an encumbrance—to my selfhood.

Identity and Community

Extensive sociological research in the field of identity theory suggests, contra this popular image of selfhood, that the self is necessarily a complex reflection of society and of one's social relationships. No bifurcation of private and communal self is possible. Identity theory understands identity to be an ongoing, interactive process made up of three distinct but inextricably related elements: role identity, social identity, and person identity—each of which depends upon the self's external relations.[1] Identity theory, however, not only claims that the social world contributes to the development of selfhood, it denies any understanding of selfhood that is either prior to or independent of the social world. The central claim of identity theory is that the self is, by definition, a reflection of the complex matrix of communities in which an individual participates. No such thing as a "black box" self, separated from the communities by which it is constituted, can possibly exist. At the same time, identity theory also suggests that individuals do not merely reflect social identity but actively participate in the construction of the social groups that, in turn, continually act as formational forces on group members. The autobiographical narrative of an individual does not reflect the discovery of some preexistent but hidden self; rather, it narrates the ongoing creation of a self through the autobiographical contingencies—including, but not limited to, the suffering—particular to the individual *in* community.

Role Identity

Role identity is the first component of identity theory. The principal claim of role identity is that individuals learn who they are, discover their "selves" in relationship to others. And in learning who they are and playing the role(s) assigned to and accepted by them, they become those people. Roles provide meaning and structure for the development of a sense of selfhood. This is most easily seen in childhood, where role playing and imitation are more widely presumed to be normative. The family—and particularly the primary caregiver, usually the mother—is the earliest social group to which a child belongs and in which the child learns to play a particular role. At its core, a role is a set of expectations. Roles are directly connected to one's particular social location, and the learning of a role involves the internalization of the attitudes, thoughts, feelings, and patterns of behavior associated with, and appropriate to, a given role. A child, for example, first learns what it is to be a son or a daughter, a brother or a sister, and a grandson or a granddaughter within the social structure of the immediate family unit.[2]

The child's social world gradually expands in concentric circles, expanding first to his or her wider kinship group, gradually to social groups tangentially connected to the kinship group, and eventually to groups beyond the kinship group and immediate community. Through kinship relations individuals are exposed to the larger communities in which the kinship group exists, and the roles internalized within the family continue to exert tremendous influence on identity as more and more roles are internalized. Pristine individuals do not go out into the wider social world unformed; rather, individuals enter into social communities with identities already both formed and forming through the roles they have learned in their kinship groups. So the child who has already learned, and is continuing to learn, the role of son or daughter—and all of the expectations and patterns of behavior that accompany that role—simultaneously begins to learn the roles of playmate, classmate, teammate, and student, as well as how these roles fit together.

Role identity, however, is not limited to childhood; there is no point in time where the learning and performing of roles are outgrown.[3] Moreover, individual behaviors are neither stagnant nor exclusively externally imposed. Though clearly an element of external coercion occurs in role playing—as in one socially imposed based on gender, race, social class, or the perception of handicap—the individual does not play a role in a strictly scripted way. Instead, the individual performs a particular way based on individual perceptions of the role expectations, as well as on the individual's relative degree of acceptance of the social expectations for the role. The playing of each role is impacted in significant ways by a person's character. While the roles played are indeed meaning-making insofar as they contribute to an individual's identity, the roles also receive meaning from the identity of the individuals who accept them, whether that acceptance is explicit or implicit.

The unique spin each person puts on any role is, in part, understood to be related to the individual counterroles with whom each person interacts. A counterrole is closely related to, and in some sense definitive of, a role. The role of son or daughter makes no sense removed from the role of parent. Similarly, without the existence of the role of child, there is no parent. It is likewise with the roles of teacher and student. The existence of one role both presupposes and makes a space for the existence of the other. Thus, roles are mutually dependent upon one another. This is the case regardless of the moral content—criminals, for example, simultaneously require and create victims; superheroes, supervillains; and enemies, one another.[4] Insofar as roles are reciprocal and dependent upon one another, so are identities. Where there are counterroles, there are counteridentities.[5] No identity exists in isolation; all identities are dependent upon, and depended upon by, counteridentities.

No individual plays a single role. Rather, every individual plays any number of roles—child, spouse, parent, sibling, teacher, pastor, friend—at the same time. Some roles remain constant over the span of many years, even a lifetime (the role of sibling, for example), while some shift or become obsolete over time. Each role has its own set of behavior expectations that interact with every other role and that in this interaction contribute its own element of identity.[6] This dynamism suggests that an individual is not a passive recipient of identity but an active agent. Part of the uniqueness, the individuality, of each person is the characteristic way in which the myriad roles are embedded in one another. An element of personal agency is integral to understanding the ways in which the roles are understood to interact (positively and negatively) with one another. This agency, however, cannot be understood to be absolute. Identity is not something one merely chooses, but it remains contingent upon a number of biographical factors—chief among them, the roles one has learned to play and the social structures that continue to create the expectations for, and assign meaning to, each role.

Social Identity

Social identity is the second component of identity theory. Social identity has two primary elements. The first is the individual's identification as a member of a particular group and with the ways in which certain social group roles—particularly nationalistic, familial, and/or religious commitments—are not merely descriptive in terms of identity formation but prescriptive as well. Both explicit and implicit expectations are attached to every social group, and in exchange for adherence to these expectations there is a transference of identity and status. Social identity is thus integrally connected to role identity, as no role exists in isolation from the social group within which the role exists. As such, social groups are meaning-making. The participation, the in-ness, of belonging to social groups, acts to organize behavior and provide a meaningful narrative for one's life. This meaning-making role of social group participation reduces anxiety levels, providing answers to the questions of what is expected at any given time.

Social identity is also norming. The norming element of social groups is dependent upon an insistence on sameness. Social groups define themselves in large part on what it is that makes the members of the group the same—Americans, Catholics, soccer players, and so on. The norming of social identity is heavily dependent upon prototypes, a norming that identifies the unachievable ideal perceived to be representative of the group. It is significant that prototypes are not real—they are a projection, the imagined ideal of a group, the ideal that no individual member can ever achieve.[7] Despite their ethereal nature, prototypes function as a social barometer, measuring one's in-ness in any given group. The closer one comes to matching the standards of the prototype, the more normative, and more accepted and admired, even the more powerful, one becomes. So, while social identity serves to minimize the existential anxiety over the "Who am I?" question, it simultaneously creates anxiety over one's failure (and perhaps more notably one's perceived failure) to live up to the accepted standards of the group.

The second essential part of group identity is concerned with the ways in which social groups interact with other groups, the ways groups define both who is in and who is out ("This is who we ar; this is what we do"), and how members of a group, collectively, understand themselves in relationship to other groups. This component of social identity concretizes an "us" and "them" approach to social relations. The power of group identity is characterized by the hyperidentification of one's sense of self—one's value as a person—with one's nationality, race, gender, or even favorite sports team. Membership in this particular group provides a sense of security and belonging. In exchange for this security of selfhood, group members pledge— sometimes explicitly, often only implicitly—a level of allegiance to this group above, and sometimes against, any other potentially competing group allegiance. Group membership becomes a quick way of categorizing people, including oneself. It is a form of human taxonomy with an evaluative sense of ranking (not unlike what the biological sciences use to classify animal species into lower and higher orders), in which one's own primary group is generally perceived as being both normative and inherently superior.

Role identity and social identity are integrally connected— roles are embedded in social groups, both in terms of what being in a particular group means by way of behavioral expectations within the group and in terms of the ways in which one learns to perceive those from outside the group. Role identity and social identity are also reciprocal. Role identity exists only insofar as there is a social group within which the role makes sense. At the same time, the fulfillment of a role provides social identity because there is no role outside of a socially constituted group. The distinction between role identity and social identity is primarily analytical, not functional or empirical. It is impossible to separate the formational aspect of role identity and social identity; they are two sides of the same coin.

Person Identity

The idea of person identity as a significant element of the formation of identity is a relative newcomer in the field of sociology. Specifically, person identity refers to "the idiosyncratic personality attributes that are not shared with other people."[8] This element of identity theory evidences the influence of the field of psychology on the work of sociologists. Person identity has to do with the way an individual perceives himself or herself as being unique and distinct from others. Person identity, however, is derived primarily from culturally normed characteristics and includes traits such as perception of relative masculinity or femininity, of aggression or passivity, of competitiveness or cooperation. Such person identity characteristics do not exist in isolation but are understood in relation to both role identity and social group identity. One perceives oneself as a caring person in one's role as a parent or because one is a nurse. Similarly, the perception of oneself as caring may be couched in relative language: I am caring, for a man; or I am caring, for a woman. The inclusion of person identity in the work of identity theorists allows for a more complex understanding of the ways in which role identity and social identity interact to form an individual identity. The person identity is the unique spin a given person puts on the particular conglomeration of roles and social groups by which that person is formed.

Person identity also makes a space for understanding the refusal to accept particular role identities deemed normative by social groups. Individuals can refuse both the limitations and the expectations presumed normative for particular roles, as has often been the case in regard to perceived gender- and/or race-appropriate roles. But even when a strict adherence to social roles is refused, person identity cannot be understood in an individualistic or isolated manner as the individual's perceptual norms—the very norms being refuted—are shaped by the roles and social groups within any given identity matrix. Rebellion against social norms and role identities is inherently dependent upon, and therefore acknowledges the reality and power of, the very norms and identities it rails against.

Identity Salience

The multiplicity of identities and the fact that identities operate never in isolation, but in interaction not only with other persons/identities in a multitude of situations but even with multiple identities within oneself, results in an exponential growth dimension to identity identification. The more roles an individual plays, the more complex the sense of self.[9] It is, in fact, possible to suggest that identity theory allows not merely for a complex sense of self but for a multiplicity of selves.[10] Rather than envisioning the self as the true core of an individual, identity theory envisions a complex set of roles that an individual can comfortably play. The uniqueness of any individual self is to be found not by removing all of the external trappings of role playing but in the unique combination of roles and the relative degree of privilege the individual gives to each role. Thus, a hierarchy of roles is inevitable. This hierarchy is what identity theorists refer to as identity salience.[11] Identity salience considers the ways in which the multiple selves of an individual interact with one another, with how a given self is privileged in a specific interaction.[12]

Salience is the likelihood that a particular identity will, in fact, be activated. For example, if one of my role identities is as a mother and another of my role identities is as an accountant and I come across a lost child in the grocery store, the salient identity to be activated will most likely be that of mother. Of course the reality is never that simple, as no one is ever only a mother or only an accountant, and many role and social identities are quite complementary. If I am, instead of an accountant, both a mother and a police officer, both roles may be activated simultaneously by the sight of a lost child. Identity salience necessarily involves countless variables as an infinite combination of role, social, and personal identities are possible. However, generally speaking, the hierarchy of identity salience suggests that the larger the number of people impacted by any particular role, the higher the salience is for that role.[13] Similarly, the greater level of commitment to a particular identity—in my own perception, my identity as parent trumps my identity as a distance runner—the greater the identity salience of that identity.

The issue of identity salience becomes particularly critical when competing identities within an individual come into conflict with one another. Take, for example, the situation of an adolescent girl having a friend over at her house.[14] With her friend the adolescent has a certain role, one in which she perceives the need to be seen as sophisticated. The necessary level of sophistication, however, directly conflicts with the girl's role as daughter to her parents. Though most people shift identities routinely through the course of daily interactions with others, choosing the identity appropriate to the situation and the counteridentities with whom they interact, such a transition is not possible when two noncomplementary identities are called upon at the same moment. The identity system necessarily maintains a delicate balance. When an individual is in a situation in which the interests and needs of two or more identities come into conflict, identities shift and change in response and reaction to this conflict. Identity salience offers an explanation for the shifting of identities made necessary by the inevitable complications of social interaction.

Social identity theory highlights the complexity of human identity and suggests that any notion of self as autonomous is misguided at best. The dynamism of identity is integrally connected to the dynamic interactions within a complex web of social relationships. Each of these social relationships contributes to transference of personal identity within which identity (both individual and communal) is continually evolving. Social identity theory suggests that an individual's reliance upon this complex web of social relations is necessary not only for the formation of identity but for its sustenance. Quite simply put, no human "being" is possible outside of being with others in community.

Toward a Theological Account of Community: Alasdair MacIntyre and Traditioned Communities

Identity theory attempts to explain the formation of individual identity as a complex, socially constructed project based on participation in any number of social groups. Identity theory does not, however, consider the purpose of the social group qua social group, nor does it take into account the explicit or implicit purpose or truth claims of any particular group. Similarly, little sustained attention is given to the telos of the group or to how participation in social groups is significant in terms of the telos of the human being qua human being. *That* human identity is dependent upon social relationships is rightly made clear in identity theory; whether, and to what extent, the nature of the group matters is not.

Likewise, identity theory has no explicit theological dimension. In fact, identity theory sees religion—and religious community—as just one of any number of social groups, the significance of which is presumed to be dependent upon the individual's relative perception. Identity theory, that is, entails a presumption of moral neutrality to group association. What is considered to be important is not the moral compass of any given group but the individual's perception of the claims of any given group upon the life of the individual. This is not to suggest that identity theory necessarily sees religious communities as freely chosen or voluntary associations—it acknowledges the complexity of any understanding of community as chosen—but it does tend to presume that religious community is inherently no more formative than any other group, nor does it presume that religious community *should* have a higher identity salience.

Rather than seeing social groups as morally neutral, Alasdair MacIntyre understands the human telos to be that of the development of virtue, and the community to be the locus of this development—a telos loaded with moral content.[15] And virtue is neither neutral nor freestanding but is instead embedded within the practices of the tradition to which the virtue belongs and in which virtue is to be exemplified. Virtue manifests itself in a consistency of character, which is to say that virtue qua virtue is exhibited in the entirety of the virtuous person's life. Virtue cannot be cordoned off into this or that arena of life. In the life of the patient person, for example, patience will be displayed in a myriad of settings, not simply as one aspect of one persona or social role the person chooses to play. The patient person will be patient whether at work, at play, or at rest—likewise with the wise person and the courageous person. Virtues are not roles that can be put on or off at will, nor can they be chosen through a moral calculus equivalent of identity salience. Herein lies one of the problems MacIntyre sees with the fragmented liberal understanding of selfhood. The stark division into social-setting appropriate roles, in addition to the division of life into discrete temporal (childhood, adolescence, adulthood, old age) and spatial (sacred or secular) realms, calls into question the unity of character necessary for selfhood as MacIntyre understands it. Is it, as social identity theory might suggest, indeed possible to be kind and compassionate in my role as friend while being shrewd and dishonest in my role as businessperson? Social identity theory not only makes a space for such a schizophrenic conception of selfhood; it *presumes* it as normative. MacIntyre, on the other hand, presumes that identity rightly formed manifests itself in a unity of character such that "I am forever whatever I have been at any time for others."[16] This claim does not deny the possibility of change, but it suggests that change makes sense only within the narrative of a given life. Given sufficient narration, change demonstrates a continuity of character that is developed through time in movement toward its telos.[17]

Narrative is what lends coherence of identity not only to an individual life, to an individual self, but to an entire community. MacIntyre denies the very possibility that identity is something objectively founded, and he suggests that individual identity is both produced by, and expressed through, the narratives individuals tell to make sense of their lives. Thus, insofar as identity is constituted in and through the narratives we tell, and therefore over which we possess a modicum of control, human beings remain self-interpreting to a degree. MacIntyre, however, understands us to be, at most, coauthors of our own lives. This is so in that these narratives are inextricably embedded in the contingent communities of which we are a part.[18] An important element of MacIntyre's claim is that a constitutive part of the self actually predates that very self. It is impossible for a self to exist isolated/apart from the history and character of the communities in which the self is born. The history and character of the communities that constitute the self provide the necessary grammar with which individual narratives may be constructed. Who I am cannot be disconnected from the family, regional, and national history into which I am born.[19] This is true in terms of language, ideas, expectations, and goals. By no means can an individual be separated from the communities that have given shape to the individual. This indicates that any individual narrative necessarily both includes and is limited by the larger narrative—the metanarrative, even—of the primary formational community.

MacIntyre's understanding of embeddedness, however, extends beyond the embeddedness within a greater communal narrative to the understanding that any given individual narrative is likewise embedded in the narrative of other individuals who similarly participate in the larger communal narrative. Such mutual embeddedness results in a degree of accountability; those whose stories overlap in varying degrees have a claim on one another's lives exactly to the extent that they have a claim on one another's stories.[20] Individual narratives are inextricably connected to—and therefore to a great extent formed by—the narratives of other individuals.[21] The narratives that construct individual lives are interlocked in an ever-increasingly complex web of relationships. The mutual embeddedness of narratives creates a rich set of narratives in which the whole is different from, and arguably substantively greater than, the sum of its parts.

Because MacIntyre understands the self to be not just socially constructed but socially *and* narratively constructed, it is important to ask what is at stake in his focus on the social construction of narrative (or on the narrative construction of social being). In a manner quite similar to that of identity theory, MacIntyre understands role fulfillment to be a significant part of identity formation. Whereas identity theory understands roles to be learned primarily, if not solely, in response to counterroles, MacIntyre suggests that it is stories that are of primary significance in the learning of roles. The narratives a community tells about how people relate to one another, about who carries out what function within the group, about what desires and emotions are acceptable, are passed on with a pedagogical purpose. Stories provide a paradigm for socially expected behavior and are therefore a crucial element of identity formation.[22] The narrative of the community and of other individuals by and through whom identity is forged cannot be separated from the narrative of the individual.

Narrative is not incidental to MacIntyre's account but integrally tied to his conception of telos. The point of the communal narrative is to narrate movement toward, through the development of virtues appropriate to, the community's telos.[23] In this way the narrative functions both to shape and to describe identity. While MacIntyre acknowledges the importance of social identity, rather than drawing a distinction between social groups and traditioned communities, he suggests that there is, in fact, no social group that can be completely removed from the traditions that gave rise to the group. Demonstrating his continued intellectual commitment to Aristotle, MacIntyre suggests that the communal telos is best exemplified through participation in the life of the local geopolitical community.[24] He suggests that the nuclear family is too small and inward-focused and the modern nation-state too large to maintain a coherent notion of the common good. In this suggestion it seems that MacIntyre is mostly right. However, the problem with understanding the local geopolitical community as the locus of virtue and narrative identity is that such communities, even if they do develop a relatively thick understanding of the common good, often lack any sense of an eschatological telos.[25]

Insofar as MacIntyre offers a critique of the conception of an unencumbered and atomistic individual identity, MacIntyre's project appears to be in line with sociological identity theory. MacIntyre refuses the Enlightenment project's understanding of the individual as a discrete moral agent acting both rationally and independently. He suggests that this liberal, largely Kantian, concept that the individual as a "democratized self which has no necessary social content and no necessary social identity can then be anything, can assume any role or take any point of view, because it *is* in and for itself nothing" is utterly mistaken.[26] MacIntyre's entire project is, in large part, a refutation of the possibility of a self that is a detached observer rather than a socially and narratively constituted moral agent.

So, while MacIntyre's project overlaps with identity theory in a significant way, MacIntyre suggests that the socially complex pluralistic world of identity theory is mistaken. Rather than seeing contemporary culture as pluralistic, MacIntyre sees it as fragmented. Whereas identity theory suggests that the complex nature of a pluralistic society results in an individual's ability to adapt, facilely shifting identities as context demands through identity salience, MacIntyre suggests that the liberal self is severely diminished by the lack of telos of the social group that has resulted from, and is symptomatic of, the fragmentation of the contemporary moral world.[27] Identity salience attempts to explain how a particular identity is privileged over any other personal identity based on a matrix of perceived import and influence; the concept of identity salience does not, however, take into consideration the existential truth claims of any given group. Social groups are presumed to be largely neutral and, if not rationally chosen, at least to some extent given rational consent. The hierarchy is one of the individual's perceptions of the relative import of the group, and is not based on a truth-claim.[28]

MacIntyre's distinction between the social group of identity theory and the traditioned community pushes toward, but does not explicitly name, the church.[29] The church, as the body of Christ, is not merely another social body among many bodies — a matter of consumer choice — but *the* social body whose narrative is the narrative of ultimate, and therefore ultimately defining, reality. Rather than envisioning the local geopolitical community as the locus of identity, for those for whom the master status is Christian, the primary community is necessarily the church.[30] Identity theologically understood, then, is grounded in relationship, much as it is in social identity theory. Unlike social identity theory, however, theologically the "with whom" of relationship becomes that which is defining. Identity as defined by the community of the body of Christ is not merely teleological in a generic sense; *it is to have one's narrative embedded within the narrative of God's story.* However, insofar as identity is grounded in participation in the community, which is the body of Christ, the primary relationship on which identity depends is that with God. Relationship with God, however, is necessarily mediated through others and is therefore subject to myriad vulnerabilities.

Suffering and Disembodiment

Both social identity theory and MacIntyre's call to traditioned communities illustrate the crucial nature of social groups for the development of individual identity. Suffering, however, threatens the very nature of community — whether the community of identity theory, MacIntyre's traditioned community, or the body of Christ — as well as the individual's relationship to the community. Profound suffering, as defined in chapter one, refers to *intense and enduring pain of a physical, psychic, or social nature, resulting from the violent actions of another human being, the memory of which is disorienting or disintegrating of personal identity, is destructive of social bonds, and that cripples the individual's capacity to imagine a future unbounded by the past.* In much the same way that profound suffering threatens the integrity of memory and consequently of personal identity, suffering also threatens the very relations with which personal identity is intertwined and upon which it is dependent. Profound suffering's damage to the memory is largely evidenced in suffering's unnarratability, the propensity of suffering to strip the sufferer of the language for expressing suffering. In addition to rendering the sufferer mute, suffering often damages the relationships that are necessary for the sharing of the experience of suffering. Suffering often ruptures the very community necessary for overcoming the effects of suffering, leading to a devastating state of self-perpetuating isolation. As a result of the sufferer's isolation, the suffering of the past continues to manifest itself in the present.

The isolation of suffering is not merely an accidental result of suffering but instead an inherent part of the logic of suffering itself.[31] Isolation embodies suffering; suffering is embodied in isolation. Bodies are not incidental to suffering but the locus of suffering. Because humans *are*, rather than merely *having*, bodies, suffering is first and foremost made possible by the very vulnerability of embodiment. The vulnerability of embodiment is the case whether suffering is physical, mental, or psychic, but is most acute in the case of physical suffering.[32] Because the body is the vehicle through which suffering is experienced — the body's sensitivity to touch is the vehicle for sensations both pleasant and painful — the isolation of suffering is also a bodily experience. Pain has a way of drawing attention to itself at the exclusion of all else, so much so that in the moment of pain "the name of one's child, the memory of a friend's face, are all absent."[33] The outside world ceases to exist in the perception of the sufferer. This is not, however, an egoistic denial of others; it is impossible to deny something that refuses to exist. In situations of intense physical pain, particularly when the pain is recurrent or prolonged, the body itself, as the locus of pain, is experienced as an enemy, as a thing to be overcome, while simultaneously being experienced as all that is.[34] The claims of the body in profound pain nullify all external claims to reality. The world is effectively reduced to the location of suffering, and yet the suffering looms as large as the universe.

This reduction of the world to the site of pain and suffering often results in a withdrawal from the source of suffering — one's own body.[35] The phenomenon of disassociation is not uncommon amongst those who have suffered acute or prolonged trauma — torture victims, abused children, and rape victims being among those most commonly experiencing (or reporting) it.[36] When the body experiences profound pain, the self is perceived as an object, an inanimate thing lacking in subjective agency. This awareness of extreme powerlessness, of a lack of agency, causes the self to be divided against itself and often renders the sufferer less able to experience his or her own embodiment. In extreme situations the disassociation results in a total lack of physical sensation such that the sufferer experiences his or her body as a detached observer, as one who is aware of what is happening but with no more bodily or emotional feeling than as if watching a television show. The more prolonged or repeated the suffering, the longer lasting the dissociative state. In fact, this lack of feeling can, and often does, long outlast the time of suffering itself.[37]

In addition to isolating the sufferer from his or her own body, suffering isolates the individual from the communal body, totalizing the experience of disembodiment.[38] Much, if not most, of the suffering that is intentionally perpetrated in interpersonal relationships (such as domestic violence or sexual assault) is experienced in isolation. No visible or tangible community is present at the time of the assault. If others *are* present, they are often either accomplices or bystanders who are either incapable of preventing the suffering or worse, insensitive to it. The absence of any physical community means that the experience of suffering is itself an experience of isolation. Or, rather, it is experienced only in the company of the one inflicting the suffering, violating the very trust that makes any meaningful notion of community possible. Consequently, when these bonds are broken, the embodied lesson is that one is both powerless and alone, and that it is the state of isolation, not the fleeting experience of community, which is real and lasting.[39] Though this in no way minimizes the physical harm of violence, this loss of community, that the self is an inherently relational entity, is a loss of identity that goes considerably deeper than the surface of the skin. The violation of trust both initiates and exemplifies the state of isolation that is manifested in a ruptured relationship with the other who is responsible for the experience of suffering. This fissure often widens rather quickly and ruptures relationships on a much broader scale than the individuals directly involved in the experience of suffering.[40] The isolation of suffering and loss of community ironically creates atomistic individuals while simultaneously destroying individual selves.

Physical aloneness is a significant part of the isolation of suffering, but profound suffering also creates a situation of psychological isolation. This psychological isolation can be imposed by both the self and others, usually a combination of both. The experience of suffering, particularly when that suffering is at the hands of an intentionally violent other, can destroy the sufferer's belief that it is possible to ever again be oneself in relationship to others. When the body has been treated as an object by another, rather than being honored as Buber's "thou," the self can be internalized as object rather than as acting subject. Though this is especially the case in situations of child abuse or long-term suffering—such as child abuse, domestic violence, or torture—it can likewise occur as a result of a one-time traumatic event. The objectification of the self has the potential to be a self-fulfilling prophecy: "This is how other people treat me; this must be who I am."

The internalized objectification is often complicated by feelings of both shame and fear—feelings that result in a conspiracy of silence. Though suffering often damages communicative ability, even when one who has suffered does not experience a loss of vocabulary or communicative skill there is often a tacit cultural agreement that unpleasant events not be discussed in polite society.[41] Perhaps the most painful burden of suffering is the silence induced by an inability to talk with another person. One of the primary motivators for this silence is the fear of social presumptions of guilt, as well as the nagging sense of self-blame. It is perhaps the cruelest irony of the suffering of interpersonal violence that it is most often the victims, and not the perpetrators, who feel shame. The shame of suffering is directly connected to the self-doubt suffering initiates; in addition to the internalized message of a lack of worth, there is the fear that if others know of what happened, they will discover that the story of violence is, in fact, the true story of one's identity.[42]

The shame and fear that often accompany suffering result from the stigmatization of suffering. The response to human suffering is often to distance oneself from it by rationalizing the suffering. Either the one who suffered must have done something to deserve it, and is therefore not worthy of compassion, or else the one who suffered, no matter how innocently, is thought to be contagious. Suffering is seen as something akin to a cultural leprosy, such that those not directly affected distance themselves in order to prevent the possibility of contamination. Avoiding those who suffer speaks more of a collective fear of suffering than it does of the character of the one who suffers, but either way—whether those who have suffered are seen as meriting suffering or as unfortunate but contaminated—the end result is that those who suffer are often abandoned by the community, secular and ecclesial, both in and to their isolation.

Incorporation: The Restoration of Community

To the extent that the body is the locus of suffering, the body must likewise be the locus of redemption. Incarnational theology necessarily refuses an instrumentalized view of the body. The body and soul are inseparable—what happens to one affects the other. And insofar as the community of the church is also a body, the physicality of that Body cannot be ignored. That is, neither individual bodies nor the ecclesial Body is peripheral to community or to suffering and therefore cannot be peripheral to redemption.

Bodies are integral to the formation of habit. And habit is a type of memory—an implicit or tacit memory—that is integral to identity because it is memory that has moved from the realm of intentional cognitive attention to the realm of automatic response. Habits both construct and alter identity.[43] One of the habits of physical suffering is a disconnection from body as the locus of suffering.[44] In the extreme, such a disconnection can manifest itself in an involuntary, sometimes pathological, dissociative state in which one who has suffered extreme violence seems to vacate the body. This disconnection is not merely a psychological response to trauma but a physiological one as well. It is, in effect, the memory of the experience of violence "inscribed on the nervous system."[45] For suffering to result in a disconnection from the body—a sort of disembodiment—does not, however, require a pathological dissociative state. Bodily habits of suffering can result in a less extreme disregard for, and lack of awareness of, the body's legitimate physical needs and sensations. However, that bodies can be trained, habituated, in such a way as to inform identity also suggests that bodies can be retrained, re-habituated, in ways that likewise alter identity. New habits can be learned. Bodies can, indeed, be re-formed.[46]

In addition to the disembodiment from one's own body, the suffering of violence also often results in a disconnection from the communal body.[47] Violence, by its very nature, ruptures communion on every level—the individual, the interpersonal, as well as the communal. What happens to an individual body cannot be separated from what happens to the communal body. Insofar as the communal body of the church is the body of Christ, restored communion, both with and within the body, is a necessary part of what redemption of violence must mean. The place where such communion is made manifest is in the practice of worship.

Contemporary worship is often domesticated. This domestication of worship seeks to control God, to limit the power of God to work in the world. Worship, however, cannot rightly be domesticated, but insofar as it is an engagement with the living God ot should be recognized as an inherently risky activity in which worshippers are changed, transformed, through the power of God.[48] The transformation of Christian worship, however, refuses the logic of power on which violence depends. For this reason, for one who has experienced violence, worship that proclaims God's no to violence may indeed be experienced as a good and safe place. Even the order of the liturgy, with its predictable patterns, provides stability and a sense of security for those who have experienced the chaos and disorder of violence. That worship refuses to allow those who have suffered to remain unchanged in their suffering is a promise; not changing is a much greater threat to those for whom violence has been formative.

Worship is often conceived as a primarily cognitive act— one from which we are to "get" something. Worship, however, is not primarily about what those who worship think, or believe, or think they believe. Rather, worship is about rightly shaping the desires—and thoughts—as well as the bodies of Christians. Whereas violence shapes bodies with an acute awareness of the pervasive power of pain, worship shapes bodies through a growing awareness of the healing power of the presence of the Holy Spirit. Worship cannot be reduced to its constitutive components; the act of worship is, indeed, greater and much more formative than the sum of its parts. Consequently, it is impossible to isolate a particular worship practice that enables those who have suffered to be reembodied. Instead, embodying worship is the result of a constellation of practices, two of which (anointing and holy friendships) are particularly well suited for redeeming both the bodies of those shattered by violence and the ecclesial body of which shattered bodies are often a part.

Anointing

Insofar as the body is the locus of the suffering of violence, it can also be the locus of healing, not in merely a metaphorical sense but in a literal, tactile sense. Because touch is the vehicle of violence and the efficient cause of the disassociation or disembodiment affiliated with the suffering of violence, touch is often the vehicle through which redemption may be experienced. That both violence and healing may involve touch—even personal, intimate touch—is incidental neither to the suffering nor to the healing. Both violence and healing entail a crossing of physical and social boundaries. The difference—and it is a crucial difference—is that violence violates boundaries against the will of the one being touched, whereas healing crosses those same boundaries with the consent of, perhaps at the request of, and always for the good of, one whose bodily boundaries have been violated.[49]

The locus of the experience of interpersonal violence is the individual body—a body that may have suffered in isolation from the community.[50] As illustrated in the preceding section, such suffering often isolates the individual, not merely from the communal body, but from one's own body as well. The body, in its failure to ward off violence and prevent suffering, is not only the locus of suffering; it is the vehicle through which suffering is experienced. The very thing that binds—that is, the body— also isolates. The ecclesial practice of anointing can offer a new story to the body that has been the locus of violence, because as an embodied act that is both particular and communal it binds the suffering body to the ecclesial body in a way that leads to communion rather than isolation.[51]

The inexpressibility of suffering is undeniably acute. However, despite the loss of temporality and agency that robs the sufferer of a vocabulary with which to express the suffering, the suffering body "is communicative. It cries out for companions, it issues a summons for the church to close the gap of isolation. Anointing cultivates an ecclesial disposition to listen for the voice that breaks through the imposed silences."[52] Anointing is a fundamentally and intentionally embodied act, an act performed on a particular body, by particular bodies, on behalf of the very particular body of the church—on behalf of Jesus. It is this particularity and intentionality that makes anointing also a fundamentally reembodying act. In the act of anointing a body that has suffered violence, the priest reclaims the site of deepest sorrow and of deepest pain and offers it a new story.

A significant element of the embodiment of anointing is that it is fundamentally an act of touch—touch of a particular suffering body.[53] In the rite of anointing, the particularity of the touch of violence is met with the particularity of the gentle touch of healing. Bodies that have been touched violently, however, often shrink from touch, regardless of how gentle. This shrinking is both literal in that the body may pull away, even unconsciously, from the touch of others and metaphorical in that the person, particularly when physical withdrawal is not possible, may withdraw into the body such that the body's ability to sense touch is decreased. Insofar as violent touch, then, has been that which binds in isolation, it is healing touch that can bind in communion. Admittedly, suggesting that touch is the route to reembodiment and ultimately of healing for those for whom touch has been traumatic is riddled with significant risks.[54] However, touch changes bodies: "In any experience of interaction with another, the body is physically changed in some way, in its posture, heart rate, skin conductance level, hormonal level, etc. Prolonged, habitual interactions can physically reconfigure the body."[55] If violent touch changes bodies in harmful ways, the touch of anointing can change bodies in healing and redemptive ways. Power dynamics that have the potential to be or become exploitative exist in and influence all relationships; ecclesial relationships are not immune to the potential for sin. However, because the only way to recover (or learn for the first time) trust that has been destroyed by violence is through a vulnerability that is met with compassion, violent touch is best responded to with the redemptive touch of love.[56]

The practice of anointing "performs the imagination of the church."[57] As such, anointing refuses the isolation of suffering—it is a communal act, an ecclesial act, whether performed within the liturgical space of worship or in the private space of the home. The priest performing the anointing not only represents, but embodies, the church: in and through the practice of anointing, the whole body of Christ is with the one who suffers. This refusal of isolation draws the sufferer into relationship in which he or she is enfolded in the arms of Jesus. Insofar as the suffering of violence ruptures trust, the isolation of violence ruptures communion, even when the community remains unaware of the violence. The practice of anointing is both a proclamatory act, which announces the redemptive and healing work of Jesus, and a performative act, which begins the healing not only of the

individual wounds of the body of the one who suffered violence
but also of the wounds that violence inflicts on the body of Christ.

Holy Friendships

The isolation of suffering extends well beyond the isolation of
disembodiment from one's own body and to a detachment from
relationship with others. The suffering of interpersonal violence
cuts at the root of identity precisely to the extent that relationship
with others constitutes a necessary element of identity. Violence
threatens to unravel the web of relations that constitute identity. This nullification of relationships brings with it an awareness of the thin line between kindness and cruelty, as well as an
acute sense of vulnerability to cruelty. Regardless of the private
nature or degree of relative isolation in which an act (or acts)
of violence may occur, such violence remains situated within a
social context, and it necessarily has social consequences. Even
violence that takes place behind closed doors, shielded from the
scrutiny of the community, is a communal event that damages
that community. In the same way the practice of anointing helps
one who has suffered to re-member his or her body, within the
body of Christ the practices of holy friendships—particularly
the attentive caring and tending of one another, body and soul—
may begin to re-member the communion ruptured by violence.[58]

The love of friends is one of the primary means by which we
are assured of God's love. Consequently, care for one another,
perhaps especially for one another's bodies, makes God's love
manifest with-in the body. In his Letter to the Galatians, Paul
admonishes the church to bear one another's burdens (Gal
6:2).[59] This bearing of burdens is too easily spiritualized with
suggestions that as Christians we are called to bear patiently
with those we find burdensome or that we are to bear burdens
in the metaphorical sense of listening to another's problems with
love and caring. And these are indeed right and salutary things

for members of the body of Christ to do. Such a minimalistic interpretation is not, however, sufficient. The bearing of another's burdens is necessarily as embodied a practice as the experience of bearing one's own burdens. This includes the burden of suffering. Holy friendships, made possible by the formation of disciples through the practices of worship, train bodies that are able both to bear another's burdens and to allow themselves to be borne when burdened.

The classical understanding is that friendship is first and foremost a relationship between equals.[60] The legacy of such an understanding tends to reduce friendships to relationships between two members of very narrowly defined, homogeneous groups. That is, friendships tend to be reserved for those with a common race, gender, ethnicity, and socioeconomic level. Christian friendship, however, is based on a common telos rather than on perceived social equality. What makes friendship possible in the Christian community is participation in the body of Christ. As such, friendship need not be restricted to a community of social equals or even to those who seem to have much in common. Because such holy friendships are countercultural refusals of the status quo, as well as of the power dynamics that make space for, and attempt to make sense of, acts of violence, such "friendships are potentially subversive—acts of genuine protest and resistance—because they dare to break free from what is most corrupting and dehumanizing in a culture in order to begin something new."[61] The glue that binds ecclesial friendships is the unity that comes from mutual participation in the body of Christ. This solidarity is not, however, the solidarity in suffering found in therapeutic survivor groups. Though survivor groups certainly have a rightful place—even in the church—what is most significant about the subversive friendships in the church is that they do not depend upon any solidarity beyond that of a common baptism.[62] By its very nature, holy friendship denies

the validity of violence and in its application often defies culturally accepted norms that would dictate whom one can befriend.[63]
The church is a community of "socially disruptive possibilities"[64]
through which the logic of violence may be refused.

Though any number of markers of holy friendships might
be named, one is the willingness to bear one another's burdens. Bearing another's burdens requires compassion. To bear
another's burdens is not mere sympathy, nor is it a paternalistic
impulse to "fix" whatever is wrong. It is, instead, to enter into
the suffering of another in a way that honors the person and
seeks to care for that person in his or her suffering. Jesus' act
of washing the disciples' feet is not merely—perhaps not even
primarily—an act to be symbolically reenacted but a call for us
to care for the very real, very bodily needs of those who suffer.
Jesus shows us "the importance of meeting each other, touch-
ing each other, with simplicity, gentleness, and great respect,
because each person is precious."[65]

The compassionate bearing of another's burdens is indeed
an act of patience.[66] This may be particularly true when the one
who has suffered is unable to receive the kindness and compassion of friendship. However, compassion toward another can
indeed be formative.[67] Friendship, like touch, changes—albeit
sometimes slowly—the body.

A second marker of holy friendship is the openness to
being borne—that is, to having another bear one's burdens.
Compassion and vulnerability are, in some respects, two sides
of a piece.[68] For one who has suffered violence at the hands of
another, particularly a trusted other, vulnerability can be a terrifying thing—a thing one may desire to avoid at all costs.[69] The
greater the violation of trust, the greater the resistance to future
vulnerability is apt to be. The recognition of vulnerability is
heightened by an awareness that past vulnerabiility has resulted

in an experience of violence. Vulnerability, however, is a necessary element of the giving and receiving of friendship.[70]

Restoration of Trust

The experience of violence disintegrates trust. This loss of trust
manifests itself both internally, within the very body that was the
locus of the suffering, and externally, within the communal body
where violence took place. The practice of worship forms bodies
that learn to trust themselves as places of healing, places that
have experienced, and continue to experience, God's presence.
Through the practices of friendship, bodies begin to learn to
entrust themselves to one another through mutual concern and
caregiving. These two practices are not an either/or; nor does one
have temporal priority over the other. In practice, both worship
and friendship occur concurrently, each shaping and forming the
other. The deeper one enters into, and makes oneself open to, the
formative power of worship, the more deeply one will be drawn
into friendship with other members of this same body. These two
practices of worship and friendship, then, work together to rees-
tablish (or perhaps establish for the first time) a degree of trust
that was damaged or destroyed by the experience of violence.
In the aftermath of violence, that which is most needed for the
healing and redemption of violence "requires engaging the reality that one fears most, other people."[71] This is so because it is
almost a tautology to suggest that trust requires trust, making it
quite difficult to repair once damaged.

The notion of trust is often thought to be exemplified by
the young child who yells "Daddy" a millisecond before leaping
from some precipice into Daddy's arms, or by the young child
who will willingly, even happily, go off hand in hand with anyone who offers a friendly smile. This notion of trust, however,
has more to do with adults' projection of trust onto the young
who are simply too naïve to recognize their vulnerability. A more

nuanced notion of trust necessarily takes into account a recognition of vulnerability, of risk — a recognition young children generally do not have.[72] Rather, what is often hailed as trust in the young child is more properly thought of as innocence, even ignorance. Children are often simply oblivious to their relative lack of power. Even when they recognize their lack of power, they remain unaware of the vulnerability that comes with this lack of power. Adults, however, are acutely aware of the vulnerability of small children.[73]

Trust properly understood is a conscious decision made not out of ignorance or naïveté but while recognizing one's vulnerability. Vulnerability is something contemporary culture is often afraid to acknowledge. A stigma, a sense of shame, is inherent in being vulnerable, perhaps most especially when that vulnerability has been exploited — for example, shame is a remarkably common response in victims of domestic violence or sexual assault. The absurdity of the shame of vulnerability is that we are all, of course, vulnerable. Even Superman has Kryptonite. Rather than seeing vulnerability as something to be denied or overcome, the Christian tradition sees vulnerability not merely as a necessary result of our fallen, sinful condition but as the glue that holds a community together. As Hauerwas writes, "The last thing the church wants is a bunch of autonomous, free individuals. We want people who know how to express authentic need, because that creates community."[74] Through intentional practices of vulnerability and compassion, such as anointing and the development of holy friendships, the ecclesial community provides a space for relationships of trust to flourish, allowing the isolation of suffering to give way to the communion for which all have been created.

5

VOCATION
The Anticipating Self

Human identity is contingent upon a complex constellation of factors. Along with memory and community, temporality is essential but often overlooked. Both the passing of time and the experience of time are crucial elements of human identity; in addition to existing *in* and *through* time, identity is also dependent upon the experience *of* time. As such, identity is not solely determined by past and present experiences (memory and community) but also contingent upon perceptions of the future—that is, upon anticipated future experiences. This element of futurity necessarily lends a degree of openness to identity, an openness that can be visualized as something akin to the poetic use of ellipsis.

Time and identity are integrally connected such that Augustine suggests that rather than speaking of past, present, and future, we might better speak in terms of past present, present present, and future present.[1] All three modalities of time exist simultaneously within the soul of the individual at any given point in time, and therefore all three are equally accessible to the individual's experience.[2] This necessarily means that identity is not a stagnant phenomenon that can be observed or dissected in an impartial or detached manner but always experienced as a relative state of flux (of becoming), since one is always simultaneously who one remembers oneself to have been in the past, who one experiences oneself to be in the present, as well as the possibilities one imagines for oneself in the future.[3]

Identity and Futurity

The ticking of a clock provides a helpful illustration of the connection between identity and temporality.[4] The experience of the present exists in the space between the tick (which is the remembered experience of the past) and the tock (the anticipated experience of the future). The self exists always in the tension, the pregnant pause, between the remembered past and the anticipated future, while attending to the experience of the present. Though this pregnant pause may be experienced as a freeze-frame photograph, it is the acute tension between memory and expectation—between the past and the future—that makes this possible. This understanding of identity suggests that, despite the ethereal nature of the future, the future—and more precisely the expectations for the future—is as integral a part of the identity of any individual or communal body as the remembered past. This image is helpful for understanding identity (and consequently the impact of profound suffering on identity) in its recognition that the past not only pushes toward the future but requires the future in order for the past to be, indeed, experienced *as past*.

The recognition of the future as an integral part of identity is largely overlooked in contemporary therapeutic settings, which, as a result of the overwhelming reliance on the analytical psychology of Freud, focus almost exclusively on the impact of the past—as something solidified in memory, particularly the time period of early childhood—in thinking of the formation of identity. A focus on the stories of the past, however, ignores the need for "future stories," which consist of the various images of the possible paths an individual's future may take.[5] Future stories are, of course, largely dependent upon both past and present but are not coterminous with them. The future stories that an individual imagines—the anticipation of what happens next, of who I will be in another year, or of what life will be like five years from now—are a determinative part of present individual identity and are connected directly to the memories of the past insofar as the imagination is shaped both by the actual experiences of past and present and perhaps even more so by the perceived trajectory from the past and into the present. Moreover, an individual's *interpretation* of the present, which cannot be isolated from the individual's experience of the present, is at least as determined by the anticipated future as it is by the remembered past.

This understanding of the critical nature of future stories reflects the essentially narrative nature of human identity. The self is the tension between the remembered experiences of the past and of the narrative presently being constructed, a narrative constructed largely in light of projections into the future. That identity is necessarily future directed is itself a teleological claim, precisely insofar as it implies that identity is movement *toward.*[6] The teleological claim of identity as moving toward does not, however, mean that an individual is somehow or other less than fully formed at any given point in time; in means that the whole of the self is only a self insofar as it exists *in* time. Identity is not restricted to the movement of a being through time, nor does it exist only where past and future meet. Identity is a complex matrix *of* time—past, present, and future—experienced simultaneously as well as linearly. Identity is not an objective thing to be manipulated and studied, but an action; being is becoming—it is being *in* time. Movement toward, as a constitutive element of identity, is neither restricted nor defined by its linearity.

The simple act of brushing one's teeth provides an apt analogy. Though brushing one's teeth involves any number of steps— grasping a toothbrush, applying toothpaste, scrubbing the teeth, rinsing, spitting, returning each item to its proper place in the medicine cabinet—no one step stands alone and can, in and of itself, be identified as the act of tooth brushing. The action is temporal and "has a unity of form through time, a form revealed only in the action as a whole." That the action of brushing one's teeth is revealed only as a whole does not, however, make any single step less fully a part of the action. To omit one step is no longer to brush one's teeth, properly understood. Similarly, the claim that identity exists in time, in the act of movement toward the future, does not suggest that at any moment in the past or present identity was somehow incomplete—nor does it imply that there will be a future point in time in which identity will become complete. Rather, it is to say that identity at any point in time always already includes the perceived movement of the individual through past and present and into the future.[7]

A narrative understanding of identity that takes into account the temporal nature of being in time both allows for the permanence of identity through time and simultaneously accounts for changes through time. To the extent that identity thus understood is not stagnant but always an ongoing activity, it is possible to see how the self changes in response not only to past and present experiences but also to expectations for the future. The self is actualized in openness to the future. Rather than locking oneself into the past, the temporality of being entails a receptive stance to the future. Because the self cannot be rightly understood only in relation to the past, the refusal to be open to the future is a refusal of one's very identity, a refusal of selfhood.

In terms of human identity, an understanding of Paul Ricoeur's notion of emplotment is critical for envisioning how the seemingly disconnected events of past, present, and future all converge in the meaningful formation of an individual self that is continuous without being stagnant.[8] Ricoeur understands time to exist in two modes: linear and phenomenological. Linear time is chronological time. It is one thing following another in linear succession; it is a strictly chronological rendering of events. The example of the present filling the space between the tick and the tock of past and present is an example of linear time. The one event necessarily precedes and makes space for the next. Phenomenological time, though not in opposition to linear time, is tensed without necessarily being linear. Phenomenological time is commonly used in storytelling where present chronological events reflect both past (i.e., flashbacks) and future (i.e., foreshadowing) events in the telling. Narrative emplotment is the coming together of linear and phenomenological time.

Narrative emplotment allows not merely a simple straightforward chronological reading of a story but its continual rereading in light of continually changing events. The past is continually reread—and therefore reinterpreted—in light of the present and perceived future, and as such it never remains stagnantly in the past. Emplotment is what makes a narrative a narrative, as opposed to a bullet-point listing of disjointed events. Through emplotment, seemingly unrelated elements are brought together and rendered meaningful. The individual is never merely a product of past memories, or of present relationships, or even of expectations for the future, but always a complex admixture of all of the above. Past memories, present relationships, and future expectations, however, are not stagnant, self-interpreting objects but always in a state of flux insofar as they are being reread, remembered, and reinterpreted by both the individual and the community.

Temporality as an integral dimension of identity allows for a fluid understanding of self in which no one event, no one time, is privileged above all others. The self, though necessarily shaped by the remembered experiences of the past and the relationships of the present (and therefore to an extent bound *to* both past and present), is not bound *by* past and present but always open to new possibilities in the future. This promise of the future is not, however, the substance of inspirational graduation speeches but the material toward which life narratives tend and from which life narratives are formed. Identity as something that is continually being reread, and therefore re-created, allows for the possibility of a future in which the stories of the past can be retold from continually new perspectives.[9] This continual retelling of the past is neither a reductionistic nor a revisionist romanticizing of the past but a reflection of lived experience in and through time. Such an understanding of identity might be thought of as an anticipatory ontology. That is, identity is shaped, to a large extent, by the anticipation of who one is becoming.

Understanding the impact of the perceived future on human identity is, in an important sense, absolutely crucial. Theologically, however, there is also a distinct sense in which this focus on the *perception* of the future falls short. As significant as the perception of the future is in terms of an individual's understanding of identity, the reality of identity is dependent not merely upon perception of identity but upon the reality of an identity that is always already determined by Christ. Human identity and human teleology are essentially eschatological. Who we are now does not determine who we will become; rather, who we are becoming—who we already are in Christ—is what ultimately determines who we are now. This notion of identity might be thought of as retroactive ontology.[10] It is this

retroactive identity—an identity founded in the promise of resurrection and of redemption—that is the ground for Christian
hope. Retro*active* identity is not, however, coterminous with the
notion of retro*spective* identity. It does not mean that I can fully
give an accounting of myself, fully come to see myself, only in
retrospect from the moment of my death—though this may be
true as well. This retroactive element of identity simultaneously reaches both further back and further forward in time
than any individual human life span. This suggests that identity is grounded in teleology, that who I ultimately am is who I
already have been determined by God to be, in and through the
resurrection of Jesus Christ. Insofar as identity is understood
as being determined by one's past and present experiences and
one's imaginings of the future, the future remains bounded by
the memories of the past. Identity understood retroactively
suggests that the future is not merely a projection of the past
and present self—just a bit older. Rather, retroactive identity
sees the past and the present self as a reflection of the promised
redeemed self of new creation.

Thus, human identity is simultaneously retroactive and anticipatory not in a way that is merely additive but in such a way as
to make the past inextricably woven into the future, and vice
versa. This understanding of identity is not a denial of the significance of past and present; rather, it is just the opposite, as both
past and present shape the ability to anticipate the future. It is to
say that identity is tensed—it is experienced *as* past, present, and
future, as well as experienced *through* past, present, and future.
Identity is not, however, limited to this linear temporality but
also reflects Ricoeur's phenomenological time. Insofar as identity
is shaped by futurity, this futurity is both retroactive (reflecting
a future event that has already come to pass) and anticipatory
(projecting itself into the future that is already perceived). That
identity is simultaneously retroactive and anticipatory as well as

simultaneously tensed (past, present, and future) suggests that identity is extremely complex and cannot be reduced to any simple reflection on past experiences or present circumstances, but necessarily reflects the hoped-for future.

Secular Hope?

The temporality of identity—the experience of being as past, present, and future—is both a teleological and an ontological claim. The added focus on futurity does not lessen the influence of memory or community on the formation of identity. Notions of the future both shape and reflect concrete cultural practices as well as the cultural perceptions of the community's own past and present. A community's perception of its telos is expressed in and through its concrete practices and habits.[11] The telos is reflected in the practices by which a community expresses its hopes and dreams for the future, even when that telos is neither explicitly stated nor broadly recognized, and even when the notion of "hope" is denuded of its explicitly theological content.

Glorification of the Past

In the absence of any promise of a future redemption, hope for the future often depends upon human attempts to honor the past. When the achievements of the past are honored, the past is perceived as living on in the present, while simultaneously inspiring future greatness. National monuments, ostensibly designed to remember those who have sacrificed in some way in the past for the sake of the common good of the future of the nation, often take on something of a religious nature. Sites such as Boston's Freedom Trail or battlegrounds like Gettysburg have become secular pilgrimage sites. Some monuments—the Lincoln Memorial, for example—have signs posted requesting respectful silence be maintained while visiting the monument as a proclamation of the sanctity of the space. The Vietnam

Veterans Memorial shares a certain resonance with Jerusalem's Wailing Wall, with family and friends seeking out the names of lost loved ones and etching them on paper. Such memorials seek to fulfill a religious need via secular means. In the absence of an eschatological telos, however, in the end the only promise such secular memorials can offer is to remember the past.

Remembrances themselves are not problematic. Not only is remembering inevitable; it is a good and right thing to do. Nonetheless, the theological problem with the memory affiliated with such monuments is twofold. First, it is problematic when remembering is an end in itself, when the memory of the past becomes a substitute for both present and future—as if by memorializing the past it can be frozen in time, in all of its glory, with no recognition of its shadow side. A second, closely related, theological problem with such national monuments is that they do not simply offer a means for remembering the past, but they inculcate a particular story told of the past, a quasi-religious story that intentionally refuses not only competing stories but a recognition of its very limited place within a much larger narrative, which has both a history and a future.

In addition to reflecting what is the next best thing to hope—a promise not to forget—the problem with such memorials is that this promised remembering takes a particular, often rather selective, form. That is, memorials do not merely reflect history; they are, in fact, a form of history writing. Communities memorialize not simply what happens and what they promise to remember but *how* they remember. Memorials are a way communities bear witness to both their history and their values, and, as such, memorials have the power to create history.[12] Memorials allow those in the present to determine how those in the future learn to remember the past.[13]

Similarly, smaller communities, families, and even individuals construct countless memorials to remember more intimate, personal losses. The act of memorialization—seen in the enacted practices of placements of a tombstone, roadside crosses, and erected memorials—is a cultural expression of the promise "you will not be forgotten."[14] Such memorials, though often explicitly mourning a loss of the future (particularly with the deaths of those who are young), implicitly mourn the loss of a sentimentalized and idealized perceived past innocence.

Memorials that attempt to glorify the past, promising a form of eternal life through memory, seem largely to be attempts to refuse powerlessness. When the trauma of the past—for example, Vietnam or 9/11—is overwhelming, memorials are a vow not to be overcome by the trauma.[15] Remembering is *not* problematic. Memorials themselves are not necessarily problematic. The Christian church has always remembered. The church remembers her saints and martyrs, and rightly so. The entire history of Israel can be seen as an act of remembrance. The liturgy of the Eucharist is a proleptic act of remembrance. Theologically, the problem is not with remembering but *with the resignation that our hope is in remembrance*; the problem is the claim that remembering the past takes the place of hope for a new creation in which all manner of atrocities will be redeemed. The loss of the past cannot be undone, but promises to remember, to honor the past, and to face the future with greater wisdom as a result of the past are a way of denying the past a power over the future. The problem with such memorials is not *that* they remember the past but that the telos of the remembering is disconnected from any hope for the future.

Transcendence in the Present

In situations where memorializing the past is perceived to be impossible or insufficient, the attempt to transcend the present is another secular expression of hope. While not grounded in any historical, confessional faith, contemporary notions of transcendence tend to reflect the peculiarly North American trend toward a disembodied and transcendent spirituality, which finds its roots most famously in the writings of the transcendentalists, Ralph Waldo Emerson and Henry David Thoreau.[16] Emerson and Thoreau popularized something of an intellectual nature-mysticism combined with a material asceticism through which, it was believed, one could transcend the mundane world and experience life more intensely, more fully. In a sense the disassociation of suffering is a psychological defense mechanism not dissimilar from the intellectual search for transcendence. It is interesting to note that whereas disassociation is recognized by psychiatrists as a pathological response to unbearable pain and suffering, in certain circles, this intellectualized attempt to transcend the everyday is praised as a higher form of consciousness.

Though admittedly less common in contemporary Western culture, interest (and perhaps belief) in reincarnation (a religio-philosophical concept historically associated with Hinduism) as a way of transcending the present appears to be expanding beyond the Hollywood world of Shirley MacLaine.[17] The growth of new age spirituality has brought with it an interest in ancient non-Western beliefs, including reincarnation. The topic of reincarnation has worked its way into the likes of popular children's card games such as Yu-Gi-Oh! and even into the work of some ostensibly Christian writers.[18] Reincarnation is an extreme form of relying on another present—a future present—in order to deal with the pain of the "present present." Such attempts to transcend the present, however, inevitably fall short of any Christian understanding of hope as they are, by their very nature, more a denial of suffering than an ontological promise.

Progress toward the Future

A third secular approach to facing an uncertain future is through a studied belief in progress.[19] Though reliance on progress is by no means limited to the so-called new atheists, the writings of the new atheists exemplify hope for the future through the power of reason and technology today.[20] This understanding of science as salvation—the myth that humanity is continually progressing forward (though toward *what* remains problematically unclear)—is a direct result of the Enlightenment. The myth of progress is expressed in two primary ways: science and history.[21] Both, however, assume movement toward a new world order as opposed to any expectation of new creation.[22]

The scientific notion of progress is, to a large extent, an outgrowth of the dual Darwinian understanding that the entire universe, including the human race, is continually evolving and that evolution favors the "fittest" of each species. Scientific advancement is thought to be both evidence for and a form of contemporary evolution. Though by no means the only way to which science is looked for salvation, this is perhaps most apparent in the fields of biotechnology and epitomized by studies in cryogenics and cloning. The Human Genome Project, whose goal was to provide a complete map of human DNA, is perhaps the most significant biomedical project of the past century.[23] The hope of the project is that by mapping the human genome the root of medical problems, whether inherited or acquired, can be determined and therefore resolved. Though the Human Genome Project does not promise an end to illness and death, the medical hope of such a project is that a deeper understanding of the development of diseases at the molecular level will enable treatments aimed at the elimination of illness, the reduction of suffering, and the prolongation of life. The Human Genome Project cannot and does not promise an end to suffering; however, it focuses hopes for a better life on the medical field's ability to minimize suffering.

The historical version of the myth of progress can be seen in the work of Georg Wilhelm Friedrich Hegel. Hegel envisioned history moving toward a particular telos in a dialectical fashion.[24] Rather than precluding the scientific myth of progress, Hegel's philosophy of history assumes it. For Hegel, whose philosophy owes a clear debt to Kant's rationalism, the telos of history is human freedom and knowledge. This same approach to historical theory can be seen in the more contemporary writings of Fukuyama, who claims that history is directional and its telos is (and always has been) liberal capitalism.[25] Fukuyama's claim is that we have now reached the "end of history," insofar as there is no sociopolitical option save liberal capitalism. Whether based on science or history, the myth of progress places its trust for a better future on human rationality and will, on the human movement forward in time toward utopia. Such hopes, though largely a reflection of post-Enlightenment idealism, are hardly novel, nor are they uncontested.[26] They do, however, suggest that if there is no suprahuman human telos, human ingenuity is the only hope the future holds.

A Theological Account of Hope

A theological account of hope is grounded in the claim that Jesus' resurrection is central to any Christian notion of hope, that any discourse of hope is necessarily an inherently theological—in fact, a christological—discourse.[27] In much the same way that human identity is simultaneously retroactive and anticipatory, so is hope. Hope necessarily looks back to the remembered event of the resurrection while remaining future oriented, looking toward the promised return of Christ. Hope is that which carries the Christian community through the in-between time from resurrection until eschaton. Hope is inherently poignant insofar as it is a recognition of becoming, of possibility, and of the gap between what is and what might be. The poignancy of this gap is the creative space of the imagination. Thus, hope is necessarily both doxological and participatory; it is the means through which God enables the church to participate in, and witness to, the kingdom of God now.

Christian hope is, first and foremost, epistemological. It is necessarily an eschatological reality grounded simultaneously in the knowledge of the resurrection of Jesus and of the promised Parousia. As such, hope is based on what is ultimate rather than what is speculative. Hope is the recognition that suffering is not ultimate. To say that hope is epistemological is, of course, to call into question the very nature of knowledge, blurring lines that had, before Jesus' resurrection, been perceived as immutable. Because Christians know Christ to be raised from the dead—in direct contradiction of all experiential knowledge of death (dead people, after all, tend to remain dead)—Christians know that death is no longer the end of life with God. Because Christ is raised from the dead, Christians, too, trust in their own resurrection. The possibility of hope is contingent upon the trustworthy character of God, not our own strength of character, and upon our trust in God's character. This trust is an anticipation of the fulfillment of God's promises, which hinges on the expressed character of God as witnessed in the resurrection of Jesus.

Hope is how the church remembers the past. The past is remembered as a past in which the new thing God is doing has already begun. Hope is the knowledge that memorializing the past, escaping the present, and striving for utopia through scientific and technological progress are *not* the best life has to offer. Fallen humanity is not merely left to its own rather feeble devices. Hope is the knowledge that new creation can happen, is happening, and will happen—that the new thing foretold by Isaiah has begun. Hope, then, is inseparable from trust in God's promise of new creation. The foundation of hope is the confession that Jesus is Lord *now*, even when Christ's lordship is hard to see, and that he is returning, to set all things right.

Hope is the form faithful waiting takes. Hope is eschatological; it anticipates the new creation promise of God. Hope is penultimate and therefore necessarily both precedes the eschaton in a temporal sense and is entirely dependent upon its coming.[28] While Christian hope is made possible only by the resurrection of Jesus, it is not to be equated with the promise of the resurrection. Rather, hope is the means and the manner by which we await redemption. "We know that the whole creation has been groaning in labor pains until now; and not only the creation, but we ourselves, who have the first fruits of the Spirit, groan inwardly while we wait for adoption, the redemption of our bodies. For in hope we were saved. Now hope that is seen is not hope. For who hopes for what is seen? But if we hope for what we do not see, we wait for it with patience" (Rom 8:22-25). Hope provides sustenance in the interim. It fills the gap, the void between the now and the not yet.

Hope is a theological expression of the subjunctive mood. Whereas the indicative language of past and present describe what *is*, hope describes what *might be*, what *ought to be*, and what, in fact, one day *will be*. Insofar as hope is based on the resurrection promise of what is yet to come, what must be waited upon, hope is necessarily future oriented; it is an orientation toward a good that can be imagined, because it has been glimpsed, even if it is not yet realized. Hope envisions that which is within the realm of the possible, though as yet unseen. Insofar as hope is recognition of what might be, the language of hope is necessarily imaginative. To say that hope is imaginative, however, is not to suggest that it is imaginary.[29] Rather, hope entails the ability to see a deeper reality than that which is most immediately apparent.[30]

Hope looks not for the undoing of suffering but for its promised redemption. The recognition of the gap between *is* and *ought* does not, however, spontaneously lead to hope. In fact, an acute recognition of this "ugly broad ditch"[31] between God's intention for the world (what ought to be) and the fallenness of the world (what is) can just as easily lead to hopelessness as it does to hope. What opens the future of *ought to be* to hope is the assurance that *ought to be* ultimately *will be*.[32] Hope exists within the proleptic promise that the resurrection is the inauguration of the new creation still to come. This new creation is not a restoration to a prelapsarian state but the promise of something new, something beyond even the wildest of human imaginings. It is the promise that what Lessing perceived as a ditch is, in fact, not a chasm that cannot be traversed but one that is being closed by Christ. As such, hope cannot be stagnant; it implies a movement toward — movement from *is* through *ought to be* toward *will be*. The ability to see what might be is only hopeful insofar as it is a glimpse of the promise of that which is to come. Hope is a leaning into the future, into the promise of the resurrection.[33] Otherwise vision is nothing more than salt rubbed in the wound of what is.

Hope is the vehicle through which we participate in doxological time. Hope is participatory; it is the manner through which the church participates in the time between resurrection and Parousia. The promise that what ought to be in fact will be requires patient endurance and inextricably links hope and temporality. Hope is the form that right relationship between the present and the future takes. All time is rightly understood as doxological; time is created for worship.[34] Hope recognizes God's sovereignty over time as well as God's movement in time. It is a willingness in spite of, and in the face of, situations of sin and suffering to wait "for the emergence of a larger moment and a larger time."[35] Such patience requires an understanding of time as a created good amongst the backdrop of God's eternality. This is so because hope is the vision of what might be as well as the commitment to live as one already fit — created, in fact — for the new creation.[36]

Suffering and Hope

Profound suffering refers *to intense and enduring pain of a physical, psychic, or social nature, resulting from the violent actions of another human being(s), the memory of which is disorienting or disintegrating of personal identity, destructive of social bonds, and crippling of the individual's capacity to imagine a future unbounded by the past.* Such suffering impacts not only the ways in which one remembers the past and participates in the present, but, at least as importantly, the experience of such profound suffering can diminish the ability to anticipate a hopeful future. Future stories—the ability to imagine what the future may entail—are, in fact, a constitutive element of identity such that the redemption of the memory of past suffering must necessarily include the promise of a redeemed future as a part of the redemption of the individual.

Suffering is a way of knowing that can never be un-known. To forget suffering is not to un-know suffering, because suffering is remembered implicitly even when it is no longer remembered in an explicitly narratable way. The epistemology of suffering—particularly of prolonged and profound suffering—can overshadow the epistemology of hope. Because the knowledge of suffering is experiential and resides in the body of one who has suffered, suffering can train the habit of expectation of suffering. Once vulnerability to suffering is known in bodily form, particularly in situations of prolonged suffering, it becomes the anticipated norm. As such, the expectation of suffering can distort the knowledge of hope that is always necessarily, at least in part, anticipatory. For this reason, hope cannot be separated from trust; hope is predicated upon a trust in the promises of God despite an expectation of suffering rooted in past experience. Hope trusts that the promises of redemption ultimately will be, even when redemption is not yet known experientially. Therefore, exactly to the extent that the epistemology of suffering has ruptured the capacity for trust, it will likewise diminish the capacity for hope.[37]

The experience and memory of profound suffering can render hope rather elusive, because suffering can destroy the imagination necessary to nourish and sustain hope.[38] Thus, suffering problematizes hope. This problematization is not merely theoretical; it is not a question of theodicy but primarily pragmatic, and it is a result of particular habits of the imagination that are cultivated by the very logic of suffering. Rightly ordered desire reflects an orientation toward both God and toward the neighbor. And desire rightly ordered is an orientation of charity. As such, desire is a positive good in that it evidences a presence, not an absence. The presence of rightly ordered desire evidences the anticipatory eschatological nature of identity. Desire is constitutive of human identity, and human identity is always simultaneously retrospective (reflecting "what the past is doing now")[39] and anticipatory (reflecting that which one is becoming). Rightly ordered desire propels the individual into the future in which the eschatological promise of who one will be is, to some extent, always already reflected in who one is now.

Profound suffering, however, can disorder desire because it ruptures the experience of temporality, which an orientation toward the future eschatological promise requires. In the same way that suffering can destroy notions of temporality, thus distorting memory, suffering can, likewise, distort perceptions of the future. A key dimension of the temporal problem of profound suffering is the refusal of the past to remain in the past. The past is not only brought into the present but also projected into the future—a future of anticipated suffering.

The sufferer—particularly in the midst of profound suffering, but in suffering's aftermath as well, because such suffering refuses to remain *past*—often desires an alleviation of suffering above all other desires. The resulting orientation toward whatever might promise to alleviate suffering can become etched so deeply in the psyche of one who has suffered that the very capacity for positive desire can be stunted.[40] In such times "the past reaches into the present and throttles desire before it can become directed toward the future."[41] Not suffering is, of course, to be desired above suffering.[42] But not suffering is no substitute for the positive good of God.[43] This desire for the alleviation of the pain of suffering is a movement away from the created positive good of rightly ordered desire to the cessation of an evil. Of course, the cessation of evil *is* good. It is, however, a minimal good. Thus, it is insufficient to the extent that desire comes to be defined in terms of an absence of suffering rather than by the presence of God. When the effects of profound suffering are overwhelming such that the *only* desire is for a cessation of suffering, the desire for the positive good of God is lost. This loss of desire for God is simply another word for despair.

In addition to leading to despair, the distortion of desire wrought by suffering can also cripple the imagination, rendering the sufferer void of any future stories other than those implanted and nourished by the event of suffering. In the aftermath of profound suffering, it may become nearly impossible even to imagine, let alone to anticipate, the eschatological promise of redemption. The very nature of suffering "destroys a person's self and world, a destruction experienced spatially as either the contraction of the universe down to the immediate vicinity of the body or as the body swelling to fill the entire universe."[44] This diminution of space is not, however, merely geographical but equally temporal, causing the sufferer's world to contract to the now. No world exists beyond the locale of the body in pain, nor is there a world beyond the moment of its infliction (or anticipation). This loss of any world beyond suffering extends imaginatively and indefinitely into the future and often leads to resignation to the inevitability of suffering.[45]

However, the complete loss of any sense of futurity is not a given in the aftermath of suffering. The loss of hope brought about by suffering is not limited to the inability to imagine the future, but, in a way that is equally problematic, it can also result in the ability to imagine only a future of a continuation of unbearable suffering. Insofar as one who has suffered profoundly in the past *does* imagine the future, it is likely to be envisioned as a hell that is merely "the ceaseless reiteration of the past."[46] The future, insofar as it is thought of at all, is filled with anticipation of more suffering. The inability—or perceived inability—to avoid a future that is simply more of the same suffering may lead to a sense of passive resignation, an acceptance of powerlessness.

Conversely, the inability to imagine a future that will be qualitatively different from past suffering can also lead to an active sense of defiance. In the absence of any perception of hope that things will be better, that any action on the part of the sufferer can make a positive difference in future experiences, an active form of resignation may be found in defiance.[47] Exactly to the extent that one has nothing to gain, one has nothing to lose, such that those with no hope for a future other than that of repeated suffering may, in turn, perpetuate the cycle of suffering.[48]

The future stories of those who have suffered—whether stories of resignation or of defiance—illustrate the ways in which the constriction of time in the midst of suffering to the "now" handicaps the ability to imagine the future. Suffering can make future stories as threatening to the integrity of the individual as memories of the past and as broken relationships of the present. When the past has been one of profound suffering, the ability to imagine a future that is in any significant way different is often destroyed. The overwhelming powerlessness against such suffering, coupled with suffering's incongruity between what is and what ought to be, often leads to a loss of hope for anything other than the repetition of past suffering that continues unabated long after the suffering itself has ceased. This loss of ability to imagine a future that will be narrated differently than the past is often the case even when the present is qualitatively better than the suffering, when, in other words, clear experiential evidence witnesses to the reality that the past suffering is *not* ceaselessly repeated.

The effects of profound suffering do not cease when the suffering stops. Or, perhaps it is more accurate to say that suffering does not stop when the violence ends, but may extend indefinitely into the future. For this reason the effects of such suffering cannot be expected simply to dissipate with time. Rather, profound suffering can result in a loss of hope that is evidenced in the despair of disordered desire, such that there is a loss of desire even for God, as well as a crippling of the imagination, rendering it impossible to imagine a future that differs from the past. Despair and resignation, however, are not so much opposites as they are two paths, often traversed simultaneously, to the same place, as both grant ultimacy to suffering and both result in a loss of perceived future as a direct result of suffering. Though the impact on identity of futurity is considerably more difficult to recognize because of its not-yet nature, the claim of this chapter is that the anticipated narrative of the future is as significant a dimension of identity as is the narrative of the remembered past. Insofar as suffering diminishes the ability of one who has suffered to envision a hopeful future, redemption of the memory of the past will necessarily entail the promise of a redeemed future.

Vocation: The Renewal of Hope

The nature of human identity is necessarily and complexly temporal. This temporality is not limited to remembered past or present experiences but also includes perceived notions of futurity. The temporal experience of suffering becomes a constitutive element of identity and is, therefore, necessarily part of the "all things" being made new in the redemption of our bodies. Suffering itself—in *all* of its temporal dimensions—must be redeemed if the individual who has suffered (and continues to suffer) is to be redeemed. Insofar as identity is rightly understood to be simultaneously retroactive and anticipatory, suffering damages the futurity of the sufferer in significant ways. Any account of the redemption of suffering must consider not merely the redemption of the past and present damage of suffering; it must address the future damage of suffering—the loss of hope—as well.

Forgiveness

The claim that forgiveness is a practice integral to the Christian faith is a noncontroversial assertion—almost a tautology. What exactly the practice of forgiveness means, however, is not always quite so clear.[49] Forgiveness is primarily the means by which Christians learn to tell a truthful story. As such it is neither a denial nor a condoning of the suffering of the past, nor is forgiveness a matter of forgetting or excusing the suffering of the past. In fact, forgiveness is at least as much about the future as it is about the past. Forgiveness addresses the suffering of the past by remembering it well in the present while rightly orientating one toward the future.[50] It is this future orientation of forgiveness that is crucial in learning to see redemption of the past.

Forgiveness is first and foremost a practice of truth telling; rightly naming the suffering of the past is integral to forgiveness. Forgiveness cannot mean pretending the past did not happen; nor can it be a matter of ignoring or forgetting the suffering of the past.[51] In fact, forgiveness is a form of active confrontation with the suffering of the past, and perhaps even with the perpetrator of the suffering. It is a confrontation that names the sin of the past as sin in order to overcome the evil of that past. Forgiveness cannot gloss over suffering but names the damage the suffering has caused. This naming of the damage of the past is, at least in part, for the sake of those who have caused the suffering. That is, the naming of sin that forgiveness requires is an acknowledgment of the personhood of the perpetrators of suffering. Honest confrontation with the perpetrator of suffering honors the humanity of the perpetrator.[52] Forgiveness hopes that in the naming of the damage of suffering the perpetrator will be moved to repentance, but forgiveness is not contingent upon said repentance.

In situations of profound suffering, the need to forgive the perpetrator will likely be obvious. However, what may be less apparent is the need to forgive others who may be indirectly implicated in the suffering. For example, telling a truthful story of the past may include the recognition that the perpetrator was enabled by others. Others who were in a position to intervene may have chosen not to know what was going on, not to get involved, not to act in order to prevent the perpetrator from acting.[53] Likewise, there may have even been bystanders, those who stood by and watched, participating vicariously in the violence rather than risking consequences for standing up on behalf of the vulnerable.[54] In some situations of profound suffering, there may have also been larger systemic networks of institutional structures or sociopolitical powers that, were the story truthfully narrated, bore a portion of the burden or responsibility for suffering.[55]

Perhaps as importantly as the forgiveness of the perpetrator and of others who may have participated in creating the conditions in which the suffering occurred, there may be a need for forgiving oneself. This is emphatically *not* to suggest that those who suffer are in some way at fault for their suffering. It is rather to recognize that a common response to profound suffering is to misappropriate guilt and shame.[56] Self-blame is, at least in part, an attempt at self-protection—that is, insofar as the victim can be to blame for the suffering, she could prevent a recurrent suffering simply by not repeating her past mistake. However, the propensity to blame oneself for such suffering is considerably more complex than protection from future suffering. Profound physical suffering creates conditions in which the body is often experienced as an object of shame and of ridicule. The body — which cannot, of course, be separated from the sense of self — may be blamed for its weakness, its vulnerability. That one is vulnerable is, of course, not something for which one can be culpable; however, in order to narrate the suffering truthfully, there may need to be an acknowledgment of one's vulnerability and an openness to forgiving oneself for vulnerability that is remembered as weakness.

To focus attention on the need to forgive oneself is not to suggest that such forgiveness is a private or individualistic reassurance of one's innocence, though (re)assurances of innocence may also be needed. Rather, the forgiveness of oneself is integrally connected to the practice of holy friendship *within* the community of the church. Forgiveness of oneself is perhaps best understood as a gift one receives in and through restorative relationships with others. Insofar as forgiveness is a matter of telling a truthful story, to forgive oneself may require having one's story re-narrated by truthful friends such that one is enabled to be the recipient of grace. As long as the story of suffering remains a private story — interpreted only by and through the lens of the one who suffered, and given both the temptations of self-blame and the human propensity for self-deception — the ability to narrate one's own story rightly is rather limited. Because of the isolating nature of suffering and because of the shame often involved, forgiveness may be made possible only in and through the sharing of the suffering such that the possibility of a different narration of the story of suffering is glimpsed.

Forgiveness tells a truthful story not merely in its confrontation with past suffering; forgiveness tells a truthful story in *how* it remembers. Forgiveness remembers the suffering of the past within the context of the broader narrative of God's story of redemption as one who has been incorporated into the body of Christ. As such, not only is forgiveness explicitly *not* a matter of forgetting; it is a way of learning to remember the past such that it is possible to "envision and embody a future different from the past."[57] Forgiveness is one of the means by which the church participates in the eschatological kingdom, the promised future, now. As such, forgiveness is a way of remembering that is simultaneously retrospective (remembering backward not only to the particular situations of suffering of one's own life, but to Jesus' life, death, and resurrection) and anticipatory (remembering forward into the future God has promised in Jesus' return).

Though forgiveness may indeed involve feelings of love for one's enemies, forgiveness is not limited to feelings but involves concrete acts of love as well.[58] Forgiveness is both an act of the will and a disposition developed by intentional immersion in the practices of the church.[59] Forgiveness is both a single practice and a constellation of practices. That is, forgiveness is first an act of obedience in which one who has been profoundly injured by another refuses to allow the injury to be the defining lens through which the other is viewed.

This act of obedience, however, is not a singularly individual act. Rather, it is an act undertaken within a community that is continually learning what it means both to be forgiven and to forgive. This is so because forgiveness is a gift that is primarily received through the communal formation of habits of speech and of worship, which rightly form, or re-form, one's ability to remember well. Because forgiveness is a habit, a disposition that has to be formed, it is rarely experienced instantaneously. In fact, forgiveness is as likely to be a retrospective judgment as it is a prospective intention.

In addition to being a practice learned in and through participation in a community that intentionally cultivates habits of forgiveness, forgiveness is a practice *of* the community. Forgiveness—like love and justice—is not an individual virtue, not something any one person, no matter how holy, can be expected to exhibit alone.[60] Forgiveness cannot be reduced to a choice that an individual must wrestle with alone, but is a practice of and for the entire body of Christ to wrestle with together.[61]

That forgiveness is necessarily connected to community is not incidental to forgiveness. Rather it is a reflection of the telos of forgiveness, which is the restoration of communion. This does not deny the painful reality that there are indeed situations of profound suffering in which the restoration of community with the perpetrator of the suffering is neither possible (e.g., in situations where the perpetrator is deceased) nor prudent (e.g., in situations where the perpetrator is unrepentant or unreformed and therefore continues to pose a threat of further violence).[62] But forgiveness recognizes this as a sign of the continued rupture in community that evidences the fall and *not* as the ultimate end to which Christ calls us. Forgiveness even in the midst of such situations that defy reconciliation—and perhaps *especially* in the midst of such situations—is a reminder that though forgiveness can neither undo the suffering of the past nor diminish vulnerability to suffering in the future, it can, in fact, imagine that there is hope for a future that is not bound by the suffering of the past. Forgiveness can begin to imagine the mending of relationships ruptured, and the memories shattered, by past suffering. Forgiveness may open a space for the possibility that the *ought to be*, in fact, *will be*—which is, of course, definitive of hope.

Forgiveness is how the church remembers in hope. Forgiveness is about "drawing out the sting in the memory that threatens to poison our entire existence"[63] such that it becomes possible to imagine a future that is no longer held captive by the past. Because profound suffering can lead to a crippling of the imagination such that it becomes impossible to remember a past that predates suffering or to imagine a future not still mired in that suffering, redemption necessarily involves a freeing of the imagination. Forgiveness, insofar as it creates a space for the activity of the Holy Spirit, can open up possibilities for the future that are simply unimaginable as long as the future remains clouded by the suffering of the past.

Bearing Witness

Not only can the memory of past suffering be redeemed such that one who has suffered is no longer bound by the memories of the past or isolated by those bonds, but it can be redeemed such that one who has suffered profoundly can bear witness to the hope of redemption. In so doing, one who has suffered profoundly can become a blessing for others.

Contemporary secular discourse regarding the naming of those who have experienced profound suffering has shifted away from that of "victim" to that of "survivor."[64] This linguistic shift has the advantage of defining one who has suffered in terms of strength rather than of weakness, in terms of activity rather than of passivity. Though "survivor" definitely has theological advantages over "victim" as well (particularly in terms of agency), it is still a theologically inadequate designation in large part because of the individualistic assumptions upon which it rests. The theological advantage of *witness* is that this designation necessarily both includes an element of testimony to the power of God working in and through situations of suffering and is simultaneously grounded in relationship. A "survivor" is understood simply as one who has lived another day. A survivor, therefore, may well live for herself alone. A witness, on the other hand, necessarily exists as a *living symbol* pointing others toward the redemption found in and through the love of Christ. As such, *witness* is fundamentally a teleological designation.

Witnessing is *not* coterminous with watching or seeing. To watch is to be a spectator, but to witness is to become, in a qualified but significant way, a participant. John Milbank claims that spectator violence, the nonparticipatory watching of violence, is perhaps intrinsically *more* violent than participation in acts of violence themselves.[65] Milbank's suggestion rests on his understanding that in watching violence the spectator remains detached, uninvolved, and therefore unaffected by the violence. Such detachment can render the spectator void of empathy for those who suffer violence. In fact, perhaps it can leave the spectator incapable of empathy, rendering the spectator more prone to actual violence. Milbank's claim is correct insofar as *watching* violence is not *witnessing* violence. To watch violence in a detached manner—or worse yet, in a voyeuristic manner, for sport or entertainment—is, indeed, itself a form of violence.[66] To *witness* suffering—whether one's own or that of another (and the one to whom suffering is narrated is, in fact, a witness to that suffering)—is not violence but a form of solidarity because to witness to suffering is to pronounce a judgment upon that suffering. It is a recognition that the suffering of violence is *not* God's intention.

One of the starkest and most disturbing images in *Night* is Elie Wiesel's description of the hanging of three prisoners—two grown men and one young boy. The entire prison camp is forced to witness the execution. Wiesel explains that the two adults die instantly, but the boy does not weigh enough to break his neck, so he dangles for nearly a half an hour, slowly suffocating. Wiesel, an adolescent himself at the time, later writes of looking into the child's eyes as he is marched past the barely still alive boy. Though Wiesel does not describe this moment as a moment of witness or as a moment of solidarity, it seems to me quite likely that in the moment, in the gaze of another suffering person, the little boy recognized an affirmation of his own humanity in the prisoners who met his eyes. Wiesel did not look on for sport; he was not a detached spectator but a witness to the incredible inhumanity of the child's suffering, and in that witness he was united with the boy in his suffering.[67]

In speaking of bearing witness to suffering, it is to this sense of solidarity, of validation of the humanity of the other, that is intended. When those who have suffered profoundly begin to recognize the redemption of their own suffering such that they can bear witness of that suffering to others, a solidarity is created through which hope for one's own future redemption is inextricably bound to the hope for the redemption of others. Bearing witness to suffering is always, then, an act of solidarity. Witness is that dimension of redemption that is primarily other—rather than self-directed. It is the dimension of the redemption of suffering through which the life of one who has suffered profoundly becomes, itself, a gift to others. This is not a gift in which the self is lost or negated, however, but a gift in and through which the self experiences fullness of being, redemption.

Bearing witness in the aftermath of profound suffering does not mean that one has forgotten the depth of one's suffering. It is not a denial of the intensity of the suffering or a naïve refusal to recognize the significant harm that the suffering has done and continues to do. Rather, bearing witness relies not on the delusion that evil has been overcome but on the epistemological hope that evil is not ultimately triumphant.[68] In fact, bearing witness recognizes that it is in remembering suffering well, in re-narration, that one is able to remember suffering not merely as an instrument of horrible pain but also as the vehicle for incredible grace. That suffering has not entirely prevailed leaves a space for hope, for a future that is not merely a replica of the past's suffering. This hope for the future never forgets or denies the contingent realities of past suffering, but it no longer grants suffering primacy or ultimacy. As such, while continually shaped by the past, hope is uniquely open to the promise of the future, to the new thing God is doing.

This openness to the future that acknowledges its continuity with the past allows for an ever-increasing recognition that change is possible, that the future is not merely a ceaseless repetition of the past. Significantly, the bearing witness of this reality to others who suffer is simultaneously to bear witness of this to oneself. The reception and embodiment of the new story—the second narrative of suffering—made possible in and through redemption necessarily involves a transformation of the self that may lead to further re-narration of one's story as well as to greater and deeper incorporation within communities of caring. The vocational dimension of redemption, while remaining largely dependent upon the other two, is also to some extent reciprocal with them, perhaps especially with the narrative dimension, as it is in the realization of the vocation of bearing witness that the new narrative of redemption is performed. The hope of witness, and the witness of hope, cannot be reduced to sentimentalism or blind optimism; it is an eschatological epistemology, a hope for new creation. Such hope for new creation, the hope to which redemption bears witness, is the hope that as those who have suffered are set free *from* the bondage to the suffering of the past, they are set free *for* a future that is bounded only by Christ's redeeming love.

Receiving Vocation

The experience of suffering—particularly profound suffering inflicted by the cruelty of another human being, though in no way being a chosen or desired experience—is a contingent aspect of a person's identity. Absolutely nothing can be done to change this. That is what it means to suggest that profound suffering is ontological—it becomes an integral part of *who* one is; it gets to core of *being* itself. One of the most enduring and pernicious ways in which profound suffering damages the identity of one who has suffered is by rendering the imagination void of hopeful future stories. Thus, the final aspect of the redemption of suffering is transforming it, such that it is not merely ontological but teleological. That is, the final (temporal) aspect of redeeming the memory of profound suffering is the transformation of that memory into a hope-filled vocation.

Vocation is, at root, *moreness*. Whereas the therapeutic response to suffering is adaptation, developing coping skills, the new life of redemption entails the reception of a new vocation. Vocation has to do with the flourishing of life, with Jesus' proclamation that he came to offer abundant life. The *moreness* of vocation is not the self-actualization of Maslow's hierarchy of needs.[69] Nor can this *moreness* be reduced to the consumeristic pursuit of happiness. Rather, vocation is the *moreness* that obviates the diminishment of sin and suffering by augmenting the self, not in an individualistic or narcissistic way, but in a way that is primarily teleological. Thus, the *moreness* of vocation has to do with becoming who one is called to be in and through the waters of baptism. The *moreness* of vocation is the means by which the individual participates in, and contributes to, the larger narrative of God's redeeming work in the world.

This *moreness* of new vocation does not forget the suffering of the past, but it finds creative and imaginative ways to integrate it into the new narrative of one's life.[70] Though it is in no way intended either to glorify or to justify profound suffering (nor does it offer anything like a rational explanation for such suffering), the promise of vocation is that somehow God can—and will—take the experience of suffering and use it as the soil in which something beautiful might grow.[71]

Vocation is something that is more often discovered than chosen. This is perhaps more acutely the case in the aftermath of profound suffering. Vocation as a dimension of the redemption of the memory of suffering is both discovered in and clarified by the redemptive dimensions of narration and incorporation. That is, as one continues to learn how to narrate suffering rightly as a part of the larger story of God, and as one learns what it means to be incorporated into the community of those striving to live into this larger story, one may receive the gift of vocation.

That vocation is largely a gift of redemption discovered often retrospectively does not lessen human agency in the crafting of vocation. Vocation as a discovered gift is inextricably intertwined with vocation as a choice to make something beautiful, even in the aftermath of the ugliness of suffering. Vocation understood in this way is dependent upon—and perhaps necessarily proceeded by (though in such a way as to be mutually reinforcing)—the development of agency and of trust. Agency and trust allow for hope to take root, filling in the creative gap between the *was* of suffering and the *will be* of redemption. The practices of forgiveness and witness—though by no means the only vocational practices—are both ultimately vocational acts.[72] Forgiveness and witness are ecclesial practices both rooted in an understanding of the vocational calling of discipleship while simultaneously transforming the identity of their practitioners. Witness recognizes that the present is already participating in the redemption of the past, while forgiveness, in its openness to the future, allows for the possibility of a future story unbounded by the suffering of the past.

Vocation is bound to community; it is never private. Though it may be experienced in an intensely personal and particular way, the *moreness* of vocation is for the common good, for the building up of the community.[73] Vocation is the means through which one who has suffered profoundly is enabled to become a blessing, a gift, to the church and to the world.

Imagining a future unbounded by the suffering of the past, and yet in which one continues to tell a truthful story of that suffering, is a supremely vocational act. The suffering, while being neither glorified nor justified, is the impetus behind the creation of something new, something that is intended to alleviate or prevent others from experiencing similar suffering. Vocation is an energy and a direction in which the telos of the reincorporation of suffering, even the aspects of suffering one might ardently wish could be forgotten, is participation in the creation of a new narrative.[74]

Just as it is not possible to speak of suffering in the abstract, it is not possible to speak of vocation in the abstract. What vocation means in the aftermath of situations of profound suffering necessarily depends on a constellation of factors, including the particulars of the suffering as well as the particularities of the individual, and upon how these factors interact with the creative and redemptive activity of God. The redemption of profound suffering—the reception of a new narrative, a new community, *and* a new vocation—is limited only by the divine imagination, and the eyes to see.

Conclusion

THE REDEEMING SELF

Faced with even the cruelest situations of suffering, the imaginative power of God to redeem human suffering far exceeds the most atrocious of suffering. Nothing—no situation of violence and suffering, no matter how profound—is so horrendous as to be beyond the scope of redemption.

Human identity is inherently tensed. Not only is identity experienced in terms of past, present, and future, but it is actually *constituted* by these temporal dimensions. All three elements of identity are simultaneously present at all times, and each contributes something unique to identity. The *past* is constituted by and made available through the vehicle of memory. The *present* is largely constructed in and through relationships with others. The *future* is present in the imaginative expectations for what is possible. These three elements cannot be separated from one another; they are mutually interdependent. This dissection is purely heuristic and allows for insights gleaned from the corresponding disciplines of psychology, sociology, and philosophy, which demonstrates how the experience of profound suffering impacts each temporal dimension—and thus the totality of identity—in predictable but unique ways long after the cessation of the instigating violence.

Redemption is the work God the Father continues to do in the world, making all things new as he draws them toward their telos, through the love of Christ and the power of the Holy Spirit. Given the profundity of suffering and its effects on identity, suffering cannot be redeemed in the abstract. Redemption as a new creation must involve the redemption of each temporal aspect in order for the individual whose identity is constituted by this temporality to be redeemed, to be made new.

Though the promise of redemption is ultimately an eschatological promise, it is one that has been initiated in the resurrection of Jesus and therefore can be seen—albeit often in only the faintest of shadows—now. The ability to see redemption now is primarily a matter of training in seeing what *is* rather than merely what appears to be. The practices of the church are a means of grace given by God to train the imagination such that the ongoing act of redemption comes into focus more clearly. Ecclesial practices are not magic, but they are a means by which God invites all, especially those who have suffered profoundly, to participate in the divine mystery of redemption. This neither denies nor diminishes the ability to recognize the profundity of suffering; rather, it enables suffering to be re-narrated as a smaller part of a much larger and greater story. This re-narration of suffering makes possible, and is made possible by, the incorporation of the one who has suffered in the community of the church where this new narration belongs.

Ecclesial practices that train Christians to see rightly are complex and interrelated. No practice stands alone. Each is constitutive of, and constituted by, a variety of other practices.

Likewise, no single practice develops the vision needed to see redemption. Rather, the gift given to the church is a constellation of practices, each of which is grounded both in the tradition of the church and in the particularity of the local congregation.

The practices of the church cannot be used for the sake of procuring redemption. Instead, the practices aid the church in the act of description. Description, of course, is not an objective or neutral act but an inherently theological and ethical act. Ecclesial practices supersede the competing therapeutic practices to the extent that they develop the imaginative habit of right vision. While therapeutic accounts of the healing of the damage of suffering offer, at best, the promise that one who has suffered profoundly can survive, can learn to move on despite the memory of suffering, the Christian narrative of redemption is one in which one who has suffered profoundly can learn to remember the past *as* a past that has been and is being redeemed. As such, the Christian narrative of redemption creates witnesses—those whose very lives become icons to the redeeming love of God in Christ active in the world through the power of the Holy Spirit.

The power of ecclesial practices to help those who have suffered learn to see—and thus live into—redemption now has applications in both the field of theology and that of pastoral care. The particular claim that we can, indeed, learn to see the redemption of the most profound situations of the suffering of human violence offers a lens to the wider theological questions of suffering. The point of the particularity has been to broaden the theological imagination. As the church learns to resituate the narratives of profound suffering within the wider context of God's continuing work of redemption, the ability to recognize—and therefore bear witness to—redemption may be heightened. Theology cannot be separated from pastoral care. Pastoral care is an inherently theological practice. Likewise, theology should be alert to its pastoral application. Learning to see theologically—learning to *see* redemption—in no way offers a therapeutic model for the pastoral care of those who have experienced traumatic suffering. However, recognizing the significance of rather ordinary ecclesial practices is intended to illustrate what is already going on, but it may be overlooked even, and perhaps especially, by those for whom such practices are routine.

Calling attention to the formative nature of ecclesial practices hopefully makes explicit what has been present but hidden all along.

NOTES

Introduction

1   To think that such suffering is new, or that humanity's inhumanity is somehow or other more severe or more graphic today than in the past, would be a mistake. Even the most cursory glance at history—or at the Scriptures—shows that such violence is not, in fact, new. The presumption that the contemporary world has achieved a level of mastery of the infliction of suffering unmatched by previous generations is a form of cultural myopic narcissism worthy of another study.

Stephen Pinker argues persuasively that not only is contemporary society not becoming progressively more violent, but by many standards the world is less violent now than at any time in recorded history. See Pinker, *The Better Angels of Our Nature: Why Violence Has Declined* (New York: Penguin, 2011).

2   Yann Martel, *The Life of Pi* (New York: Harcourt, 2001).

3   That learning to tell a truthful story is a crucial component of Christian theology and ethics is one of Stanley Hauerwas' primary claims and is evident throughout his corpus. See especially *Sanctify Them in the Truth: Holiness Exemplified* (Nashville: Abingdon, 1998).

4   I begin also with the presumption that the formative experience of suf-
     fering is a past-tense event—recognizing that the questions are radically
     different in ongoing situations of violence and abuse.

5   The Gospels, as well as the letters of Paul, speak of salvation in all three
     temporal senses—salvation is past tense, present tense, and future tense.
     Salvation and redemption are not strictly coterminous. For the purposes
     of this project, *salvation* is intended as an exclusively eschatological event,
     whereas redemption is intended as freedom from the bondage to past sit-
     uations of sin and suffering in the form of new life; it is our participation
     in that eschatological event now.

6   That redemption comes by and through having the eyes to see is illus-
     trated beautifully in Lois Lowry's young adult series, The Giver Quartet.
     In this series, Jonas is a young man who discovers he has the ability to
     "see beyond." This gift allows him to see things others cannot—things as
     simple as color and as complex as peace. This ability is a gift that sets him
     apart from the community and yet through which his community ulti-
     mately receives redemption. Lois Lowry, *The Giver* (New York: Houghton
     Mifflin, 1993); *Gathering Blue* (New York: Houghton Mifflin, 2000); *Mes-
     senger* (New York: Houghton Mifflin, 2004); and *Son* (New York: Hough-
     ton Mifflin, 2012).

7   In *The Politics of Jesus*, John Howard Yoder says that the present not only
     leads us to the future but is, itself, only intelligible insofar as it partic-
     ipates in God's eschatological promises. Yoder, *The Politics of Jesus: Vicit
     Agnus Noster*, 2nd ed. (Grand Rapids: Eerdmans, 1994), 241.

8   This is both a counterpoint to Dante's exhortation to abandon hope upon
     entering hell and an extension of John Howard Yoder's claim that all his-
     tory is doxology and that doxology is "a way of seeing; a grasp of which
     end is up, which way is forward." Yoder, "To Serve Our God and to
     Rule the World," in *The Royal Priesthood: Essays Ecclesiological and Ecumenical*
     (Scottdale, Pa.: Herald, 1998), 129.

9   This is contra Miroslav Volf's claim that there are some memories that are
     simply so horrible as to be irredeemable. For Volf, the memory of suffer-
     ing is antithetical to the notion of heaven to the extent that the memory of
     suffering limits the eternal experience of joy. Volf, *Exclusion and Embrace:
     A Theological Exploration of Identity, Otherness, and Reconciliation* (Nashville:
     Abingdon, 1996), chap. 3.

     The claim of this project is that there is no suffering that is irredeem-
     able. Therefore, rather than limiting joy, the memory of suffering is trans-
     formed into the memory of redeemed suffering—which is an altogether
     different type of memory.

Chapter 1

1   This is true such that not only do core tenets of every major religious
    tradition address questions of suffering but attempts to explain suffering
    could, in fact, be said to be causative agents of religion. John Bowker,
    Problems of Suffering in Religions of the World (New York: Cambridge Univer-
    sity Press, 1970).

    It is important to recognize and even to honor the impulse toward a
    desire for an explanation of suffering as a universally human impulse that
    is honored in every major religious tradition in ways appropriate (in vary-
    ing degrees) to that tradition while at the same time refusing the premise
    that suffering acts as a causative agent of the Christian faith.

2   What follows is my own somewhat loose interpretation of Aristotle on
    causality. Aristotle's treatment of causality can be found in *Physics* II 3 and
    Metaphysics V 5.

3   In other words, to understand fully the essence of the stemware requires
    seeing the stemware through quadra-focal lenses that take each cause
    into account. To leave any one cause out is to see only part of what it
    means for a lead crystal piece of stemware to be a lead crystal piece of
    stemware.

4   The reality of vulnerability is complex. In the aftermath of disasters or
    in the face of horrific suffering, vulnerability is often understood to be
    something bad, something to be avoided. So the overwhelming political
    response to 9/11 was a heightening of the nation's security alert level and
    a strengthening of military power, a collective promise that never again
    would we allow ourselves to be attacked. But minimizing vulnerability
    requires a degree of power, power that remains in the hands of the few,
    of those who are less vulnerable. In August of 2005, Hurricane Katrina
    slammed into New Orleans, making it nearly impossible for Americans
    to remain blind to the relationship between poverty (social and economic
    vulnerability) and incommensurate suffering. There are a number of
    studies on the correlation of socioeconomic status (including dynam-
    ics of race, gender, and nationality) and vulnerability to suffering. See,
    e.g., Brenda B. Lin and Philip E. Morefield, "The Vulnerability Cube:
    A Multi-dimensional Framework for Assessing Relative Vulnerability,"
    Environmental Management 48, no. 3 (2011): 631–43; and Andrew Curtis,
    Jacqueline Warren Mills, and Michael Leitner, "Katrina and Vulnerabil-
    ity: The Geography of Stress," *Journal of Health Care for the Poor and Under-
    served* 18, no. 2 (2007): 315–30.

    Vulnerability is inevitable; it is part of the human condition. And
    though suffering is only possible insofar as one is vulnerable, vulnera-
    bility is not inherently bad. Vulnerability can also be a powerful conduit
    for change and transformation, for mercy and for grace. Brene Brown

is a sociologist who writes of the social power of vulnerability in *Daring Greatly: How the Courage to Be Vulnerable Transforms the Way We Live, Love, Parent, and Lead* (New York: Gotham, 2012). And Kristine Culp offers a theological argument in favor of vulnerability as the basis of our life before God. *Vulnerability and Glory: A Theological Account* (Louisville, Ky.: Westminster John Knox, 2010).

However, many feminist theologians, social theorists, and philosophers resist the characterization of vulnerability as a positive good, arguing that such a characterization places those already at greatest risk for oppression and violence at even greater risk. For a collection of essays that address the complexities of feminism and vulnerability, see Catriona Mackenzie, Wendy Rogers, and Susan Dodds, eds., *Vulnerability: New Essays in Ethics and Feminist Philosophy* (New York: Oxford University Press, 2013).

5   Insofar as suffering has an internal logic, the grammar of that logic is sin. In what follows I hope neither to clearly separate sin from evil nor to simply collapse the categories. Though it is true that "to say 'evil' is not just to say 'sin' with a loud voice" (Samuel Wells, *God's Companions: Reimagining Christian Ethics* [Malden, Mass.: Blackwell, 2006], 113), the experience of sin and evil are inextricably linked. Any doctrine of sin must account for evil, and any theodicy must include a doctrine of sin. Sin and evil are *both* implicated in suffering. Thus sin and evil must both be considered theologically in order to consider the possibility of the redemption of suffering.

6   Robert W. Jenson argues (rightly) that "righteousness" is the proper scriptural and theological category, and that Scripture speaks of sin in a variety of different ways. What these ways have in common is that they are contrary to righteousness. Jenson, *Systematic Theology* (New York: Oxford University Press, 1997–1999), 1:72.

7   The distinction between venial and mortal sins is one of degree. Mortal sins are those sins that separate one completely from God's grace and, if not forgiven and absolved, result in damnation. Venial sins, on the other hand, are understood to result in a state of partial loss of grace. Unforgiven venial sin is not thought to result in damnation but, rather, will be purged in purgatory.

8   The seven deadly sins can be either mortal or venial, depending upon the situation. They are understood to be deadly not because of their severity but because they are understood to be the sins from which other sins flow. For more on the seven deadly sins, see William H. Willimon, *Sinning like a Christian: A New Look at the Seven Deadly Sins* (Nashville: Abingdon, 2005); and Rebecca Konyndyk DeYoung, *Glittering Vices: A New Look at the Seven Deadly Sins and Their Remedies* (Grand Rapids: Brazos, 2009).

9   Throughout the history of the church, theologians have attempted to determine the essence of sin. One way sin has historically been cast as a

noun is as perversity. This view of sin has arguably had the greatest influence on all subsequent thinking of sin as the doctrine has been further developed by a number of later theologians. Sin as perversity is derived primarily from the work of St. Augustine, who sees sin as primarily a matter of the will. The will, rightly ordered, is ordered toward the good, toward God. But Augustine understands humans to be created with the freedom to choose the good or to choose evil instead. Augustine describes sin as nothing more or less than the choice for evil over good. Such a choice for sin, though made possible by human freedom, is itself a choice for bondage. The terms *freedom* and *free will* are often used interchangeably. For Augustine, however, freedom is always the ability to choose the good, whereas free will is agency, the ability to make decisions and choices. Insofar as the will is able to choose anything less than the good, it is not, in fact, free—it lacks freedom. The difference between free will and freedom is the difference between an act freely chosen (that is, without compulsion) and an act of freedom, a choice for the good. Insofar as the will is actually free, it will in fact choose the good as only the will bound to sin chooses sin. Free will, therefore, cannot be understood to be the source or cause of sin; it is instead simply the material condition that makes sin possible. Augustine, *On Free Choice of the Will*, trans. Thomas Williams (Indianapolis: Hackett, 1993), 3.19.53. For Augustine this choice for sin is necessarily rooted in the will, in perversity, and in pride.

Much like Augustine, Reinhold Niebuhr conceives of sin largely in terms of pride. Also like Augustine, for Niebuhr it is not necessarily that sin is pride as it is that pride is the form sin often takes. Whereas Augustine sees sin as primarily rooted in a willful perversity, Niebuhr understands it to be rooted primarily in anxiety. Fallen humanity attempts to usurp God's power rather than accepting its place as created being. Niebuhr's account of sin does not render sin necessary or inevitable. Rather Niebuhr's branch of Christian Realism holds that charity, instead, is always ideally possible, though he finds it highly improbable precisely because it is an ideal. The chasm between the ideal and the real, between what could be and what appears to be, is the cause of human anxiety that inevitably leads directly to sin. See Niebuhr, *The Nature and Destiny of Man: A Christian Interpretation*, 2 vols. (Louisville, Ky.: Westminster John Knox, 1996).

For Karl Barth, sin is primarily not perversity or immorality but a refusal of grace. Barth speaks of sin as pride, sloth, and falsity, but at the root he sees each of these as being hostility to grace born out of ingratitude. It is both interesting and instructive that Barth does not address the question of sin on its own. Sin is addressed in *Church Dogmatics* as subsections under the Doctrine of Reconciliation because sin, Barth holds, cannot be recognized outside of God's gracious gift of reconciliation, Barth understands this starting place to be significant. By placing the conversation of sin in the context of a greater conversation of reconciliation Barth reframes the discussion. Barth follows Augustine in suggesting that sin makes no sense, that it is theologically absurd. In fact Barth even suggests that sin is an ontological impossibility. Again, following Augustine, Barth understands the real to be that which endures, that which God will sustain eschatalogically. Sin, therefore, while having very real effects and existing in a transitory fashion, is, in an ontological sense, not possible as it is not something ultimately sustained by God and therefore cannot endure in the eschaton. Insofar as sin is impossible and yet it is, Barth refers to sin as the impossible possibility. See *Church Dogmatics* IV/2, 495.

George Hunsinger, in *How to Read Karl Barth: The Shape of His Theology* (New York: Oxford University Press, 1991), suggests that the key to distinguishing between Niebuhr and Barth lies in their respective understandings of "impossible possibility." Whereas Barth's theological project was thoroughly theocentric and christocentric, Niebuhr's was thoroughly anthropocentric. For Barth this means that God is the objective measure for reality, so when Barth thinks of what it means for something to be real he holds it in opposition to that which is unreal, which he understands to be anything in opposition to God's grace—i.e., sin. Niebuhr, on the other hand, based his conception of the real on what he saw evidenced in human beings and human relationships. His anthropological assumptions made sin the self-evidently real that he saw in opposition not to the unreal but to the ideal. For Niebuhr love is the human ideal, but sin is the human reality. Love, therefore, is for Niebuhr the "impossible possibility" instead of sin. Niebuhr, *An Interpretation of Christian Ethics* (New York: Harper & Brothers, 1935).

10   John Wesley also couches sin primarily in verbal form. Wesley distinguishes between "sins properly so-called" and "sins improperly so-called." Sins properly so-called are willful transgressions of known divine command and deserve punishment, whereas sins improperly so-called are unintentional transgressions of God's law. Implicit in this distinction is the claim that sin is, first and foremost for Wesley, as it is for Aquinas, a morally bad act. Wesley understands both types of sin to require the atoning grace of Jesus, but juridical culpability applies only to sins properly so-called. He conceded that the sins improperly so-called might in fact be sins, but he held that insofar as they are not a deliberate and knowing violation of God's law they are not sin in the sense that the Bible uses the word. Wesley held essentially the same position on reason and will held by both Aquinas and Augustine, though he did not deny that the fall damaged the freedom of the human will. Wesley held that the human will

was capable of making choices for the good and could therefore be held responsible for the intentional choices made. See Albert C. Outler and Richard P. Heitzenrater, eds., *John Wesley's Sermons: An* Anthology (Nashville: Abingdon, 1991).

11 However, there are a variety of ways to understand the cause of the son's suffering. Mark Allan Powell, for instance, suggests that the text actually offers three different, equally valid, explanations for the son's suffering: he squandered all he had in dissolute living, no one would give him anything to eat, and there was a famine in the land. These alternate interpretations of the son's suffering render suspect any simple causal effect between the son's behavior and his subsequent suffering. Powell, *What Do They Hear? Bridging the Gap between Pulpit and Pew* (Nashville: Abingdon, 2007), chap. 2.

12 I am aware that many New Testament scholars consider this passage a later interpolation rather than a part of the original Johannine text. Regardless, it is a part of the Christian canon and tradition and is interesting to consider in light of the present discussion.

13 These are interesting stories to consider precisely because Jesus calls into question the assumption that the sinful act necessarily correlates to the suffering of divine punishment. However, they seem to stand in contradiction to John 5, where Jesus heals the paralyzed man by the sheep gate and then tells him, "Do not sin any more, so that nothing worse happens to you" (John 5:14).

14 J. Louis Martyn understands the condition of sin to be such that it has morphed into a power, an invading power that has infiltrated the good creation, leaving all of creation in bondage to this alien power—or condition—of sin. See Martyn, *Galatians* (New York: Doubleday, 1997).

Walter Wink offers the most complete and well-known argument of sin as "powers and principalities." Wink understands the powers to be a part of the fallen creation, a created good that has been turned toward evil. The powers, as Wink understands them, are more than the sum of their parts. The powers take on a new life, a new power that is invasive and accounts for experiences of systemic evil. See esp. Wink, *Naming the Powers: The Language of Power in the New Testament* (Philadelphia: Fortress, 1984).

15 Luther suggests we even sin when we do good. Martin Luther, *Luther Works: With Introductions and Notes*, Vol. 25, *Lectures on Romans, Glosses and Scholia*, ed. Jacob Preus (St. Louis, Mo.: Concordia, 1972), 276.

16 Sin as intention is best illustrated by Immanuel Kant. Kant understands moral law to be autonomous from divine (or human) will. The moral law is a priori and as such cannot be verified through sensory experience but can be intuited and confirmed as both necessary and universal by

means of reason. Kant's ethic is exclusively deontological. We do the good because it is our duty to do so. And precisely because it is our duty, we are capable of, in fact, doing the good. It would make no reasonable sense to suggest that what ought to be done cannot, in fact, be done. However, in Kant's thinking it is not merely the carrying out of one's moral obligation that is necessary. It is equally necessary to do one's duty precisely because it is a duty. Said differently, for Kant the intention behind the doing of the right action is a key ingredient to making the moral act moral. To do the good for the wrong reason (i.e., in order to be happy, to be thought well of, etc.) is to sin. The only moral reason for performing a moral act is because it is one's duty, because it is the right thing to do. Insofar as other motivations and deliberations enter into moral acts, the acts themselves become corrupted. Kant, *Critique of Pure Reason*, trans. J. M. D. Meiklejohn (London: Henry G. Bohn, 1855).

Sin as being relationally challenged has its roots in the creation story. Genesis tells the story of humanity as being relationally constituted. Adam and Eve are created in relation to God and to one another. The separation between Adam and Eve and the enmity between their offspring and the serpent are perhaps most often interpreted as being a result of sin. That is, the rupture in relationship is understood as a punishment for their disobedience. However, a careful reading of Genesis 3 suggests that the rupture in relationship is not a result or punishment for sin but rather the form of their sin. The cunning of the snake and the subsequent disobedience of Adam and Eve are best seen as symptoms of the rupture of sin. Much like Augustine's claim that sin makes no sense, that it is absurd, and Barth's claim that sin is the impossible possibility, there is no rational explanation of the presence of sin in the garden that causes Adam and Eve to relate to God and to one another in a sinful manner.

The recognition that sin is a descriptor of human relationships, particularly as they are damaged in and through violence, as a result of the fall has been explored by a number of contemporary theologians, most notably Marjorie Hewitt Suchocki, *The Fall to Violence: Original Sin in Relational Theology* (New York: Continuum, 2004); and Matt Jenson, *The Gravity of Sin: Augustine, Luther and Barth on* Homo incurvatus in se (New York: T&T Clark, 2006).

17 Paul Tillich explains that though most Christians have been taught to think of sin in terms of action, a catalogue of dos and don'ts, to speak of sin as an act is to miss the point entirely; in fact to speak of sin in such a way is to trivialize its reality. This power within us to sin is the human condition in which the resultant state of sin is one marked primarily by isolation, not only from one another but even from ourselves. Not only can Tillich not accept sin as merely a verb; he also cannot accept sin as

merely a question of fallen will, precisely because in sin "we experience a power that dwells in us and directs our will against itself." Sin, then, is a description not of an individualistic struggle to will and do rightly, but it is a description of the diminution of the flourishing of human relationship intended by God. See Tillich, *The Eternal Now* (New York: Scribner, 1963), chap. 4.

Rudolf Bultmann's conception of sin is even more explicitly existentialist than Tillich's. For Bultmann sin has to do with the way in which one is oriented toward one's self. The human condition is one of being bounded by time and, moreover, by one's experience of time. Authenticity and self-actualization are humanity's telos, which is symbolized in freedom. However, insofar as any individual understands him/herself in terms set by the prevailing culture rather than the individual's freedom, the individual experiences a form of bondage in which the self is frozen in time, as it were, responding to new situations from an outdated and inauthentic perspective. For Bultmann sin is largely a matter of being defined by one's past in such a way as to limit one's freedom to exist rightly in the present and to be oriented rightly toward the future. Such bondage to the past represents a lack of authentic self-understanding and creates an internal state of anxiety. See Bultmann, *Existence and Faith: Shorter Writings of Rudolf Bultmann*, trans. Schubert M. Ogden (New York: Meridian, 1960).

18   Stanley Hauerwas challenges the secular notion that all suffering, particularly that which can be attributed to finitude, is to be categorically avoided and that medicine is the primary means by which suffering can ultimately be alleviated. The problem with the contemporary approach to medicine as the redemptive means by which suffering is to be ultimately relieved is that it rests on the presumption that autonomy is a—if not the—primary human virtue. Contra this notion of autonomy, Hauerwas repeatedly offers the L'Arche communities as exemplars of the Christian response to the vulnerability of what is perceived as the suffering of human finitude. See Hauerwas, *Suffering Presence: Theological Reflections on Medicine, the Mentally Handicapped, and the Church* (Notre Dame, Ind.: University of Notre Dame Press, 1986); idem, *Naming the Silences: God, Medicine, and the Problem of Suffering* (Grand Rapids: Eerdmans, 1990); and Stanley Hauerwas and Jean Vanier, *Living Gently in a Violent World: The Prophetic Witness of Weakness* (Downers Grove, Ill.: InterVarsity, 2008).

19   Vulnerability, of course, is not limited to humanity but applies to all of creation. Finitude, therefore, is not limited to the vulnerability of humanity but includes the suffering of all that is. Therefore, suffering as a result of various ecological and weather-related disasters as well as suffering within the animal kingdom would fall here as well.

20 Susan Nelson Dunfee refers to this as "ambiguous creation," and Karl Barth as the "shadow side" of creation. The problem with both is the implication that the suffering of finitude is necessarily built into the fabric of creation rather than a reflection of the perversion of God's created intent. See Dunfee, "The Sin of Hiding: A Feminist Critique of Reinhold Niebuhr's Account of the Sin of Pride," *Soundings: An Interdisciplinary Journal* 65, no. 3 (1982); and Barth, *Church Dogmatics* III/3, 50.

The suffering of human finitude and the suffering of human cruelty are equally as difficult to distinguish from each other. Human cruelty—or at least human hard-heartedness—often contributes to the suffering of human finitude, as it is those who are already most vulnerable in society (the poor, the elderly, the sick, and young children)who are most often also the victims of human cruelty.

21 Or, if they are to be spoken of in terms of "natural," this must be understood in a carefully qualified sense that they are a part of the "natural" world postfall and are therefore not a part of the natural world as God created and intended it. This, of course, leaves open questions about God's role in the face of disasters. In what is both a deeply theological and profoundly pastoral text that responds to questions of God's presence or absence in the midst of the Asian tsunami of 2004—a tsunami that killed upward of a quarter of a million people—David Bentley Hart insists that natural disasters cannot be attributed to God. Furthermore, he insists that these evils and their concomitant suffering have no divine purpose—that they can neither be attributed to God's inscrutable will nor be explained as a form of divine retribution—but are, rather, overwhelming material evidence of the rebellion of all of creation. Hart, *The Doors of the Sea: Where Was God in the Tsunami?* (Grand Rapids: Eerdmans, 2005).

22 A brief chronological narrative account of the history of the church's martyrs that illustrates this view of suffering can be found in Mark Camp Water, *The New Encyclopedia of Christian Martyrs* (Grand Rapids: Baker, 2001).

23 See, e.g., Acts 5:41: "As they left the council, they rejoiced that they were considered worthy to suffer dishonor for the sake of the name." See also 2 Thess 1:4-5. Luther considered suffering to be a necessary component of the Christian life. In fact he includes suffering as one of the definitive "marks of the church." See Mary E. Hinkle, *Signs of Belonging: Luther's Marks of the Church and the Christian Life* (Minneapolis: Augsburg Fortress, 2003), chap. 8.

Of course, seeing suffering as a mark of special election is not restricted to Christian teachings. Folk wisdom—as evidenced by expressions such as "Only the good die young"—often suggests that a select few, by virtue of their innocence, are special enough to suffer in unmerited and poignant ways. This is a common response to the suffering of young children who are diagnosed with life-threatening illnesses as well as in response to early and unexpected deaths of adults considered to be still in their primes.

24 Suffering for Jesus' sake may indeed be the calling of a Christian, but to conflate one's own suffering with the redemptive work of Christ is troublesome both because it minimizes the human need for Christ and because it creates a space for the exploitation of the vulnerable by those in positions of greater power. Nancy Pineda-Madrid explores ways that the misguided glorification of martyrdom unjustly perpetuates suffering for vulnerable groups, particularly poor women of color, in *Suffering and Salvation in Ciudad Juárez* (Minneapolis: Fortress, 2011).

   Traditional Roman Catholic teaching understands *any* suffering, not just that which results from persecution for faithful discipleship, to be redemptive insofar as it is offered up in union with Christ's sufferings. Liguori Publications, *Catechism of the Catholic Church* (Liguori, Mo.: Liguori, 1994), §1505.

25 Elizabeth A. Castelli offers a pre-Constantinian overview of the Christian experience of martyrdom. In it she argues that martyrs are formed by the particular communities of which they are a part and that the stories of the martyrs played a crucial role in shaping the church in the midst of persecution. Castelli, *Martyrdom and Memory: Early Christian Culture Making* (New York: Columbia University Press, 2004).

26 Alice Sebold's novel *Lucky* gets its title precisely from such a response. While a college freshman, Alice is violently sexually assaulted. A police officer who comes to the hospital to take her statement, upon seeing how badly she is beaten, tells her she is "lucky" that she was not hurt even more severely, that she is, in fact, lucky to be alive. As Alice, of course, experienced her assault as anything but lucky, the title of the book is intended to be bitterly ironic. Sebold, *Lucky* (Boston: Back Bay, 1999).

27 See, e.g., Heb 12:7-11. Though, at times suffering is imaged as a warning for others. For instance, in the fifth chapter of Acts, Ananias and Sapphira sell a plot of land and lie to the church about the proceeds and are immediately struck dead. Clearly neither Ananias nor Sapphira learned much from their suffering, but the community did, "and great fear seized all who heard what had happened" (Acts 5:5). In his healing miracles, Jesus, at times, appears to associate sin and suffering, equating healing with the forgiveness of sins. In his healing miracles, such as when Jesus heals the paralytic, Jesus appears to associate sin and suffering, equating the healing with the forgiveness of sins (Matt 9, Mark 2, and Luke 5). However, in speaking of the eighteen who are killed by the tower of Siloam, he refuses any direct calculus between the two (Luke 13:1-5).

Likewise, in the Gospel of John, Jesus refuses the equating of blindness with sin (John 9:3).

28 "Theodicy" is theological shorthand for the theological questions surrounding the problem of evil. If God is both benevolent and omnipotent, then how and why do sin, evil, and suffering exist? The three statements "God is good," "God is powerful," and "Bad things happen" can be experienced as logically incoherent. Theodicy is the theological attempt to reconcile the seeming contradiction. Though the term was coined by Gottfried Leibniz in 1710 as a title to a treatise dedicated to wrestling with the problem, the history of theodicy is as ancient and as complex as Scripture. St. Augustine (and a large strand of Western Christianity following Augustine) argued that at the moment of creation there was no sin, no evil, no suffering. But that in the fall of Adam and Eve sin entered the world and thus "original sin" is one of the oldest theodicies. Irenaeus, on the other hand, argued that God allowed for the presence of sin and evil because, though humans were created in God's image and likeness, this image and likeness had to be grown into. Wrestling with sin and evil (and having the free will to do so) allows humans to mature spiritually. For more on the distinction between Augustine and Irenaeus, see John Hick, *Evil and the God of Love* (New York: Palgrave Macmillan, 2010), chap. 11.

Free will, which is crucial to Irenaeus' theodicy, is further developed by Alvin Plantinga. Plantinga suggests what is known as the "free will defense," which argues that God created humans as moral agents with whom God wants to be in relationship and thus we cannot be forced to act in accordance with the will of God (a self-limiting power) as a forced will is not a free act of a moral agent. Plantinga, *God, Freedom, and Evil* (Grand Rapids: Eerdmans, 1977), chaps. 4 and 8.

The so-called new atheists claim that their atheism is grounded purely in science and reason; a key common thread through the various new atheists' philosophies is the claim that belief in God, as expressed through the practice of religion, is the primary cause of moral evil. (The new atheist, in other words, would deny the validity of what follows.) It is possible, however, to argue that the problem of theodicy—particularly in terms of natural evil—underwrites at least some of the concerns of contemporary atheism. That there is no rational, compelling explanation for suffering plays a significant role in the atheist argument: "In a universe of blind physical forces and genetic replication, some people are going to get hurt, other people are going to get lucky, and you won't find any rhyme or reason in it, nor any justice. The universe we observe had precisely the properties we would expect if there is, at bottom, no design, no purpose, no evil and no good, nothing but blind pitiless indifference."

Richard Dawkins, *River out of Eden: A Darwinian View of Life* (New York: Basic, 1995), 133. See also Dawkins, *The God Delusion* (New York: First Mariner, 2006); and Christopher Hitchens, *God Is Not Great: How Religion Poisons Everything* (New York: Hachette, 2007).

29 The book of Job is perhaps the most oft-referenced scriptural story of suffering. In the story Job's friends try to make sense of Job's suffering by determining both an efficient and a final cause—the sin that would give the suffering some semblance of sense. The presumption is that suffering must have a root cause and that this cause can be discovered. Further, the assumption seems to be that if the cause of suffering can be discovered, it can be remedied, alleviating present suffering and preventing similar future suffering. However, David B. Burrell claims that using the book of Job to find meaning for suffering is misguided because the key exegetical point of Job is that in the midst of inexplicable suffering Job speaks *to* not *about* God. The witness of Job—and the greater witness of Scripture—is that God is present with humanity in suffering, that God's response to human suffering is not explanation but incarnation. Burrell, *Deconstructing Theodicy: Why Job Has Nothing to Say to the Puzzle of Suffering* (Grand Rapids: Brazos, 2008).

30 In what is arguably the most well-known and influential book to wrestle with questions of unjust and unprovoked suffering since the book of Job, this is precisely what Harold S. Kushner attempts to do. Unable to find an intelligible explanation for his own suffering of the loss of a son, Kushner determines that the only explanation for suffering is found in a combination of totally random bad luck and a limitation in God to prevent all suffering. Kushner, *When Bad Things Happen to Good People* (New York: Schocken, 1981).

   Despite its widespread popularity and use in pastoral circles both Jewish and Christian, Kushner's explanation is theologically inadequate. He presents himself a false dichotomy in the face of suffering—"I can worship a God who hates suffering but cannot eliminate it more easily than I can worship a God who chooses to make children suffer and die, for whatever exalted reason" (147). Any theological explanation that pits God's goodness against God's omnipotence is based on a false premise and is therefore logically bound to be inadequate.

   Similarly, Kenneth Surin rightly argues against the free will defense of Plantinga. Surin argues that the free will defense is misguided, as is any attempt at theodicy, insofar as it is intellectual gymnastics designed to exculpate God. Rather than defending God, who needs no human defense. The message of Scripture is not a defense of God but a call to conversion, turning again to the one who continues to draw us into relationship. Surin, *Theology and the Problem of Evil* (Eugene, Ore.: Wipf & Stock, 1986).

31 Hannah Arendt explores notions of power, force, violence, and vulnerability, and suggests that the use of violence is necessarily antithetical to genuine power, especially when used against the vulnerable. Reliance on physical force or violence is an admission that one is, in fact, otherwise powerless. Thus, no amount of power can make one impervious to suffering. Arendt, *On Violence* (Orlando, Fla.: Harcourt, 1969).

32 Questions of power and vulnerability are necessarily complex as all notions of power are inextricable from the social and political contexts within which they exist. Likewise, what it means to be vulnerable is not absolutely clear-cut but to a large extent a context-laden experiential reality. In her essay "Kenosis and Subversion," Sarah Coakley addresses the theological dangers of either demonizing or glorifying vulnerability, with particular attention to the deleterious impact of each on a well-reasoned, orthodox Christian feminism, suggesting that either extreme necessarily entraps the conversation in victimology. Coakley offers a third way of viewing vulnerability, something she refers to as the "paradox of power and vulnerability" in which, following Foucault, she suggests that no one is without both power and vulnerability, and thus, discourse on power and vulnerability can never be a matter of simple division by gender, race, class, or any other category. Rather, in "Creaturehood before God," Coakley speaks of dependence—upon God, upon one another individually, and upon society as a whole—as integral to what it means to be created by God. The vulnerability is created by God and, subsequently exploited, does not suggest that the exploitation of vulnerability is God's created intention for God's creatures. Coakley, *Powers and Submissions: Spirituality, Philosophy and Gender*, Challenges in Contemporary Theology (Malden, Mass.: Blackwell, 2002); as well as her *God, Sexuality, and the Self: An Essay 'On the Trinity'* (Cambridge: Cambridge University Press, 2013).

33 There is a growing recognition within the medical profession of the significance of the stories behind illness and injury as illustrated by the relatively new study of "Narrative Medicine." See, e.g., Lewis Mehl-Madrona, *Narrative Medicine: The Use of History and Story in the Healing Process* (Rochester, Vt.: Bear, 2007); and Rita Charon, *Narrative Medicine: Honoring the Stories of Illness* (New York: Oxford University Press, 2006).

34 For more on overcoming suffering, see Dorothee Sölle, *Suffering* (Philadelphia: Fortress, 1975). Sölle divides suffering into three phases. The first is one of "mute suffering" in which the sufferer is unable to give expression to the suffering. The second is a stage of lament in which the suffering is expressed, sometimes in little more than cries of pain. This stage, however, is critical because Sölle suggests that it is only in lamenting suffering

that the sufferer can begin to envision that circumstances might be different. And the final stage is one in which the sufferer seeks to change the situation causing the suffering.

I find Sölle's breakdown of the phases of suffering to be helpful and instructive, and to some extent they will guide my thinking in this project. However, for Sölle the onus of alleviating the suffering is primarily on the sufferer, and God is understood to be a powerless participant in our suffering. While affirming God's presence in human suffering and with the sufferer, I want to suggest that God's very presence is the power to heal the suffering. The onus for change is not on the sufferer but on God and, to a lesser extent, on Christ's body on earth, the church.

35 Though in this study the use of the word "trauma" is not restricted to its medical or psychiatric technical sense, insofar as trauma necessarily results in wounding, not mere injury, the following works on trauma study inform the thinking on the importance of considering context in relation to suffering: Serene Jones, *Trauma and Grace: Theology in a Ruptured World* (Louisville, Ky.: Westminster John Knox, 2009); Shelly Rambo, *Spirit and Trauma: A Theology of Remaining* (Louisville, Ky.: Westminster John Knox, 2010); Cathy Caruth, *Trauma: Explorations in Memory* (Baltimore: Johns Hopkins University Press, 1995); idem, *Unclaimed Experience: Trauma, Narrative, and History* (Baltimore: Johns Hopkins University Press, 1996); and Judith Lewis Herman, *Trauma and Recovery* (New York: Basic, 1997).

36 American Psychiatric Association, *Diagnostic and Statistical Manual of Mental Disorders: DSM-IV* (Washington, D.C.: American Psychiatric Association, 2000), 309.81.

37 American Psychiatric Association, *Diagnostic and Statistical Manual of Mental Disorders: DSM-III* (Washington, D.C.: American Psychiatric Association, 1987), 236 (emphasis added).

38 According to the 2010 Center for Disease Control (CDC) report, nearly 20 percent of all women in the United States have been raped while 36 percent of women and 29 percent of men have been victims of intimate partner physical domestic violence. See M. C. Black et al., *The National Intimate Partner and Sexual Violence Survey: 2010 Summary Report* (Atlanta: Centers for Disease Control and Prevention, 2011). What these statistics suggest is that at least a quarter, perhaps as much as one-third, of the U.S. population has experienced, or will experience, traumatic violence at some point in their lives—problematizing the defining of trauma as something outside the statistical norm of human experience.

The *DSM-V* has significantly expanded its treatment of trauma and "stressor-related disorders" in recognition of the statistical frequency of trauma-related psychological problems. American Psychiatric

Association, *Diagnostic and Statistical Manual of Mental Disorders: DSM-V* (Washington, D.C.: American Psychiatric Association, 2013).

39   The suggestion that trauma is normal (i.e., commonly experienced) risks the implication that it is, therefore, normative (i.e., an intended part of the created order). This is, of course, the logic that David Hume refuted in his dictum that an ought cannot be derived from an is. Hume, *A Treatise of Human Nature* (1739–1740). Aside from, and of considerably greater theological import than, the logical flaw of the suggestion that trauma is normal, however, is the recognition that such goes against the scriptural witness that God created the world good and desires, not trauma and suffering, but abundant life for all of God's creatures. That profound suffering may be statistically within the realm of the normal does not imply that it is within the realm of God's desires.

40   I recognize the complexity of intentionality. Humans have a remarkable capacity for self-deception and are often only semi-aware—at best—of intentions. Furthermore, much human cruelty can, and is, masked by a belief that the intentions behind the act are, in fact, good. However, in speaking of the problem of profound suffering, I restrict my focus to the narrower category of cruelty that is experienced by the sufferer as having been knowingly and willfully inflicted. This narrower focus is not to deny the very realness of the suffering of natural disasters, car accidents, or impersonal events. It is, instead, to suggest that the most profound, the most damaging, and the most difficult to redeem suffering is that which is experienced as a personal assault.

41   "Physical pain is able to obliterate psychological pain because it obliterates all psychological content, painful, pleasurable, and neutral." Elaine Scarry, *The Body in Pain: The Making and Unmaking of the World* (New York: Oxford University Press, 1985), 34.

Similarly, Leonard Shengold speaks of child abuse as a form of "soul murder" because of the psychic terror caused when extreme physical pain is inflicted by those whom the child should be able to trust most. Shengold, *Soul Murder: The Effects of Childhood Abuse and Deprivation* (New York: Ballantine, 1989).

42   Illness, though physical, is not profound suffering per my definition. Because it is not intentionally inflicted, illness does not necessarily include elements of psychic or social suffering. It is, in fact, quite possible for situations of illness to be experienced in ways in which little or no psychic or social suffering occurs, and perhaps even in ways that bring about psychic or social healing.

43   Psychologists have long recognized the role of shame and secrecy in complicating recovery from trauma. For a helpful recent collection of essays directed toward clinicians and addressing the problem of shame and

secrecy, see Jeffrey Kauffman, ed., *The Shame of Death, Grief, and Trauma* (New York: Routledge, 2010).

44 The poignancy and power of novelists such as Alice Walker and Toni Morrison, for example, is in large part due to their remarkable ability to narrate profound suffering against the Dickensian backdrop of insidious societal violence of poverty and prejudice without the triumph of the human spirit theme prevalent in Dickens.

In *The Bluest Eye*, e.g., the preadolescent girl Pecola is savagely raped by her father. This rape, and the subsequent destruction of Pecola's identity, is the foreground of the novel. But the novel's setting makes clear that the racism, sexism, and poverty of Pecola's environment are a crucible for the violence of suffering. Morrison, *The Bluest Eye* (New York: Holt, Rinehart & Winston, 1970).

45 This is, in a sense, analogous to Elijah's demonstration of YHWH's power to the priests of Baal. Elijah challenges the priests to make sacrifice to Baal and call fire down on the altar. When Baal does not reply, Elijah mocks the priests, suggesting that perhaps their god is asleep or has wandered away from them. Then, Elijah makes a similar sacrifice on an altar to YHWH but has the altar drenched with water first, such that a trench of water surrounds the altar. Only after the altar is saturated does Elijah pray to YHWH, and "then the fire of the LORD fell and consumed the burnt offering, the wood, the stones, and the dust, and even licked up the water that was in the trench" (1 Kgs 18:20-39). Elijah's point in going to these extreme measures in preparing the altar was to illustrate that any fire was, indeed, an act of YHWH as no other god could possibly be capable of such a demonstration of power. Similarly, the choice to focus on situations of profoundest suffering is to suggest that the redemption of these situations is never a matter of time healing all wounds or even of the best of human therapeutic intentions and interventions but always evidence of the power of God's redemptive love.

Chapter 2

1 However, that the world is not as it should be is the beginning point for much of liberation and feminist theology and ethics. Though by no means an exhaustive list, for the early classics in liberation theology, see Paulo Freire, *Pedagogy of the Oppressed*, trans. Myra Bergman Ramos, 30th anniv. ed. (New York: Continuum, 2000); and Gustavo Gutiérrez, *A Theology of Liberation: History, Politics, and Salvation* (London: SCM Press, 1998). For contemporary work that continues to argue theology and ethics explicitly from a perspective that the world, particularly in its acceptance of violence against the vulnerable as normal, is not as it is intended by God to be, see Miguel De La Torre, *Doing Christian Ethics from the Margins*, 2nd ed.

(Maryknoll, N.Y.: Orbis, 2014); Pamela Cooper-White, *The Cry of Tamar: Violence against Women and the Church's Response*, 2nd ed. (Minneapolis: Fortress, 2012); and Elizabeth Gerhardt, *The Cross and Gendercide: A Theological Response to Global Violence against Women and Girls* (Downers Grove, Ill.: InterVarsity, 2014).

2   In Jeremiah, God is speaking to Judah in exile. Walter Brueggemann understands this passage to be pointing Judah to God for Judah's future because Judah is in utter despair of the possibility of a future in exile: "Precisely in a situation of hopelessness, Yahweh is announced to be the one who will overcome hopelessness and open a new possibility to Judah." Brueggemann, *A Commentary on Jeremiah: Exile and Homecoming* (Grand Rapids: Eerdmans, 1998), 259. Similarly, in situations of seemingly irredeemable suffering, it is God—and only God—who is able to overcome hopelessness and offer the possibility of new life, of new creation, to those who have suffered.

3   "Hope is what you get when you suddenly realize that a different worldview is possible, a worldview in which the rich, the powerful, and the unscrupulous do not after all have the last word." N. T. Wright, *Surprised by Hope: Rethinking Heaven, the Resurrection, and the Mission of the Church* (New York: HarperCollins, 2008), 75. I explore theological virtue of hope and its role in redemption in much greater detail in chap. 5.

4   The terms "redemption" and "salvation" are often used interchangeably. I will use "salvation" to refer to the ultimate eschatological reality and "redemption" to refer to the ongoing experience of this reality. This distinction is, in a sense, purely heuristic. Though in this project I do not focus on eschatology proper, everything I claim in this project is true only to the extent that the eschatological promises of the gospel are true. This project is an extended close reading of St. Paul's declaration that "now is the day of salvation" (2 Cor 6:2) in which I consider what the outworking of the promise of salvation looks like.

    Hans Schwarz suggests that there is a reciprocal relationship between eschatology and all other human understanding. How we understand the eschatological promise of the gospel shapes how we see, understand, and even experience reality. And how we see, understand, and even experience reality shapes our eschatology. My hope is that in learning to see, understand, and even experience suffering as something that is being redeemed, we are enabled to recognize the "now" of salvation. See Schwarz, *Eschatology* (Grand Rapids: Eerdmans, 2000).

5   "I am about to do a new thing; now it springs forth, do you not perceive it?" (Isa 43:19). In the context of Isaiah, this new thing YHWH is doing "is a new Exodus, an emancipation from Babylon not unlike the ancient emancipation from Egypt. The new thing, however, is not a thin, isolated

historical event. It is rather a cosmic transformation . . . that will make new life possible." Walter Brueggemann, *Isaiah 40–66* (Louisville, Ky.: Westminster John Knox, 1998), 59.

6 Robert Jenson offers the following identification of the Christian God: "God is whoever raised Jesus from the dead, having before raised Israel from Egypt." Jenson, *Systematic Theology*, 1:63. That God brings new life out of suffering does not make suffering a prior condition to redemption. God's power in the Exodus was not contingent upon Israel's enslavement; it was God's refusal to allow Pharaoh to thwart God's plans for God's people. Similarly, the crucifixion of Jesus was not a necessary part of the divine drama as if God needed Jesus to die in order that God could demonstrate divine power in and through the resurrection. The resurrection is not the act of a manipulative bully but a divine refusal to allow violence and death to get the last word. Likewise, to suggest that God brings new life out of suffering does not mean that God wills suffering so that God can swoop in heroically and heal those who suffer. Rather, it is to suggest that suffering may be the material God uses *not* because God needs our suffering but because suffering is the reality in which we find ourselves and thus it is where God finds us. God takes the raw materials of our lives—even the rawest of materials—and uses this to create new life.

7 For Karl Barth the reality of redemption hinges on nothing other than the event of Jesus; our apprehension of this event is, in many ways, inconsequential. Barth's claim that redemption is achieved in the event of Jesus has the potential to be interpreted as an overly realized eschatology, as a claim that redemption now is merely the inevitable outworking of an eschatological reality. That this is possibly so does not, however, mean that it is necessarily so. The claim that redemption is an objective reality is a recognition of both God's sovereignty and good will. That redemption is *not* self-evident is a denial of an overly realized eschatology. Clearly the kingdom of God is not yet fully realized. My appropriation of Barth's understanding of redemption as an objective reality, independent of empirical evidence, is a statement of faith and hope even (perhaps especially) in the midst of situations of profound suffering that seem to render such faith and hope naïve at best. See Barth, *Church Dogmatics* III/2, 586; IV/1, 547; IV/2, 296; IV/3, 1050; and idem, *The Epistle to the Romans*, ed. Sir Edwyn Clement Hoskyns (London: Oxford University Press, 1933).

8 That salvation comes through Jesus is the primary claim of the Christian faith. How this is so, however, is less clear. There are a number of models of atonement, each of which focuses on different aspects of the Christ event—incarnation, life, crucifixion, and resurrection—as the locus of salvation. It is instructive that the church has never embraced

any particular doctrine of atonement. For an overview of atonement theory, see David A. Brondos, *Fortress Introduction to Salvation and the Cross* (Minneapolis: Fortress, 2007); and William C. Placher, *Jesus the Savior: The Meaning of Jesus Christ for Christian Faith* (Louisville, Ky.: Westminster John Knox, 2001).

9 Miroslav Volf, e.g., suggests that the memory of suffering—not the suffering itself—calls into question the possibility of redemption. He insists that by definition heaven means no memory of suffering or, conversely, that the memory of suffering precludes the possibility of redemption. See Volf, *Exclusion and Embrace : A Theological Exploration of Identity, Otherness, and Reconciliation* (Nashville: Abingdon, 1996), esp. p. 135; and idem, *The End of Memory: Remembering Rightly in a Violent World* (Grand Rapids: Eerdmans, 2006).

   In *Imagining Redemption*, David Kelsey tackles this question directly, suggesting that if redemption is to have any meaning it must include even the most difficult situations of human suffering. Kelsey addresses this by asking what difference Jesus makes now, on Earth—not merely in heaven or in the eschaton. Kelsey's brief but insightful book is an extended treatment of his claim that there is "no Christian point of view . . . abstracted from the messy particularities of life," and that whatever difference Jesus makes, he must make both within and to those messy particularities. Kelsey, *Imagining Redemption* (Louisville, Ky.: Westminster John Knox, 2005), 4.

10 Koine Greek has two ways to render the English "but." The first is *de*, which is a mild conjunction used in much the same way as "on the other hand" in English. The Greek *alla* is a much stronger translation of "but," implying a sharp contrast that often may be translated as "on the contrary." The "but" of redemption is the theological equivalent of *alla*. Redemption is not "on the other hand" of suffering but instead "on the contrary." It is the big, divine "but"—the absolute and direct contradiction of suffering, a refusal to allow suffering to have the final, authoritative word.

11 For more on the various scriptural images of redemption/salvation and their theological implications, see Brenda B. Colijn, *Images of Salvation in the New Testament* (Downers Grove, Ill.: InterVarsity, 2010); and Brondos, *Fortress Introduction to Salvation and the Cross*.

12 James D. G. Dunn provides a thorough exploration of the eschatological tension via Paul's use of the aorist and the progressive in the writings of Paul in *The Theology of Paul the Apostle* (Grand Rapids: Eerdmans, 1998), chap. 6, §18. And Leander Keck frames the temporal tension in terms of a dialectic of participation and anticipation: "Participation accents the present accessibility of the future; anticipation accents the futurity of that in

which one participates." Keck, *Paul and His Letters* (Minneapolis: Fortress, 1988), 79.

13 See, e.g., Rom 8:24 and Eph 2:8.

14 This experience of the "not-yet" of redemption is the labor pains of which St. Paul speaks: "We know that the whole creation has been groaning in labor pains until now; and not only the creation, but we ourselves, who have the first fruits of the Spirit, groan inwardly while we wait for adoption, the redemption of our bodies" (Rom 8:22-23).

15 Wolfhart Pannenberg calls this "eschatological ontology." Pannenberg claims that the future, not-yet-realized eschatological reality is already exercising a degree of causation on the present, existential reality. In other words, what we are becoming in the future can be experienced in the present through anticipation. Pannenberg uses the example of a flower, a zinnia: "A zinnia is already a zinnia as a cutting and remains one during the entire process of its growth up to blossoming, even though the flower bears its name on account of its blossom. If there were only a single such flower, we could not determine its nature in advance; and yet over the period of its growth it would still be what it revealed itself to be at the end. It would possess its essence through anticipation, though only at the end of the developmental process would one be able to know that this was its essence." See Pannenberg, *Metaphysics and the Idea of God* (Grand Rapids: Eerdmans, 2001), 105. Ted Peters, likewise, speaks of ontology as retroactive. See Peters, *Anticipating Omega: Science, Faith, and Our Ultimate Future* (Göttingen: Vandenhoeck & Ruprecht, 2006).

This project is the logical extension of bringing together Barth's claim that redemption is an objective reality through the past event of Christ with Pannenberg's and Peters' understanding of ontology as founded on an anticipated future event. Because all things—including profound suffering—are being made new, and because we can trust this is so in and through the Christ event, we are being redeemed.

16 The Gospel of Luke, in particular, suggests that our participation in the promised eschatological future hinges on our reception of Christ. In Luke 17:21 Jesus says, "the kingdom is among you." Luke's Jesus seems to be claiming that wherever Jesus is, the kingdom of God—and thus redemption—is also. In his theological commentary on Luke, David Lyle Jeffrey suggests, "It does not, at least in this passage, seem to refer to an eschatological reward, but to immanent participation in the shared life of Christ." Jeffrey, *Luke*, Brazos Theological Commentary on the Bible (Grand Rapids: Brazos, 2012), 137.

17 The understanding that salvation takes place primarily within human history—within our history, now—is a central tenet of much liberation theology. Jon Sobrino makes this most clear, in *Jesus the Liberator:*

A *Historical-Theological Reading of Jesus of Nazareth* (Maryknoll, N.Y.: Orbis, 1993), see esp. "Excursus 1: The Kingdom of God in Present-Day Christologies." However, a number of theologians have similarly understood redemption to be an ongoing present reality. Martin Luther, for example, speaks of salvation as a process by which sick persons "are sick in fact but healthy in hope and in fact . . . they are beginning to be healthy, that is, they are 'being healed.' " *Luther Works*, 25:336.

18   That redemption is happening now also necessarily means it is happening here. N. T. Wright suggests that this is at least part of what we pray in the Lord's Prayer, "thy kingdom come, on earth as it is in heaven." The kingdom of God cannot be relegated either to a future time or to a far-off place. See his *Jesus and the Victory of God* (Minneapolis: Fortress, 1996), esp. part 2. An understanding of the kingdom of God being realized here and now is also evident in the work of Albrecht Ritschl. Ritschl stresses that the kingdom of God is realized in history, not external to it. Ritschl, *The Christian Doctrine of Justification and Reconciliation*, ed. H. R. Mackintosh and A. B. Macaulay (Edinburgh: T&T Clark, 1902), chap. 7, §53·

19   E.g., Rudolf Bultmann understands Christian eschatology—along with most Christian doctrine—to be mythologized. And John Dominic Crossan in a similar manner suggests that the resurrection—along with most of the details of Christ's life as they are relayed in the Gospels—is primarily a metaphor. For what is perhaps the clearest account of Crossan's understanding of the metaphor of the resurrection, see Robert Stewart, ed., *The Resurrection of Jesus: John Dominic Crossan and N. T. Wright in Dialogue* (Minneapolis: Fortress, 2005).

20   Perhaps the most well-known argument for a realized eschatology comes from C. H. Dodd, who suggests that the eschaton is not the awaited return of Christ but instituted by Christ and lives on in and through the church. Dodd, *The Parables of the Kingdom* (New York: Scribner's Sons, 1961).

In his earlier work, Jürgen Moltmann, too, risks the accusation of an overly realized eschatology. However, in his more recent *The Coming of God*, Moltmann has made a marked shift away from a realized eschatology, noting that redemption is about "the new creation of all things." A new creation that is both ongoing and yet to come. Moltmann, *The Coming of God: Christian Eschatology* (Minneapolis: Fortress, 1996), xi.

21   Actually the whole world lives in this time between the times. The Christian church is simply aware of the tension in a way the world is not. Though this is not a study in ecclesiology, I take the ontological reality of the church for granted. Likewise, this is not a study in sacramentology. However, when I speak of "the church," I do so presuming a diachronic community of faith, which is always already formed by the constitutive

Christian sacramental practices of baptism and Eucharist. I address taking the ontological reality of the church for granted at greater length in chap. 4.

22 See Isa 43:19; 2 Cor 5:17; Rev 21:1.

23 Though this project does not address questions of universal salvation, the claim that redemption is an objective reality is, indeed, a claim with universal implications. Because redemption is cosmic, it must be universal. That Jesus is Lord and that God is redeeming all things are not contingent claims. As will be apparent, it is mistaken, I believe, to equate redemption with a geographical and temporal conception of heaven as some other time and place to which a select faithful few will escape the trials and tribulations of this age and world. Rather, redemption is God's way with and in the world. It is God's continued choice to reconcile creation with God.

The teaching that redemption is an objective reality for all of creation has a long, but complex, history within the Christian tradition. E.g., Gregory of Nyssa taught that Christ's work transformed *all* human beings insofar as it transforms human nature. At the same time, however, Gregory held that baptism is necessary for salvation. Similarly, both Irenaeus and Anselm taught that redemption was an objective, universal reality but that only some—those who accept Christ in faith—subjectively experience this salvation. And Karl Barth claimed, "The sanctification of man, his conversation to God, is, like his justification, a transformation, a new determination, which has taken place *de jure* for the world and therefore for all men and women. De facto, however, it is not known by all men and women, just as justification has not de facto been grasped and acknowledged and known and confessed by all men and women, but only by those who are awakened to faith." Barth, *Church Dogmatics* IV/2, 511.

Following this line of thinkers, the argument I am making in this project is that redemption is happening, objectively speaking. That this is so does not, however, make it empirically or existentially so. The task of the church is to bear witness to God's healing and redemptive activity such that those who have been subjected to profound suffering, and therefore cannot see the activity of God, are enabled to develop the eyes to see the redemption that is always already in process.

24 Throughout the history of the church, no single doctrine of redemption has been agreed upon. Though a number of atonement theories try to explain *how* Christ's death and resurrection is salvific, all the church—as a whole—has agreed upon is *that* Christ's incarnation, life, death, and resurrection make redemption possible. My claim here is that it is the incarnation that exemplifies God's commitment to redeeming all of creation, but especially humanity. Both Athanasius and Anselm argued that

the incarnation was absolutely necessary. For Anselm (see *Cur Deus homo*, 1.10) our redemption depends upon God becoming human so that God can bridge the gap between the human and the divine in some form of substitutionary atonement that satisfies God's justice. For Athanasius (see *On the Incarnation* §§4, 6) our redemption depends upon God becoming human so that humanity can become one with God. Anselm, though not without his critics, has exerted a much greater influence over the Western/Latin church, whereas Athanasius has had a greater influence in the theology of the Eastern/Greek church.

However, in *Church Dogmatics*, Barth seems to reflect Athanasius more than Anselm: "The incarnation thus does not merely involve Christ's assuming human nature per se; rather it involves 'God's participation in man'" (IV/1, 551–52). It is God's participation in all of humanity that is important for this project. The incarnation means that there is no aspect of humanity—including even the most profound suffering—that is not assumed, and thus redeemed, in the incarnation.

25 See Rom 8:19-23.

26 "The root problem lies not in our sins, but in the power called the present evil age, for the present evil age has the strength to enslave us, indeed to enslave us all. . . . The salvific verb, then, is not 'forgive,' but rather 'snatch out of the grasp of.'" J. Louis Martyn, "The Apocalyptic Gospel in Galatians," *Interpretation* 54, no. 3 (2000): 253–54.

27 Martyn, "Apocalyptic Gospel," 253–54.

28 For Paul "the present evil age has not been simply followed by the new creation. Nor do the two exist in isolation or, let us say, at some distance from one another. On the contrary, the evil age and the new creation are dynamically interrelated . . . by the motif of invasion." J. Louis Martyn, *Theological Issues in the Letters of Paul* (Nashville: Abingdon, 1997), 99.

Douglas Atchison Campbell similarly argues that the correct reading of Paul is apocalyptic. For Campbell the significance of such a reading is that it sees salvation primarily retrospectively. That is, salvation has happened. God has acted decisively in Jesus. The emphasis is on the saving work of Jesus as it has already occurred. Campbell, *The Deliverance of God: An Apocalyptic Rereading of Justification in Paul* (Grand Rapids: Eerdmans, 2009). Though any apocalyptic reading of Paul necessarily denies a strictly forensic reading as is often associated with Luther, countering this so-called Lutheran forensic reading of Paul is most acutely evident in Campbell's work.

More recently Beverly Roberts Gaventa brings together essays from a variety of New Testament scholars that explore the implications of an apocalyptic reading of Paul's Letter to the Romans, in *Apocalyptic Paul:*

Cosmos and Anthropos in Romans 5–8 (Waco, Tex.: Baylor University Press, 2013).

29 N. T. Wright argues that the apocalyptic reading of Paul adhered to by Martyn, Campbell, Gaventa, et al. is problematic insofar as it is irreconcilable with any understanding of covenant theology: "God is doing a new thing. Jesus bursts onto the scene in a shocking, unexpected, unimaginable fashion, the crucified Christ offered as a slap in the face to Israel and the world, folly to Gentiles and a scandal to Jews." Wright, *Paul in Fresh Perspective* (Minneapolis: Fortress, 2005), 51.

David Shaw does an excellent job of tracing the rhetorical and theological shifts in this ongoing debate in New Testament scholarship. Though both the covenant and the apocalyptic reading grew out of a refusal for a strictly forensic interpretation of Paul, the two have become increasingly seen as opposing lenses through which to read and interpret Paul. See Shaw, "Apocalyptic and Covenant: Perspectives on Paul or Antinomies at War?," *Journal for the Study of the New Testament* 36, no. 2 (2013): 155–71.

However, I remain unconvinced that the two are logically incompatible. Viewed prospectively, the apocalypse of Christ was not the obvious next step of the story of Israel, it was not the inevitable second scene of a play, but it was beyond the scope of anything the world might have dreamed or imagined. However, if viewed retrospectively the apocalypse of Christ seems to make perfect sense, even to be obvious. In other words, though the apocalyptic revealing of Christ could not have been predicted based on the narrative of the Hebrew Scriptures and tradition, it was in keeping with the narrative of the covenant and allows—even demands—that narrative to be read in a whole new light.

30 That this new creation is not automatic, not a natural postmortem occurrence, makes the use of butterflies as a symbol of Easter theologically problematic. This does not necessarily render butterflies a useless metaphor, but it does mean that some pastoral, educational work needs to be done to help people recognize the radical unexpectedness of new creation. Redemption is a radical gift, not a biological (or even metaphysical) given.

John Milbank distinguishes between gift and given. A given simply is; it is something we take for granted. A gift does not have to be; it is something we are asked to receive graciously. But there is no logical necessity for a gift, no reason that we ought to expect it. Milbank suggests that life and grace and incarnation are gifts, that sin and evil and violence are the refusal of these gifts, and that the Holy Spirit, the church, and redemption are gifts given again and again by God despite humanity's repeated refusal of God's good and gracious gifts. Milbank, *Being Reconciled: Ontology and Pardon*, Radical Orthodoxy Series (New York: Routledge, 2003).

31 Insofar as the bondage, the source of much suffering, from which humanity needs redemption is relational, redemption is necessarily also relational. Thus, redemption, in addition to being a cosmic overcoming of the
power of sin, entails an overcoming of that which inhibits relationship.
A relational understanding of redemption refuses any notion of redemption in the abstract. The redemption of God is necessarily experienced
as a communal liberation from relationships of oppression and exploited
vulnerability.

Though by no means limited to liberationist thinkers, and despite the
wide diversity of concerns represented by liberationist thinkers, this
understanding is most clearly evident in the work of some feminists and
liberation theologians. The significance of the work of these theologians
is that it gives voice to the particularity of redemption on a sociopolitical
level. For more on the redemptive nature of liberation from the bondage
of social class, see, e.g., Jon Sobrino, *Christology at the Crossroads: A Latin
American Approach* (Maryknoll, N.Y.: Orbis, 1978); idem, *Jesus the Liberator*;
and Leonardo Boff, *Jesus Christ Liberator: A Critical Christology for Our Time*
(Maryknoll, N.Y.: Orbis, 1978). For more on the connection between
redemption and liberation from oppressive patriarch structures, see, for
example, Joanne Carlson Brown and Carole R. Bohn, eds., *Christianity,
Patriarchy, and Abuse: A Feminist Critique* (Cleveland, Ohio: Pilgrim, 1989);
Catherine Mowry LaCugna, ed., *Freeing Theology: The Essentials of Theology in
Feminist Perspective* (San Francisco: HarperSanFrancisico, 1993).

32 It is important to note, however, that the doctrine of justification by faith
through grace is not an exclusively Lutheran doctrine. Many others,
including John Wesley and John Calvin, incorporated Luther's basic
assumptions into their own thinking, resulting in a much more complex
development of the doctrine that has continued to be the primary lens
through which much of the Protestant church has understood redemption. For more on the history of the doctrine of justification, see Stephen
Westerholm, *Perspectives Old and New on Paul: The "Lutheran" Paul and His
Critics* (Grand Rapids: Eerdmans, 2004); and David A. Brondos, *Paul on
the Cross: Reconstructing the Apostle's Story of Redemption* (Minneapolis: Fortress, 2006).

33 Martin Luther, "Lecture on Romans 1515–1516," in *Luther Works*, 25:291.
This state of being curved in upon oneself "is not only a lack of a certain
quality in the will. . . . It is a propensity toward evil. It is a nausea toward
the good, a loathing of light and wisdom, and a delight in error and dark-
ness, a flight from and an abomination of all good works, a pursuit of
evil." *Luther Works*, 25:299.

34 However, redemption and forgiveness are not coterminous. That redemption is necessarily individual and that it entails individual forgiveness of

sin does not equate redemption with forgiveness of sin. Rather, it necessitates that forgiveness of sin be a part of whatever redemption of the individual means. However, in situations of profound suffering, redemption, while still including forgiveness, must mean something different, something more. Redemption of individual instances of profound suffering, however, can never be isolated from the understanding of redemption as an objective reality, a reality that, because it is cosmic in scope, necessarily envelopes both the social and the personal.

35   That the Christian focus on forgiving those who sin against you, turning the other cheek, and loving one's enemies victimizes those already most vulnerable is, of course, one of the most significant criticisms of many liberationist theologians, particularly feminists. See, e.g., Brown and Bohn, *Christianity, Patriarchy, and Abuse*; and Phyllis Trible, *Texts of Terror: Literary-Feminist Readings of Biblical Narratives* (Minneapolis: Fortress, 1984).

36   Luke's portrayal of a Jesus who comes to bring redemption for the marginalized is explored in Rudolf Schnackenburg, *Jesus in the Gospels: A Biblical Christology* (Louisville, Ky.: Westminster John Knox, 1995), 186–209.

37   In speaking of redemption for the marginalized, Jon Sobrino says that Jesus "does not simply offer consolation; he offers justice. In other words, he does not propose to leave people as they are and simply console them in their plight; he proposes to re-create their present situation and thus do 'justice' to them." Sobrino, *Christology at the Crossroads*, 120.

      In this project, one of the questions I am asking is what redemption looks like when justice is impossible. Some situations of suffering are so profound, so inhumane, that it is nearly impossible to imagine a way in which the suffering could be righted by justice. Justice is a necessary component of redemption, but justice only rights the future. I am suggesting that God's re-creation also redeems the past and this is, at least in part, what makes the redemption of the future possible. So, while my project is deeply influenced and inspired by the work of liberationist thinkers, I am asking a slightly different set of questions.

38   In her 1970 essay "The Personal Is Political" Carol Hanisch argued that there is no way to divide private/political spheres, that what happens on the political front is intensely personal, and that what happens in the so-called private sphere has deep social and political implications. This is true of redemption as well. The cosmic, universal act of redemption is theologically prior to, and the cause of, social and personal redemption; the social and personal are the logical corollaries of cosmic redemption — the Doppler effect of redemption. However, the personal may be experientially prior — in other words, it may be that it is only through the experience of the redemption of individual situations of suffering that one

comes to see the cosmic activity of God. That the personal may be experientially prior does not make it theologically so.

39 In his famous *Letter from Birmingham Jail*, Martin Luther King Jr. wrote,
"We are caught in an inescapable network of mutuality, tied to a single
garment of destiny. Whatever affects one directly, affects all indirectly"
(April 16, 1963). Though King was speaking of the injustice of racial
inequality, his recognition of the interconnectedness of humanity gets at
the heart of the image of redemption I am painting.

40 Mark Allan Powell similarly suggests that the content of salvation
is "determined in each instance by the needs of the person or persons
involved." The Gospels do not tell generic stories of redemption, but
instead they narrate the particular redemption stories of very particular people with very particular needs. While this does not suggest that
redemption is a private, relativistic event, it does suggest that redemption
is always personal and always particular. Powell, "Salvation in Luke--
Acts," *Word & World* 12, no. 1 (1992): 5.

41 Most New Testament scholarship has interpreted the beatitudes as either
an eschatological warning or an entrance requirement to the kingdom
of God. See Douglas R. A. Hare, *Matthew*, Interpretation: A Bible Commentary for Teaching and Preaching (Louisville, Ky.: Westminster John
Knox, 1993), 35. Richard Lischer, however, suggests that they may be
better read as eschatological signposts, evidence that the kingdom of God
is at hand. See Lischer, "The Sermon on the Mount as Radical Pastoral
Care," in *The Theological Interpretation of Scripture*, ed. Stephen Fowl (Malden, Mass.: Blackwell, 1997), 294–306.

Similarly, Stanley Hauerwas says, "The sermon, therefore, is not a list
of requirements, but rather a description of the life of a people gathered
by and around Jesus, . . . Jesus is indicating that given the reality of
the kingdom we should not be surprised to find among those who fol-
low him those who are poor in spirit, those who mourn, those who are
meek." Hauerwas, *Matthew*, Brazos Theological Commentary on the
Bible (Grand Rapids: Brazos, 2006), 61.

42 Description matters. E.g., an adolescent boy has several abdominal scars
from a knife wound received at the hands of a grown man he had never
even met. This description is likely to conjure up images of inner-city,
back-alley violence. But, if the fact that the child had acute appendicitis
and that a surgeon saved his life is added to the narrative, the image is
drastically changed. Description matters. It shapes how we apprehend
reality.

43 George Lindbeck distinguishes three modes of doing theology: cognitive, experiential-expressivist, and cultural-linguistic. The cognitive emphasizes doctrine, making truth claims of objective reality. The

experiential-expressivist interprets doctrine by way of personal feelings and experiences. And the third, the approach Lindbeck proposes as stronger than either of the other two, he calls the cultural-linguistic approach. The cultural-linguistic approach understands theology as analogous to language. The cultural-linguistic approach denies neither cognitive truth claims nor personal experience, but it locates these within the broader framework of the story of a particular tradition with its own language and set of symbols. Lindbeck, *The Nature of Doctrine* (Louisville, Ky.: Westminster John Knox, 1984).

Similarly, Alasdair MacIntyre suggests that no tradition can be understood externally. All traditions—including religious traditions—make sense only within the particular narrative of that tradition. Redemption can, thus, only be understood within the particular story of God's creative and redeeming work. See MacIntyre, *After Virtue: A Study in Moral Theory* (Notre Dame, Ind.: University of Notre Dame Press, [1981] 2007).

44 Iris Murdoch suggests that we can only act in a world we can see, and we can only see a world we have learned to describe. Murdoch, *The Sovereignty of Good* (New York: Routledge & Kegan Paul, 1970). Expanding upon this, one of the primary themes of Stanley Hauerwas' Introduction to Christian Ethics course is his claim that we can only see a world we have first learned to describe. And, therefore, how we learn to describe the world is a crucial concern of Christian ethics.

45 For this reason Alasdair MacIntyre observes that humans are inherently storytelling creatures. MacIntyre, *After Virtue*, 216. For more on narrative and identity, see Paul Ricoeur, *Time and Narrative*, 3 vols. (Chicago: University of Chicago Press, 1984–1988); and for more on the significance of narrative theology, see Stanley Hauerwas and L. Gregory Jones, eds., *Why Narrative? Readings in Narrative Theology* (Eugene, Ore.: Wipf & Stock, 1997).

46 This is precisely the claim made and explored in much of Robert Coles' work. See esp. *The Call of Stories: Teaching and the Moral Imagination* (Boston: Houghton Mifflin, 1989).

47 This is the criterion for narrative suggested by Michael Root in his essay "The Narrative Structure of Soteriology," in Hauerwas and Jones, *Why Narrative?*, 273.

48 This argument is brilliantly articulated by Alasdair MacIntyre in his essay "What Is a Human Body?," in *The Tasks of Philosophy: Selected Essays* (New York: Cambridge University Press, 2006), 1:86–103.

49 Throughout his vast corpus, N. T. Wright repeatedly argues that resurrection is not about life after death but about life after life after death and that redemption has to do with God's plan for a new creation in which humans have an ongoing, integral role in accomplishing God's

will eternally as a part of this new creation. While I find Wright's image instructive and helpful (and theologically appealing), my focus is on the particularity, not on the universality. The particular is (and will be) a logical corollary of the universal claim that Wright makes. But the suggestion that redemption will mean that all of humanity will be creatively engaged in doing God's will does not offer an answer either to Kelsey's question of what difference Jesus makes now or to the question of whether or not all suffering—no matter how profound—is being redeemed. For me, inherent in the claim that redemption is an eternal reality is the claim that all time will be redeemed—even time of suffering.

50   E.g., organizations such as Mothers Against Drunk Driving (MADD) where parents who have lost children in car accidents involving an intoxicated driver work hard both to educate the wider community to the dangers of drunk driving and to give a face to the pain such accidents cause.

51   I.e., that these dimensions overlay nicely on the temporal paradigm of identity, this overlay is predominantly heuristic and not absolute—each dimension of redemption significantly alters the experience of temporality.

52   In his recent novel, Abraham Verghese offers a remarkably eloquent fictional, albeit not explicitly theological, account of the redemptive vocation that can come from the seemingly discarded bits of a troubling past. Verghese, *Cutting for Stone* (New York: Alfred A. Knopf, 2009). In the novel, Sr. Mary Joseph Praise "believed that her job was to make her life something beautiful for God" (33). And though the book begins with her death, in many ways the entire novel is arguably the story of the beautiful something Sr. Mary Joseph Praise made for God.

53   Much of this project is implicitly—if not explicitly—indebted to Rowan Williams' refutation of the suggestion that the only way to heal the most profound suffering is through an unmediated experience of God's power. This project is an exercise in seeking to see the ways in which the Holy Spirit is at work in the world through the practices of the church. See Williams, *Wrestling with Angels: Conversations in Modern Theology*, ed. Mike Higton (Grand Rapids: Eerdmans, 2007), chap. 13; and idem, *On Christian Theology* (Malden, Mass.: Blackwell, 2000), chap. 15.

54   Contra Wittgenstein, some experiences, especially experiences of profound suffering, are so overwhelming as to defy language. This would seem to suggest that profound suffering that cannot be narrated cannot be incorporated into a narrative. However, not all narrative is discursive. Art, music, and even some forms of theatre are examples of nondiscursive elements of every cultural narrative. The church, through its redemptive practices, offers a new narration of profound suffering—a narration that can incorporate both discursive and nondiscursive practices.

55 Paul Ricoeur, *Figuring the Sacred: Religion, Narrative, and Imagination* (Minneapolis: Augsburg, 1995), 238.

56 Christopher Kavin Rowe offers a compelling argument that this is the central narrative of the book of Acts. See Rowe, *World Upside Down: Reading Acts in the Graeco-Roman Age* (New York: Oxford University Press, 2009).

57 See MacIntyre on practices: "By a 'practice' I am going to mean any coherent and complex form of socially established cooperative human activity through which goods internal to that form of activity are realized in the course of trying to achieve those standards of excellence which are appropriate to, and partially definitive of, that form of activity, with the result that human power to achieve excellence, and human conceptions of the ends and goods involved, are systematically extended." MacIntyre, *After Virtue*, 187. That redemption is made manifest in and through the practices of the worshiping body of Christ is reflective of what MacIntyre refers to as internal goods. The recognition that the end of all ecclesial practices is right worship is crucial.

58 Paulo Freire distinguishes between practices that domesticate and practices that liberate. Practices of the church that make redemption visible, that enable those who have suffered to embody redemption now, are necessarily transformative and liberative practices. See Freire, *Pedagogy of the Oppressed*.

59 There has been a recent surge of interest in, and recognition of, the importance of practices in the life of the church. For examples of the significance of a number of other ecclesial practices, see Craig R. Dykstra, *Growing in the Life of Faith: Education and Christian Practices* (Louisville, Ky.: Westminster John Knox, 2005); and Diana Butler Bass and Joseph Stewart-Sicking, eds., *From Nomads to Pilgrims: Stories from Practicing Congregations* (Herndon, Va.: Alban Institute, 2006).

60 That such a vision is an act of the imagination in no way implies that such vision is false or imaginary. Rather, the practices of the church enable Christians first to see the world as it actually is and second to be conformed to this right vision.

61 Ecclesial practices are mutually interdependent. Though the practices can be spoken of individually and various elements of particular sacramental practices are explored in isolation, none of the practices of the church stand on their own. All are a part of a complex constellation of practices in such a way that the whole is far greater than the sum of its parts.

    Practices are inherently communal. Not only are ecclesial practices not rightly separated from one another; they cannot be separated from the community in which they have developed. This does not mean that every practice must be engaged in within a group setting. It does mean that even when a practice is engaged in by an individual, the community is present with the individual through the practice itself.

The practices of the church are repeated, both diachronically in that they are a part of a traditioned community and synchronically within the life of the individual community, and even within the life of the individual. Practices must be attended to. They do not just happen, but are cultivated in such a way as to be formative of particular habits. By extension, the practices of the church are the primary means by which Christians are invited to participate in the ongoing work of Christ in and for the world.

Chapter 3

1 And, of course, the recall of such concrete bits of information that have been stored in one's memory banks does constitute a type of remembering. Though the idea that memories are objectively preserved, something akin to family photographs, in pristine condition is complex and problematic, which will be a critical point in relation to questions of memory and suffering.

2 This statement necessarily raises the question of identity amongst those with impaired memory such as Alzheimer's patients, a question that, although important, is well outside the boundaries of this project. For a theologically astute and pastorally sensitive discussion of identity and memory in those who suffer from Alzheimer's disease, see David Keck, *Forgetting Whose We Are: Alzheimer's Disease and the Love of God* (Nashville: Abingdon, 1996).

3 This is not to say that individual and communal memory are the same. They are, in fact, rather different. However, despite the particularities of communal memory, communities—in a way analogous to individuals— are formed by and through their memories. See Paul Connerton, *How Societies Remember* (New York: Cambridge University Press, 1989).

4 For more on the science of memory, see V. Elving Anderson, "A Genetic View of Human Nature," in *Whatever Happened to the Soul? Scientific and Theological Portraits of Human Nature*, ed. Warren S. Brown, Nancey Murphy, and H. Newton Malony (Minneapolis: Fortress, 1998). For more on how memory relates to our experiences of God, see David Hogue, *Remembering the Future, Imagining the Past: Story, Ritual, and the Human Brain* (Cleveland, Ohio: Pilgrim, 2003). For an overview of the anatomy and physiology of the brain written for a scientific lay audience, see David J. Linden, *The Accidental Mind* (Cambridge, Mass.: Belknap, 2007). For more on the vulnerabilities of memory, see Daniel L. Schacter, *The Seven Sins of Memory: How the Mind Forgets and Remembers* (Boston: Houghton Mifflin, 2001). And for an overview of recent research in neuropsychology,

see idem, *Searching for Memory: The Brain, the Mind, and the Past* (New York: Basic, 1996).

5 The distinction between operant-conditioned and emotive responses to stimuli is primarily one of voluntariness. E.g., buckling a seat belt upon getting into a car is a learned response. It is often done absentmindedly simply in order to avoid hearing the dinging reminder sound the car makes; this is operant conditioning. Buckling your seatbelt—though it may in fact become an automatic response, one that has the force of habit and is no longer consciously willed—remains on some level a willed choice. On the other hand, emotive responses to stimuli—e.g., blinking in response to bright lights or startling in response to sudden loud noises—are involuntary. Such emotive responses are closely related to reflexes but are not purely neurological reflexes as they vary from person to person, and this variation is accounted for by biographical contingencies.

6 Studies show that amnesiacs with little or no ability to retain explicit memory do not suffer an equal loss of implicit memory as even one with no cognizant short- or long-term explicit memory often remembers motor skills (how to dress or ride a bike) as well as retains operant-conditioned learning (they respond appropriately to emotional cues)—for example, by demonstrating fear responses to the same stimuli they responded to prior to the onset of amnesia. See Linden, *Accidental Mind*, chap. 5.

7 Some forms of autism are characterized, in part, by an impressive degree of recall of disconnected facts while lacking the coherence of a narrative that allows one's own story to be linked with that of others. This is, of course, not to suggest that someone with autism lacks identity. In fact both *Rain Man* and *The Curious Incident of the Dog in the Night-Time* are in large part about the main character's struggle with identity. Rather, it is to suggest that the struggles faced by those with autism (and perhaps equally acutely the struggles faced by their families and friends) in terms of identity and relationship illustrate the critical nature of the interplay between the explicit and implicit memory. This is beautifully illustrated in Mark Haddon, *The Curious Incident of the Dog in the Night-Time* (New York: Doubleday, 2003).

8 Alasdair MacIntyre understands the self to be one "whose unity resides in the unity of a narrative which links birth to life to death as narrative beginning to middle to end." In fact, he suggests that the telling of stories is a crucial aspect of what it means to be human, that humans are inherently storytelling creatures—"Deprive children of stories and you leave them unscripted, anxious stutterers in their actions as in their words." MacIntyre, *After Virtue*, 216.

9 Rowan Williams says, "The self is—one might say—what the past is doing now. . . . It is continuity; and so it is necessarily memory—continuity seen

as the shape of a unique story, my story, which I now own, acknowledge as mine. To be a self is to own such a story: to act as a self is to act out of the awareness of this resource of a particular past." Williams, *Resurrection: Interpreting the Easter Gospel* (Cleveland, Ohio: Pilgrim, 2002), 23.

10   The theater of the absurd being the exception that proves the rule.

11   There are a number of narratologists who convincingly make this claim. For a representative sample, see Wayne C. Booth, *The Company We Keep: An Ethics of Fiction* (Berkeley: University of California Press, 1988); Peter Brooks, *Reading for the Plot: Design and Intention in Narrative* (Cambridge, Mass.: Harvard University Press, 1984); Lisa Zunshine, *Why We Read Fiction: Theory of Mind and the Novel* (Columbus: Ohio State University Press, 2006); Keith Oatley, *Such Stuff as Dreams: The Psychology of Fiction* (Malden, Mass.: Wiley-Blackwell, 2011); and Jonathan Gottschall, *The Storytelling Animal: How Stories Make Us Human* (New York: Houghton Mifflin, 2012).

This claim of the significance of narrative, however, is not uncontested. Crispin Sartwell, e.g., argues that the contemporary academic focus on narrative is misguided for two primary reasons. The first is that he believes that all narratives break down at some point, and the second is, without dismissing the liberative possibility of narrative, he sees narratives as potential vehicles of oppression. In lieu of narratives, Sartwell, a self-professed anarchist as well as a philosophical nihilist, wants to celebrate what he sees as the inevitable collapse into incoherence of all narratives, something of a metaphysical entropy. See Sartwell, *End of Story: Toward an Annihilation of Language and History* (Albany: State University of New York Press, 2000).

12   This claim is, likewise, not uncontested. Per MacIntyre's understanding of the narrative nature of life, narrative necessarily has a telos. MacIntyre, *After Virtue*, 217. Ricoeur similarly understands narrative necessarily to have a telos. However, for Ricoeur the telos is not necessarily known, nor is it stagnant. That is, the telos and the narrative exist in relation to one another such that the telos can be changed by the narrative itself. Ricoeur's account of narrative is considered more fully in chap. 4. See Ricoeur, *Time and Narrative*. And, of course, some postmodern thinkers reject the validity of the concept of narrative altogether. See Jean-François Lyotard, *The Postmodern Condition: A Report on Knowledge*, Theory and History of Literature 10 (Minneapolis: University of Minnesota Press, 1984).

13   Disordered or disoriented time cannot be rightly remembered. One of the problems of the memory of suffering, as we will see later in the chapter, is that because of its disordered nature, though suffering is not forgotten, it is not remembered rightly.

14 David C. Steinmetz offers this image as an analogy for the historical work done by the contemporary biblical exegete. See Steinmetz, "Uncovering a Second Narrative: Detective Fiction and the Construction of Historical Method," in *The Art of Reading Scripture*, ed. Ellen F. Davis and Richard B. Hays (Grand Rapids: Eerdmans, 2003).

15 Miroslav Volf, e.g., focuses on the importance of telling the story of the past truthfully because of what he understands to be the nature of the relationship between truth telling and justice. For Volf, to remember inaccurately, perhaps especially when it comes to painful memories, is not merely to fail to do justice to the memory and the circumstances surrounding it but, in fact, a miscarriage of justice. Moreover, Volf suggests that memory, by definition, must be truthful—otherwise it is fabrication and not memory. For Volf, to remember inaccurately is, in fact, not to remember at all. However, Volf's formal correspondence understanding of truth seems to miss, or perhaps even deny, the truth embedded in the narrative nature of memory. See Volf, *End of Memory*, esp. 49ff.

16 The four gospels are an example of this distinction. Each is a narrative, carefully crafted by its author to convey what the author understands to be most critical for the intended audience.

17 Gerard Genette makes precisely the same distinction in delineating between the literary notions of narrative and story. For Genette, "story" is concerned with historicity and "narrative" with the conveyance of deeper truth. See Gerard Loughlin, *Telling God's Story: Bible, Church, and Narrative Theology* (New York: Cambridge University Press, 1996), 52–63. It is, however, the point behind the semantic distinction, rather than the particular word ascribed to each meaning, that is helpful.

18 The genres of autobiography and memoir stand, for this reason, in stark contrast to more formal works of history.

19 For a compelling account of the inherent interrelatedness of story and storyteller, see Richard Bauckham, "Reading Scripture as a Coherent Story," in *The Art of Reading Scripture*, ed. Ellen F. Davis and Richard B. Hays (Grand Rapids: Eerdmans, 2003), 42.

20 Stephen E. Fowl suggests reading and interpreting Scripture in precisely this way. He refers to this as underdetermined, which he distinguishes from a determinate interpretation (the assumption that there is one clear meaning of any given text that is true for all people in all places at all times) and an anti-determinate interpretation (the deconstructionist assumption that there can, in fact, be no meaning for any given text other than that ascribed to it by the reader). An underdetermined reading honors the work of the historical-critical exegete while remaining open to the ongoing presence of the Holy Spirit in the process of interpretation.

Fowl, *Engaging Scripture: A Model for Theological Interpretation* (Malden, Mass.: Blackwell, 1998), chap. 2.

21   See Schacter, *Seven Sins of Memory*, in which he explains that the more active the amygdala (which registers strong emotions such as fear and anger), the guiltier the memory will be of the "sin of persistence." That is, more emotionally fraught memories will not only be more deeply embedded in the memory; they will be more likely to continue to recur in an unwanted manner. Such intrusive memories seem to be less prone to distortion than less emotively stored memories as, contrary to folk wisdom, such are the memories that are most likely to be preserved in something akin to a storage container than are memories less embedded by strong emotion.

22   The question of reliability of memory necessarily brings up the phenomenon of false memories. In terms of reliability, a number of studies suggest that there is a key distinction between recurrent memories (such as the flashbacks and nightmares common in those who suffer from PTSD) and the therapeutic or hypnotic retrieval of suppressed traumatic memories. Though this is in no way to suggest that retrieved memories are necessarily false—there are undoubtedly a significant number of people for whom the retrieved memory is of genuinely horrendous suffering— studies suggest that recurring, invasive memories are considerably more reliable than retrieved memories. Such flashback-type memories tend to be of a telescoping nature. That is, they are rarely a complete memory but are often just a snippet of a very intense memory. They bring into focus one very particular segment of a larger event but often occur in such a way that the rememberer has little context in which to situate the memory. The limited scope of the memory is partially responsible for its accuracy. Rather than retaining an entire narrative, often because the narrative is incomprehensible, the brain has taken something of a Polaroid of an emotionally overwhelming moment and preserved it. The lack of context explains both the disruptive nature of such memories and their reliability.

   In *Trauma*, Caruth explores the ways in which the nature of unintegrated memories of trauma are unaltered by virtue of the fact that they have not been integrated into one's narrative memory (153ff.). And in *Accidental Mind*, Linden describes studies of suggestibility in preschool-aged children that show that whereas preschool-aged children are very susceptible to "remembering" events that have been reinterpreted through adult intervention, and are therefore no longer true accounts, even a very young child's spontaneous recall of an event is highly reliable (126). And Schacter examines some of the same studies and comes to the same conclusion in his discussion of the "sin of suggestibility." Schacter, *Seven Sins of Memory*, chap. 5.

It is important to note that these studies compare the facticity of recurring invasive memories with therapeutically retrieved memories, not with memories that have remained intact from the time of the event. And none of these studies suggest that accurate memories cannot be retrieved by therapeutic means. Rather, the point seems to be that recurring invasive memories, by their very nature, have an extremely high degree of reliability. The problem of assigning a primacy of reliability to recurring, invasive memories is not in suggesting that such memories are reliable but in the implication that the healing of such invasive attacks of memory would, to some extent, render them less reliable. Recurring invasive memories are a living nightmare for those who experience them, and the lessening of their occurrence is considered one of the criterion for recovery from PTSD. Yet the analysis of these studies—particularly that done by Caruth—suggests that once a memory is narrated by the conscious mind rather than the subconscious, it becomes more prone to errors of memory. Healing means fogetting. Or at least not remembering correctly anymore. Not only is this counterintuitive; it is logically misguided and theologically untenable.

23 As Scarry famously notes, "Intense pain is world-destroying . . . in the most literal way possible, the created world of thought and feeling, all the psychological and mental content that constitutes both oneself and one's world, and that gives rise to and is in turn made possible by language, ceases to exist." *Body in Pain*, 29–30.

24 Dorothee Sölle notes that not only is suffering a result of powerlessness but the experience of powerlessness is precisely what makes suffering suffering. Sölle, *Suffering*, 11.

25 Perhaps this is most readily apparent in its inverse claim. The development of language skills does not merely coincide with the development of increased agency in a young toddler; it is a primary form the developing child's agency takes.

26 This lack of agency is often noted in child abuse victims who exhibit what is popularly known as "frozen watchfulness." This is a state of hyperarousal in which the child is acutely aware of her surroundings and of the actions and moods of others, especially adults (particularly those who may be perceived as a threat), while simultaneously exhibiting no signs of agency but appearing totally lethargic and passive. In this state of frozen watchfulness, children not only remain motionless for unnaturally extended periods of time but are also often rendered mute.

27 Rambo understands this distortion of temporality to be the source of pathological reactions to trauma precisely because "the central problem

of trauma is a temporal one. The past does not stay, so to speak, in the past." Rambo, *Spirit and Trauma*, 19.

28 Suffering forces the attention of the sufferer intently upon the immediate now. Nancy Venable Raine, e.g., in describing the hours during which she was raped, says, "At that moment, time disappeared into a continuous present." Though clearly the event had a beginning, middle, and end, it was experienced as interminable, outside of time such that it even defied temporality. Raine, *After Silence: Rape and My Journey Back* (New York: Three Rivers, 1998).

29 In situations of predictable repeated events of suffering such as child abuse, domestic violence, or torture, time is often instead frozen in the moment immediately preceding the moment of most intense physical pain, as the anticipation of the pain one is helpless to prevent is often more terror-inducing than the actual infliction of pain.

30 Profound suffering thus results in experiencing life as a perverse rendition of *Groundhog Day*, directed by Harold Ramis (Columbia, 1993).

31 Raine notes, "My history had been ruptured—the woman who had not been raped could never return" (*After Silence*, 80). She suggests that because the brain's neurochemistry is altered by traumatic experiences of overwhelming violence, one can never be the same after such an event because the brain is no longer the same brain.

32 Valerie Saiving Goldstein speaks of the habit of hiding as something of a mirror opposite of sin traditionally understood as pride. Goldstein, "The Human Situation: A Feminine View," *Journal of Religion* 40, no. 2 (1960).

33 Basing criteria for healing on presuffering functioning makes a certain level of sense for some instances of suffering—one-time physical or sexual assaults or military-service–induced PTSD, for instance. However, this notion of healing is rendered problematic in situations of long-term, childhood suffering (and perhaps long-term suffering of any nature) where there is no "before" to compare to an "after."

34 The classic text in the recovery of trauma victims is Judith Lewis Herman's *Trauma and Recovery*. Herman describes healing from severe trauma in terms of meeting three distinct needs: the establishment of safety, coming to terms with memories, integration into community. These stages need not, however, be thought of in strictly linear fashion; there is, rather, a spiral nature to recovery in which any new insight or movement in one area necessarily alters one's location in terms of each phase.

As is the case with most, if not all, contemporary notions of stages or phases of recovery, Herman's understanding of stages reflects the work of Elisabeth Kübler-Ross, *On Death and Dying* (New York: Macmillan, 1969). For Kübler-Ross there are five stages of grief through which a grieving person is expected to move. The movement is not necessarily understood to be strictly linear, but it is understood to be predictable and ordered. The five stages are easily remembered by the acronym DABDA, which stands for denial, anger, bargaining, depression, and acceptance.

35 This acute awareness of one's vulnerability to future similar suffering is seen perhaps most acutely in victims of sexual violence. For a poignantly insightful account of this, see Alice Sebold's autobiographical story of a violent rape and the further violence of the legal system faced by those who prosecute their attackers. Sebold, *Lucky*. For more on the effects of childhood sexual violence including, but not limited to, a heightened awareness of the vulnerability of oneself and others, see Ellen Bass and Laura Davis, eds., *The Courage to Heal: A Guide for Women Survivors of Child Sexual Abuse* (New York: Harper Perennial, 1994).

36 This also is routinely seen in rape victims who struggle to come to terms with questions of complicity and guilt that are made more complicated by the cultural ambivalence toward victims of crime in general, let alone toward victims of sexual crimes.

37 The retelling of one's story is understood to be an absolutely crucial step in recovery by the vast majority of therapists who work with trauma survivors. There are however, a growing number of dissenting voices who are concerned that the retelling of stories of suffering primarily serves to keep the wound fresh and alive rather than letting it die a quiet death. See, e.g., Babette Rothschild, *Eight Keys to Safe Trauma Recovery: Take-Charge Strategies to Empower Your Healing* (New York: W. W. Norton, 2010); and Timothy D. Wilson, *Redirect: The Surprising New Science of Psychological Change* (New York: Penguin, 2011).

38 However, insofar as memory is an integral part of one's identity, to forget, particularly to forget something as formative as past trauma, is to lose a significant dimension of one's identity. In the aftermath of her brutal sexual assault, Nancy Raine equates forgetting with the annihilation of her past. And she suggests, "[T]he annihilation of my past would be a suicide" (*After Silence*, 112).

There is a popular sense that there is an appropriate, albeit fluid, period of time during which it is acceptable to grieve for suffering, but there is an unspoken expectation that once this acceptable time has passed any continued recognition of suffering is seen as a form of self-pitying, a nursing of old wounds that is, at the very least, selfish and perhaps even a sign of emotional instability. Such notions deny the reality that memory, perhaps especially the memory of suffering, perdures beyond the will, and thus such notions, no matter how well intentioned, are capable of exacerbating suffering.

39 For more on the problematic linkage of forgiveness with forgetting, see L. Gregory Jones, "Behold, I Make All Things New," in *God and the Victim:*

Theological Reflections on Evil, Victimization, Justice, and Forgiveness, ed. Michelle D. Shattuck (Grand Rapids: Eerdmans, 1999); and idem, *Embodying Forgiveness: A Theological Analysis* (Grand Rapids: Eerdmans, 1995). This is by no means to suggest that forgiveness is not an integral part of the healing of suffering. It is, rather, to suggest that forgiveness can neither be instrumentalized nor predicated upon forgetting. Forgiveness as genuine restoration to/of community is addressed in chap. 4.

40 For an interesting account of redemption and memory representative of this perspective, see Flora A. Keshgegian, *Redeeming Memories: A Theology of Healing and Transformation* (Nashville: Abingdon, 2000).

41 This is not to suggest that all suffering will be remembered in all of its particularity for all time. Miroslav Volf offers a helpful distinction between forgetting and non-remembering. Forgetting is the inability to recall an event, even when one makes an effort to do so. What Volf calls "the gift of non-remembering" is not forgetting; it is the gradual recession of a memory out of the foreground of consciousness and into the background. The event can still be recalled if desired but no longer presents itself unbidden. Volf understands this as a gift because he sees the recession of painful memories as an important step in the healing of memories, particularly those he sees as irredeemable. However, his account of memory, though insightful, approaches memory as a purely cognitive event. See Volf, *Exclusion and Embrace*.

There is an element of forgetfulness or of non-remembering (à la Volf) that can occur in even cases of the most horrendous suffering. It is, rather, to say that such fading of the memory is not something one wills. (Volf, in fact, refers to it as a grace.) The willful suppression of memories, insofar as it is possible, is repression, not forgetting. The issue with admonitions either to remember or to forget is that they place yet another burden on the one who suffers.

42 "I am the master of my fate: I am the captain of my soul." This is the concluding line to William Earnest Henley's poem "Invictus." See Sir Arthur Thomas Quiller-Couch, ed., *The Oxford Book of English Verse, 1250–1918* (Oxford: Clarendon, 1961), 1019.

43 David L. Stubbs, *Numbers*, Brazos Theological Commentary on the Bible (Grand Rapids: Brazos, 2009), 248–49. The daughters of Zelophedad are introduced in Num 26:33 as little more than a genealogical note. The point is merely made that Zelophedad had no sons. In chapter 33, however, the significance of Zelophedad having no sons becomes a prominent concern in terms of inheritance practices, and the daughters are portrayed in an uncharacteristically assertive manner—one that Stubbs praises as simultaneously being both rightly bold and rightly obedient. The daughters of Zelophedad were bold in their willingness to challenge

the unjust authority structures that would, in essence, leave them with no inheritance and no means of sustenance. And yet they were obedient to the commands of God and the authority of the community in their willingness to restrict their marriage prospects to descendants of Joseph, assuring that their inherited land remained in the tribe of Israel.

44 See Ellen F. Davis, *Getting Involved with God: Rediscovering the Old Testament* (Cambridge, Mass.: Cowley, 2001), 17.

45 In this sense lament is not theodicy. Whereas theodicy attempts to tidy up suffering by explaining it, making it make theological sense, lament holds seemingly incompatible truths (that God is both all powerful and good and yet suffering happens) in a cognitive tension. Lament makes space for the rawness of suffering without diminishing its import by trying to explain it.

46 See, e.g., Nicholas Wolterstorff, *Lament for a Son* (Grand Rapids: Eerdmans, 1987), 81.

47 Walter Brueggemann, "The Rhetoric of Hurt and Hope: Ethics Odd and Crucial," *Annual of the Society of Christian Ethics* (1989): 74.

48 "I struggle indeed to go beyond merely owning my grief toward owning it redemptively. But I will not and cannot disown it. . . . Lament is part of life." Wolterstorff, *Lament for a Son*, 6.

49 This is, at least, theoretically true. The reality may well be that few communities actually incorporate lament into the communal liturgy. Lament psalms are rarely used in the lectionary and are often elided when they are used as if to protect the people of God from the expression of unpleasant emotions in worship. Unfortunately, with the exception of the occasional use of lament hymnody such as that found in African American spirituals, liturgical expressions of lament are generally cordoned off from wider ecclesial expression and reserved for the more private practices of confession and commendation for the dying, truncating the development of a faithful practice of lament.

50 Anderson, *Whatever Happened to the Soul?*, 50.

51 The Psalter is not, however, the only means the liturgy has for teaching lament. Scripture, particularly the Old Testament, offers a number of examples of lament. The Exodus passages are full of them, as, of course, is the book of Job. Rebekah Eklund, in her dissertation "Lord, Teach Us How to Grieve: Jesus' Laments and Christian Hope" (Duke Divinity School, 2012), argues for the importance of lament in the New Testament as well, particularly in the prayers of Jesus.

In addition to Scripture, lament is also practiced and taught through the hymnody of the church, something that is perhaps reflected best in African American spirituals. For more on lament and hymnody, see Bert

Polman, "The Role of Lament in American Musical Life: Concerto in Three Movements," *Calvin Theological Journal* 36 (2001).

52 "The Psalms are a kind of First Amendment for the faithful. They guarantee us complete freedom of speech before God, and then (something no secular constitution would ever do) they give us a detailed model of how to exercise that freedom, even up to its dangerous limits, to the very brink of rebellion." Davis, *Getting Involved with God*, 8–9.

53 Mic 6:8.

54 Samuel Wells speaks of the need for the church to be with the poor, the excluded, and the marginalized because this is where the church meets Jesus; it is how the church prepares itself for the fullness of the kingdom of God. Wells, *Improvisation: The Drama of Christian Ethics* (Grand Rapids: Brazos, 2004), chap. 10.

55 This is not to suggest that power or privilege prevent suffering. It is, however, to suggest that there is a correlation between vulnerability and suffering and that those in positions of power and privilege who have not experienced profound suffering may be less able or inclined to identify with those who suffer than those who find themselves in more vulnerable positions.

56 "[T]o repent does not mean to be filled with guilt, sorrow or shame; rather, to repent is to completely rethink and reassess one's life in light of Jesus and his message." Paul J. Wadell and Patricia Lamoureux, *The Christian Moral Life: Faithful Discipleship for a Global Society* (Maryknoll, N.Y.: Orbis, 2010), 101.

57 John Howard Yoder argues, "[T]o repent is not to feel bad but to act differently." Yoder, *The Original Revolution: Essays on Christian Pacifism* (Scottdale, Pa.: Herald, 2003), 31. While Yoder is correct that repentance involves acting differently, to repent, it seems, is to *think* and even to *remember* differently, and it is to *feel* differently. To feel badly about wrongs committed but to remain unchanged in behavior and thought is to be condemned to a perpetual cycle of sin and sorrow. Such private sorrow is distinguished from lament precisely by its lack of telos. Sorrow is internalized—turned in on the self—whereas lament cries out to God in expectation.

58 However, the ecclesial practice of penance is often misunderstood in precisely this way. The role of penance, rightly understood, is to restore right relationship with God and within the community. As such, penance cannot be separated from repentance. In this process the role of penance is not merely punitive but intended to be transformative. Penance is designed to allow for concrete practices that aid one in overcoming sinful habits. However, in the popular imagination (both Roman Catholic and Protestant), penance is often cheapened and reduced to a mere

punishment, robbing it of its intended transformative nature. For more on the theology of the Roman Catholic practice of penance—more properly called the Sacrament of Reconciliation—see Sean Fagan, "Penitential Practices," in *The New Dictionary of Sacramental Worship* (Collegeville, Minn.: Liturgical, 1990).

59   Jones, *Embodying Forgiveness*, 169. Similarly, Susan Dunfee suggests that this sin of diminishment is one that pertains particularly to women. In arguing against Niebuhr's conception of sin as primarily male pride, Dunfee suggests that for women sin is often experienced in the form of hiding—hiding from one's freedom in Christ, from one's call to embrace selfhood. As such, Dunfee suggests the need to repent of the sin of having no self. See Dunfee, "Sin of Hiding," 324.

My suggestion in this project is that while Dunfee's claim that women are more often guilty of the sin of hiding than of pride, this sin of hiding is in no way limited to women but may be a direct result of the experience of violence. Given the high incidence of violence against women, that women would be more often in need of repenting for diminishment than men may well be true, but the causative agent is not, it seems, one of gender necessarily but one of the experience of violence.

60   That this is true is in part a reflection of the reality that, with the exception of Jesus, there are no wholly innocent victims. (Though there are, of course, situations—e.g., child abuse, sexual assault, muggings—in which the victim is innocent in the particular instance.) However, by suggesting that repentance is a necessary response to suffering, I am primarily suggesting that repentance is the faithful posture of discipleship. All of the Christian life is a turning toward Christ. Situations of suffering simply cry out for this turning, for the renunciation of the grammar of sin that makes the logic of suffering possible, in a unique and poignant way.

61   Jones refers to this reframing of memory as "remembering well," by which he means coming to remember in such a way as to "envision and embody a future different from the past." Remembering well is a deliberate agential act, not something that just happens, and as such is a habit that can be acquired through specific practices such as lament and repentance. Jones, *Embodying Forgiveness*, 149.

62   This notion of agency is largely dependent upon Stanley Hauerwas, who explores the interconnectedness of agency and character. Hauerwas, *Character and the Christian Life: A Study in Theological Ethics* (San Antonio: Trinity University Press, 1975), 21. This recognition that agency and character are of a piece suggests that the habits that shape character necessarily give shape to agency. A logical extension of this recognition is that habits of worship play an integral part to the development of a proper theological account of agency.

Chapter 4

1 The following account of identity theory comes from Peter J. Burke, *Identity Theory*, ed. Jan E. Stets (New York: Oxford University Press, 2009); Steph Lawler, *Identity: Sociological Perspectives* (Malden, Mass.: Polity, 2008); and Michael A. Hogg, Deborah J. Terry, and Katherine M. White, "A Tale of Two Theories: A Critical Comparision of Identity Theory with Social Identity Theory," *Social Psychology Quarterly* 58, no. 4 (1995): 255–69.

2 There are a plethora of texts addressing the significance of family systems and roles. For a lay-accessible overview of family systems theory, see Roberta M. Gilbert, *The Eight Concepts of Bowen Theory: A New Way of Thinking about the Individual and the Group* (Falls Church, Va.: Leading Systems, 2004). For an engaging and nontechnical look at the significance of siblings and birth order in the formation of identity, see Kevin Leman, *The Birth Order Book: Why You Are the Way You Are* (Old Tappen, N.J.: F. H. Revell, 1985).

3 This is not to say that identity theory is opposed to developmental notions of identity formation. In other words, though roles change as individuals go through various life stages, that we learn and perform roles is a constant. The classic study of identity formation as a lifetime of movement through stages of growth is Erik H. Erikson, *Identity and the Life Cycle* (New York: Norton, 1980).

4 This understanding of roles and counterroles as mutually subsistent is the concept upon which much Western epic literature is based. The mythological force behind this is the presumption that it is necessary to keep such relationships in a state of constant tension. This is, in essence, the story of George Lucas' Star Wars series (Lucasfilm, 1977–2005); The Lord of the Rings series by J. R. R. Tolkien (Boston: Houghton Mifflin, 1954–1955); and, e.g., the more recent Harry Potter series by J. K. Rowling (New York: Arthur A. Levine, 1999–2009)—equal but opposite forces, each depending on the other for its very existence. Until, that is, the force of good is shown to overthrow, and therefore obliterate (but just barely), the force of evil.

5 The relational role and counterrole of identity are at the heart of the Trinity. The Father and the Son are eternally in a particular relationship with one another that is mutually dependent and sustaining. God the Son makes no sense without God the Father and vice versa. For more on the mutuality of the relational aspect of the Trinity, see Mary Ann Fatula, *The Triune God of Christian Faith* (Collegeville, Minn.: Liturgical, 1990).

6 "Different forms of identity, then, should be seen as interactive and mutually constitutive, rather than 'additive.'" Lawler, *Identity*, 3.

7 Think, e.g., of the power the fashion industry wields to distort conceptions of ideal body types through the use of exceptionally thin models as

well as the increasingly widespread use of photo retouching technology. Though not single-handedly responsible for eating disorders, the connection between the marketing of such prototypes and the occurrence of anorexia and bulimia is hardly coincidental. For more on the social construction of eating disorders, see Maree Burns and Helen Malson, eds., *Critical Feminist Approaches to Eating Dis/Orders* (New York: Routledge, 2009).

8   Burke, *Identity Theory*, 124.

9   William James, in fact, claimed, "[W]e have as many 'selves' as we have others with whom we interact." Burke, *Identity Theory*, 131.

10 Pamela Cooper-White offers a compelling feminist argument in favor of understanding identity as multiplicity. Cooper-White, *Braided Selves: Collected Essays on Multiplicity, God, and Persons* (Eugene, Ore.: Cascade Books, 2011). Similarly, Rita Carter—in *Multiplicity: The New Science of Personality, Identity, and the Self* (New York: Little, Brown, 2008)—offers an engaging exploration of the complexity of the multiple roles any given person plays and the role of memory in forming a unique and coherent identity out of what are always diverse, and often seemingly contradictory, roles.

11 "Identity salience represents one of the ways, and a theoretically most important way, that the identities making up the self can be organized. Identities, that is, are conceived as being organized into a salience hierarchy. This hierarchical organization of identities is defined by the probabilities of each of the various identities within it being brought into play in a given situation. Alternatively, it is defined by the probabilities each of the identities have of being invoked across a variety of situations. The location of an identity in this hierarchy is, *by definition*, its salience." S. Stryker and R. T. Serpe, "Commitment, Identity Salience, and Role Behavior: Theory and Research Example," in *Personality, Roles, and Social Behavior*, ed. W. Ickes and E. S. Knowles (New York: Springer-Verlag, 1982), 206 (emphasis in original).

12 Carter claims that this multiplicity of selves is a necessary and good psychological adaptation to complex contemporary lives. She further argues that the line between a pathological development of multiple personalities and the necessary multiplicity is much vaguer than portrayed in such popular film and literature as *The Three Faces of Eve* (dir. Nunnally Johnson, 1957) and *Sybil* (dir. Daniel Petrie, 1976). Though her suggestion is more nuanced than this, the primary determinative factor between pathological and normal multiplicity is one of cognizance and communication. That is, in cases of pathological multiple personality disorders, the divide between the various selves is absolute in a way that is not the case in normative multiplicity.

192 Notes to pages 86–90

13   Hogg, Terry, and White, "Tale of Two Theories," 258. This idea of iden-
     tity salience assumes that it is the perception of the individual that deter-
     mines which role(s) take priority and are therefore most determinative
     of one's identity. However, Hogg, Terry, and White also point out that
     there are some characteristics—referred to as "master statuses"—that
     override all other characteristics in the social definition of the self. These
     master statuses are neither choices nor based on one's perception of rela-
     tive impact or importance. Hogg, Terry, and White suggest that race and
     gender identity often function as such master statuses, suggesting that the
     socially constructed nature of both race and gender are externally applied
     by the dominant group as a means of social control.
14   This example comes from Burke, *Identity Theory*, 130–31.
15   MacIntyre, *After Virtue*.
16   MacIntyre, *After Virtue*, 217.
17   Human character, however, is admittedly not always so consistent.
     Though it may well be a case of the exception proving the rule, there are
     any number of instances where, after the commission of some heinous
     crime, the immediate response of those who know the perpetrator is one
     of shock and disbelief, claiming how "out of character" this act is. This is
     to suggest that while there is, as a rule, a consistency of character, human
     behavior is far too complex to be reduced to character. The psychological
     field of deviant behavior is concerned not merely with behavior that devi-
     ates from the cultural norm but also with behavior that deviates from the
     individual's norms.
18   "For the story of my life is always embedded in the story of those commu-
     nities from which I derive my identity. I am born with a past; and to try to
     cut myself off from that past, in the individualistic mode, is to deform my
     present relationships." MacIntyre, *After Virtue*, 221.
19   Malcolm Gladwell describes a study of the prevalence of feuds through
     the nineteenth century and of the continued relatively high level of
     aggression demonstrated by men from the Appalachian regions. The
     study suggests that the roots of the patterns of aggression displayed can
     be traced, via immigration patterns, to the culture that existed among
     Scottish highland herders, in which the defense of one's honor—as well
     as of one's property and possessions—was a cardinal virtue. Gladwell's
     point is that cultural legacies do, in fact, matter. They shape, often in
     ways that are far from obvious, beliefs, behaviors, even emotions. Such
     a suggestion does not imply a cultural determinism, but it does suggest
     the complexity of identity formation. Gladwell, *Outliers: The Story of Success*
     (New York: Little, Brown, 2008), chap. 6.
20   "I am forever whatever I have been at any time for others—and I may
     at any time be called upon to answer for it—no matter how changed I

may be now." MacIntyre understands this accountability, however, to be bi-directional: "I am not only accountable, I am one who can always ask others for an account, who can put others to the question. I am part of their story, as they are part of mine." MacIntyre, *After Virtue*, 217–18.

21 Individual narratives are, of course, inextricably woven together with any number of narratives in a way that is considerably richer and more complex than the reciprocity of roles suggested by social identity theory recognizes.

22 The difference between communal paradigmatic stories and the group prototypes of identity theory is that the stories are, in fact, intended to be imitable. For more on the power of stories to form identity and influence patterns of thought and behavior, see Booth, *Company We Keep*; and Coles, *Call of Stories*.

23 MacIntyre, *After Virtue*, 216–17. Without a teleological understanding of human life, MacIntyre suggests that Nietzsche's subjective will-to-power becomes the inevitable, rational moral choice.

24 Alasdair C. MacIntyre, *Dependent Rational Animals: Why Human Beings Need the Virtues*, The Paul Carus Lecture Series 20 (Chicago: Open Court, 1999), chap. 11.

25 That geographical communities often lack any sense of telos does not mean that they do so by definition. Amish and Hasidic communities may both represent communities in which the geopolitical and religious communities are, at least by intention, coterminous. Many immigrant communities may likewise be an exception to this tendency.

26 MacIntyre, *After Virtue*, 32 (emphasis in original).

27 Identity theory's social group is a much looser concept than MacIntyre's traditioned community. Social groups are broadly defined as any group to which one belongs and that is therefore, to varying degrees, formative. Examples include race, ethnicity, gender, and social class, but also things such as affinity for particular ball teams or participation in civic groups like the Lions Club or the Masons. Even more loosely, social groups include one's circle of friends and acquaintances. Such groups are not stagnant or isolated, and may overlap in any number of ways, such as mutual affiliations and friends. Some social groups are freely chosen and the association is rather loose, whereas some are a biological given and the association is more or less absolute, though its influence may still be loose, depending on a seemingly infinite number of variables. Of course, some of these social groups—e.g., the church—may also be traditioned communities in the MacIntyrean sense, but many would not. Social groups can be considerably broader than MacIntyre's community—racial and ethnic groups, for example. On the other hand, social groups can likewise be considerably narrower than

MacIntyre's community—affiliation with a particular social clique, for example. The distinction between the two is not absolute, as there are some social groups, such as the military, in addition to the church that may also be traditioned communities. The important distinction is that the social group as understood in identity theory does not, *by definition*, have a telos. This does not, however, mean social groups necessarily lack a telos; it means only that a telos is not definitionally required for a social group to be formative of individual identity.

28 Identity theory, however, fails to recognize the moral fragmentation that MacIntyre describes. In fact, as a formulation of one of the social sciences, identity theory presumes a moral neutrality that MacIntyre rejects. That is, identity theory is itself embedded within the tradition of the Enlightenment, a tradition that allows identity theorists to believe they are engaging in an exclusively descriptive, and therefore objective, task of naming the process by which identity is formed without recognizing the normative claim inherent in such an act.

29 This notion is by no means foreign to MacIntyre and in fact seems to be, in many ways, the obvious end toward which MacIntyre's quest for another St. Benedict points.

30 That this is ontologically true and should, therefore, be empirically the case does not, however, translate into it empirically being the case. There are many Christians for whom baptism is empirically no more significant an identity claim—and is perhaps even less of an identity claim—than race, gender, national origin, sexual orientation, or even consumer preferences.

31 Isolation is a strategic dimension of suffering perfected in totalitarian states and abusive families alike. In *Torture and Eucharist: Theology, Politics, and the Body of Christ* (Malden, Mass.: Blackwell, 1998), William T. Cavanaugh claims that isolation, the disruption of community, was the explicit intent of the Pinochet regime's practice of torture. The resultant state of fear and mistrust that separated neighbor from neighbor and often caused even immediate family members to withdraw from one another was not incidental to the practice of torture but an integral part of its logic. Suffering, however, does not have to come in the form of state-sponsored torture in order to be disruptive of community. Suffering qua suffering is isolating. See esp. chap. 1.

32 Elaine Scarry emphasizes that there is an important distinction to be made in terms of agency. Suffering that is willingly undergone—for example, in the case of the martyrs or in the case of certain painful medical or dental procedures—does not necessarily have the same isolating impact as suffering that is imposed against one's will and over which one has no power.

The isolation is connected to the violation of bodily boundaries. Scarry, *Body in Pain*, 34.

33   Scarry, *Body in Pain*, 30.

34   "It is the intense pain that destroys a person's self and world, a destruction experienced spatially as either the contraction of the universe down to the immediate vicinity of the body or as the body swelling to fill the entire universe." Scarry, *Body in Pain*, 35.

35   Nancy Raine describes this loss of embodiment in the midst of being raped. Though she was blindfolded and never saw the rapist, she felt that she was somehow or other removed from the person being raped and was able, in a sense, to "see" the rapist as if hovering from a position somewhere above her bed. "Whatever part of me was 'watching' did not feel alive because it no longer seemed to possess a body." Raine, *After Silence*, 11.

36   "Through disassociation the consciousness seeks to withdraw, as it were, from this pain and shame, abandoning the body, its feelings, and especially its vulnerability to being affected by others." G. Simon Harak, "Child Abuse and Embodiment from a Thomistic Perspective," *Modern Theology* 11, no. 3 (1995): 323.

Turning such suffering into a mental game of detachment is a well-attested survival technique among long-term torture and abuse victims. See, e.g., Andrea Warren, *Surviving Hitler: A Boy in the Nazi Death Camps* (New York: HarperCollins, 2001).

Though it is necessarily beyond the scope of this project, such disassociation is not limited to the one who suffers. In his haunting play, *Death and the Maiden*, Ariel Dorfman interestingly portrays a level of detachment or disassociation—likened to a form of possession—necessary for the psychic survival on the part not only of the one being tortured but also of the torturer. Dr. Mirando confesses, "A kind of—brutalization took over my life, I began to really truly like what I was doing. It became a game. My curiosity partly morbid, partly scientific. How much can this woman take? More than the other one? . . . She is entirely in your power, you can carry out all your fantasies, you can do what you want with her," Dorfman, *Death and the Maiden* (New York: Penguin, 1992), 59.

37   In the aftermath of her brutal rape, Nancy Raine recalls, "It was living with Novocain in the heart, condemned to life on the glassy surface of the emotional horse latitudes. I felt cut off from everything . . . even from the memory of emotional life." Raine, *After Silence*, 61. Though there is not necessarily a direct causal link between suffering and perpetrating violence, there is often a connection. The inability to feel one's own physical pain can, in time, lead to a loss of, or lack of, capacity for empathy, setting up the potential for the cycle of violence to continue.

38 Kai Erikson suggests that trauma actually has both a centripetal and a centrifugal force. That is, there is a way in which the isolation of suffering can become a link, a force that unites, insofar as in the presence of another who has suffered similarly there can be a sense of relief at not needing to explain one's suffering. However, she also notes that such community based on estrangement can, in the end, reinforce the isolation of suffering. Her essay implies that while there is a place for "survivor groups" in the healing of suffering, this is only the case if they are able to serve as a transition item. Solidarity in suffering is still a state of isolation from the wider community. Erikson, "Notes on Trauma and Community," in Caruth, *Trauma*, 186.

39 The resulting sense of isolation from the violation of trust is largely impacted by the perceived strength of the bonds of trust that are broken. That is, the sense of isolation that follows in the wake of a violation of trust of a loved one or of a trusted caregiver is often considerably more profound and long lasting than the violation of trust of a relative stranger.

40 William Cavanaugh suggests that the result of such suffering is a literal destruction of the victim's social world and a creation of isolated individuals. His reference to the individual is not, however, to the post-Enlightenment ideal of the self-made person but to a fragmented individual, bereft of the necessary links to a community: "A person's self and a person's world are constructed largely of interpersonal relationships—links to others, both significant and peripheral—which help define who one is. In torture's shattering of self and world, those relationships are undone, and the victim is left isolated and alone, that is, without the resources to reconstitute a shared life, and therefore an integrated self." Though Cavanaugh is speaking specifically of a state-sponsored campaign of torture, his insights into the destruction of relationship brought about by intense suffering are not restricted to cases of torture. Cavanaugh, *Torture and Eucharist*, 43.

41 Nancy Raine writes of the moment she first recognized the reluctance of public discourse on the issue of rape. When she first speaks publicly—at a gathering of women writers,—after publishing a piece related to her rape, she is told, "I thought your article was well written. . . . But let's face it, no one wants to hear about such terrible things." Much of the impetus of Raine's book is a refusal to stop speaking simply because the topic is unpleasant and therefore potentially offensive. Raine, *After Silence*, 118.

42 The prevalence of fear and shame in the aftermath of suffering is widely documented in psychological literature as well as in anecdotal accounts. For a psychological approach, see especially the aforementioned Herman and Caruth. For more on the connection between suffering and shame, see Michael Lewis, *Shame: The Exposed Self* (New York: Free Press, 1992).

For a poignant personal account, see Alice Sebold, *Lucky* (Boston: Back Bay, 2002). For an interesting and compelling mixture of the two, see Susan J. Brison, *Aftermath: Violence and the Remaking of a Self* (Princeton, N.J.: Princeton University Press, 2002). Brison is a philosophy professor who experienced a brutal sexual assault. In this book she not only recounts the assault and its aftermath but considers the effects of violence more generally. She suggests that an important distinction needs to be made between character self-blame and behavioral self-blame. Character self-blame is the internalization of the suffering in such a way that one assumes that there is a personality flaw that caused the suffering, that one in some way merited the suffering by virtue of one's character. Such self-blame is necessarily destructive. Behavioral self-blame can, however, in a limited way, prove to be helpful. Behavioral self-blame is directly connected to the loss of control, the loss of agency, of suffering. If there is some element, no matter how small, that one might have been able to control, if only x, y, or z, then there can be a sense of control over preventing such suffering in the future. Brison insists, e.g., that this sense of behavioral self-blame led her to enroll in a self-defense course, which she found to be therapeutic. Brison, *Aftermath*, 73–77.

43 Aquinas understands habit to be developed in and through the body but to manifest itself in the soul. That is, the body is the way Aquinas understands the formation of habit, but the soul is habituated by the body, and what is significant for Aquinas is that body-formed habits shape the nature of the soul. Aquinas, *Summa Theologica* I-II.50.

44 This disconnection includes but is not limited to the problem of disassociation. Herman suggests that involuntary pathological disassociation is an area in need of much more research. The phenomenon of disassociation is well documented while remaining little understood. See Herman, *Trauma and Recovery*, 238–39.

45 Jamie Kalven, *Working with Available Light: A Family's World after Violence* (New York: Norton, 1999), 244.

46 Admittedly, a focus on the human body as locus of suffering, and therefore of redemptive activity, may seem to reinforce the contemporary fixation on bodies, which is itself a form of gnostic disembodiment. This gnostic obsession with the human body is, however, a focus on the body as an object, a thing one possesses rather than a part of who one is. And as a thing that continually requires improvement in a consumerist culture, the body is, in effect, instrumentalized. Honoring the body as the locus of suffering, however, is precisely the opposite; it is the insistence that rather than seeing the body as a means to an end, the body is integral to the end, the telos, which is an embodied redemption.

47   In the 1970s, Orthodox priest Fr. George Calciu was imprisoned, tortured, and held for long periods of time in isolation in Romania. He describes a friendship he develops with a cockroach—a relationship he remembers as redemptive: "He was amazing. . . . Little by little I began to talk to him, and he actually came to visit me for weeks. . . . I was saved in my ability to remember my language by this cockroach." Fr. Calciu's story is found in Frederica Mathewes-Green, *At the Corner of East and Now: A Modern Life in Ancient Christian Orthodoxy* (New York: Jeremy P. Tarcher/ Putnam, 1999), 227.

48   Annie Dillard asks, "Does anyone have the foggiest idea of what sort of power we so blithely invoke? The churches are children playing on the floor with their chemistry sets, mixing up a batch of TNT to kill a Sunday morning. It is madness to wear ladies' straw hats and velvet hats to church; we should all be wearing crash helmets. Ushers should issue life preservers and signal flares; they should lash us to our pews." Dillard, *Teaching a Stone to Talk: Expeditions and Encounters* (New York: Harper & Row, 1982), 40.

49   That the place of violation may also be the place of healing is beautifully illustrated in the story of Maggy Barenkitse. Maggy, a Tutsi born in Burundi who adopted seven children (four Hutus and three Tutsis), was working in the bishop's house in the village of Ruyigi in 1994 when a group of armed Tutsis entered the bishop's residence, stripped Maggy, and tied her to a chair from which she witnessed the slaughter of seventy-two villagers—many of them family and friends. After the massacre, Maggy found and saved twenty-five Hutu children in addition to her own seven children. Determined not to allow the events of that October morning to harden her heart, Maggy built an orphanage aptly named *Maison Shalom*. At the site of the massacre, Maggy had a swimming pool installed for the children. The swimming pool is clearly and intentionally a baptismal reminder. The pool's location at a site of profound violence and unspeakable suffering is healing because the pool provides the children (and the larger community) with the cleansing opportunity to learn a new story—one in which the violence they have witnessed and suffered is not the determinant story of their lives. The swimming pool allows new memories to be crafted, memories of swimming in the waters of grace. Such memories do not undo or erase the memories of violence and suffering, but in the writing of a new story they do refuse to allow the suffering to be the only story of Ruyigi. For Maggy's story, see Emmanuel Katongole, *The Sacrifice of Africa: A Political Theology for Africa* (Grand Rapids: Eerdmans, 2011), chap. 9.

50   That the individual body is the locus of suffering does not diminish the communal aspect of suffering. In situations of systematic widespread

torture and genocide such as that experienced in Chile, Sudan, and Rwanda, the suffering of the individual body, though acutely particular, is also in many ways merely a microcosm of a much greater communal suffering. For those baptized into the body of Christ, such individual suffering can never be isolated from the suffering of the entire body, for as St. Paul writes in 1 Cor 12:26, "If one member suffers, all together with it." That this is not always recognized as being empirically true does not render it less ontologically true.

51 Robert Webber and Rodney Clapp claim, "To take a new story is to take a new life." Pushing this a bit further would suggest that in situations of suffering, a new story provides a new body. It is also important to note that this discussion of the practice of anointing presumes a community in which practices of baptism and Eucharist are normative formational practices. That is, anointing is not an isolated act but one way to embody the life of a community formed and fed at font and table. Webber and Clapp, *People of the Truth: The Power of the Worshiping Community in the Modern World* (San Francisco: Harper & Row, 1988), 75.

52 John Kiess, "A Grammar of Touch: The Theo-political Significance of the Sacrament of Anointing during Northern Ireland's Troubles" (unpublished paper).

53 Though the ecclesial practice of anointing most traditionally includes the use of oil, my focus is on the practice of touch as a healing act. This may take the form of a liturgical healing service in which the individual is, indeed, anointed with oil, but the healing power of touch is in no way limited to such formalized practices of touch. For more on the theology of a liturgical practice of anointing, see Peter E. Fink, ed., *The New Dictionary of Sacramental Worship* (Collegeville, Minn.: Liturgical, 1990), 49–57.

54 Cristina L. H. Traina argues that touch is as necessary to life as food, that there is, in fact, a threshold of touch below which predictable harm, both physiological and psychological, occurs. Importantly, she notes that even children who have been sexually and physically abused, and therefore tend to be more touch averse than their nonabused peers, "slept more and were more alert, social, and less depressed after a one-month course of fifteen minute daily massages." Traina, "Touch on Trial: Power and the Right to Physical Affection," *Journal of the Society of Christian Ethics* 25, no. 1 (2005): 14.

55 Harak, "Child Abuse and Embodiment," 317.

56 However, it is also possible for the rite of anointing to allow for a range of comfort with physical touch, such that for someone for whom touch is more threatening than healing, prayers of anointing may be offered without touch. Such a rite allows for the body to be positioned within the ecclesial body in ways that can also be healing. Though there is no

calculus by which this can be determined, it is conceivable that the rite of anointing may be repeated with a regularity and an intentionality such that, in time, anointing touch can indeed be a physical touch that allows the space of the body to be reclaimed and re-membered into the shalom of Christ.

57 This expression is borrowed from John Kiess. In addition to the rite of anointing of individual bodies, the church's imagination may be ritually performed in the anointing of spaces. E.g., if the violence suffered is the result of a home invasion, the priest may anoint the home, reclaiming the space as a space of peace and of love rather than of anger and of violence.

58 "Holy friendships" is a term used by L. Gregory Jones and Kevin R. Armstrong to speak of the transformative nature of friendship. Jones and Armstrong, *Resurrecting Excellence: Shaping Faithful Christian Ministry*, Pulpit & Pew (Grand Rapids: Eerdmans, 2006), 60–78. I am appropriating the term without assigning to it the same definition offered by Jones and Armstrong. I am using the term as a way of differentiating friendships based on communion with Christ from friendships based on perceived social equality and homogeneity. I do so in part to avoid using the terms "spiritual" or "soul friend" as these imply the practice of spiritual direction, which, though an important ecclesial practice, is not to what I am referring. For a beautiful meditation on friendship, see Saint Aelred of Rievaulx, *Spiritual Friendship*, ed. Lawrence C. Braceland and Marsha L. Dutton, Cistercian Fathers Series 5 (Collegeville, Minn.: Liturgical, 2010); and for an excellent introduction to the practice of spiritual direction, see Tilden Edwards, *Spiritual Friend* (New York: Paulist, 1980).

59 In their essay, "Memory, Community, and the Reasons for Living: Reflections on Suicide and Euthanasia," Stanley Hauerwas and Richard Bondi suggest that being a burden is a part of community living. That is, community means mutual interdependence such that ending one's life to prevent becoming a burden makes no sense because there is absolutely nothing wrong with being a burden. *The Hauerwas Reader*, ed. John Berkman and Michael G. Cartwright (Durham, N.C.: Duke University Press, 2001), 593.

60 Aristotle, *Aristotle's Nicomachean Ethics*, ed. Robert C. Bartlett and Susan D. Collins (Chicago: University of Chicago Press, 2011).

61 Paul J. Wadell, *Becoming Friends: Worship, Justice, and the Practice of Christian Friendship* (Grand Rapids: Brazos, 2002), 73.

62 Herman suggests that survivor groups are often an integral part to the healing/recovery process for victims of violence. However, she also notes that such groups are, at best, penultimate means of recovery. What is ultimately required for healing is integration into a wider social network in which one can learn to establish social bonds based on common

humanity rather than common victimization and in which one can learn to recognize and empathize with the suffering of others. Herman, *Trauma and Recovery*, chap. 11. This is to suggest not that the church be seen as a survivor group but that the church as the body of Christ is a unique body in which redemption can be experienced in a way that goes beyond the psychosocial healing based on the recognition of common humanity.

63 By this I am both thinking of the insistence in some circles that outside of marriage same-gendered friendships are the only legitimate friendships and thinking of the friendships between people who society might have at odds with one another—think, for instance, of the increasing prevalence of Gay-Straight Alliances forming in public high schools or of the cultural disbelief that members of the Nickel Mines community have befriended the family of the shooter, Charles Roberts.

64 Wadell, *Becoming Friends*, 75.

65 Jean Vanier, *The Scandal of Service: Jesus Washes Our Feet*, Arche Collection (New York: Continuum, 1998), 38.

66 Parker J. Palmer tells the story of a time when he was suffering from depression and one friend came by his house every day, sat with him, and rubbed his feet. Unlike the friends who tried to talk to him or cheer him up, this friend simply provided presence and physical contact. Palmer credits this friend with seeing him through his bout with depression. Though Palmer was suffering from depression rather than from a violent physical assault, he recognized that his friend's act of daily foot massage was an embodied act of burden bearing. It was an act that honored the preciousness of Palmer's body and therefore of Palmer himself. Palmer, *Let Your Life Speak: Listening for the Voice of Vocation* (San Francisco: Jossey-Bass, 2000), 60–61.

67 "How I act toward others affects them not externally but internally, and that means I can render someone lovely, or I can bruise them deeply. How I relate to others to a large extent determines who they will be. I can touch the promise of their lives and lure it to fullness, or I can crush or destroy them—my agency has that awful, splendid power." Paul J. Wadell, *Friendship and the Moral Life* (Notre Dame, Ind.: University of Notre Dame Press, 1989), 162.

68 That this is only partially true reflects the ability of compassion to outlast resistance.

69 The critical nature of vulnerability and its right reception is addressed brilliantly in Brown, *Daring Greatly*.

70 In *Resident Aliens*, Stanley Hauerwas and William Willimon offer an example of a willingness to be vulnerable in a holy friendship that seems, by cultural standards, to make little sense. They tell the story of a woman who is assaulted in her yard and is urged by her therapist to find someone

outside of her family and aside from her pastor to whom she can tell her story. Much to the surprise of her pastor she chooses to talk to a man who is a recovering alcoholic. When asked why, she answers, because he has been to hell and back, "I think he will know what it has felt like for me to go there. Perhaps he can tell me how he got back." Hauerwas and Willimon, *Resident Aliens: Life in the Christian Colony* (Nashville: Abingdon, 1989), 110.

71   Serene Jones, *Trauma and Grace: Theology in a Ruptured World* (Louisville, Ky.: Westminster John Knox, 2009), 18.

72   Harak points out that in loving intimate relationships young children remain largely unaware of the power differential between themselves and their caregivers. Harak, "Child Abuse and Embodiment," 320. In time, of course, young children do become aware of their relative lack of power. However, for children in intimate relationships where their lack of power has not been used against them, they tend to see adults as those with greater, even magical, powers to do all manner of good, from fixing broken toys to healing scrapes and bruises.

73   This is not in any way to deny the significance or importance of a child's openness to adults. This innocent stage of lack of awareness of vulnerability is crucial for the child to develop trust more properly understood. This may rightly be thought of as the foundation upon which trust can be built, but it is not trust itself. If this stage of relative innocence is necessary for the development of trust, this implies that for those whose vulnerability is exploited at an early age, the future development of trust is rendered impossible, thus granting ultimacy to the power of sin rather than to the redeeming and transforming power of God.

74   Stanley Hauerwas, "Abortion, Theologically Understood," in *Hauerwas Reader*, 612.

Chapter 5

1   Augustine, *Saint Augustine: Confessions*, trans. R. S. Pine-Coffin (New York: Penguin, 1961), book XI.

2   Slightly more than fifteen hundred years later, Martin Heidegger became one of the first philosophers to articulate a sustained discussion of temporal ontology. Heidegger suggests that being (by which he intends not just human beings but being itself) takes place in time. Because there is no being outside of time, there is therefore no identity outside of that which is experienced in time. Heidegger speaks of humanity's "thrownness" into time, an act that necessarily, then, means that identity is "caught" between the remembered and contingent past and the anticipated and open future. By "thrownness" Heidegger refers to the contingency of history in which beings find themselves, contingencies that are always already existent, offering both possibilities for life as well as the inevitability of death. For

more on Heidegger's understanding of the temporal nature of identity, see Heidegger, *The Concept of Time*, Athlone Contemporary European Thinkers (London: Athlone, 2011); and idem, *Being and Time* (New York: Harper, 1962).

Gadamer, a student of Heidegger, further emphasizes the importance of openness. In discussing the importance of history, Gadamer argues for the necessity of an openness to the past that overcomes the admittedly wide temporal gap between past and present. Hans-Georg Gadamer, *Truth and Method* (New York: Seabury, 1975). The same claim, it seems, needs to be made in relation to the future.

3   For Heidegger, it is this embracing of the possibility of the future—as opposed to being bound by the status quo—that is what it means to be authentic, and authenticity is his understanding of human telos.

4   Though speaking of literary theory rather than of temporal ontology, this illustration comes from Frank Kermode, *The Sense of an Ending: Studies in the Theory of Fiction with a New Epilogue* (New York: Oxford University Press, 2000), esp. 44–46.

5   The notion of "future stories" comes from Andrew D. Lester, *Hope in Pastoral Care and Counseling* (Louisville, Ky.: Westminster John Knox, 1995). Though Lester speaks primarily of the pastoral situations of grief that arise at the loss of a loved one, whether through death, divorce, or serious illness, his insight that images of the future are a constitutive part of present identity, and that grief, insofar as it renders such future stories void, is aptly applied to situations of violence and suffering as well.

6   Alasdair MacIntyre suggests that there is no present "which is not informed by some image of the future which always presents itself in the form of telos—or a variety of ends or goals—toward which we are either moving or failing to move in the present . . . our lives have a certain form which projects itself toward our future." MacIntyre, *After Virtue*, 215–16.

Insofar as Heidegger considers—and then rejects—a theological account of teleology, his account of being in time is problematic. Whereas I think his insight that human identity is inherently temporal is critical, his rejection of a teleological basis for this connection between temporality and identity is lacking because it fails to account for the created nature of time. Though it is beyond the scope of this project, a fuller consideration of the temporal nature of human identity not only would need to consider not the fact that identity is experienced in and through time, and is made up of time, but would also need to take into account the created nature of time as a gift given for the sake of temporal beings.

7   See Stephen Crites, "The Narrative Quality of Experience," *Journal of the American Academy of Religion* 39 (1971): 292.

8   For more on Paul Ricoeur's understanding of time and narrative emplot-
    ment, see Ricoeur, *Oneself as Another* (Chicago: University of Chicago
    Press, 1992).

9   This understanding of identity is perhaps analogous to Zeno's paradox
    of motion. The paradox of motion states that if, e.g., one is to cross the
    room, the distance from one side of the room to the other must first be cut
    in half. Once half the distance has been traversed there is a new starting
    point, a new zero, so to speak. It is from this point that one now must
    again cut the distance in half. With each movement there is a new starting
    point, one in which the distance already traversed as well as the distance
    still to be traversed meet. The observation that with each step forward
    there is a new starting point—with both a different history and a different
    future, while it is still the same person making the journey—is, perhaps,
    a helpful image. The paradox is in the theoretical observation that such
    cutting in half of physical distance can continue ad infinitum, a concept
    known as asymptotic theory in statistics. Asymptotic theory is perhaps
    also a helpful way of envisioning the movement through time toward
    one's telos. It is, theoretically, possible to get closer and closer to who one
    actually is without ever—this side of the eschaton—fully realizing one's
    identity. Zeno's paradox is from Plato's "Paramenides" and is explained
    in a helpful way in John Lechte, *Key Contemporary Concepts: From Abjection
    to Zeno's Paradox* (London: SAGE, 2003).

10 See, e.g., Peters, *Anticipating Omega*.

11 MacIntyre, *After Virtue*, esp. chaps. 14 and 15. MacIntyre, of course,
    argues that post-Enlightenment Western civilization has lost its sense of
    telos, that the modern, or postmodern, Western world is fragmented, with
    little or no sense of direction or purpose.

12 The power of memorials to create, rather than merely represent, history
    is evidenced, for example, by the proliferation of "Heritage not hate"
    bumper stickers throughout the South in a post–Civil-Rights era. This
    is a way in which memorializing the past serves the purpose of rewriting
    and reinterpreting the past in light of the values of the present, not of the
    values of the past.

13 Elaine Ramshaw suggests that in addition to the proliferation of memo-
    rials in contemporary society there is a sense in which the increasing ten-
    dency toward memorials that are both larger and more spontaneous (and,
    not insignificantly, less institutionalized) is emblematic of a fragmented
    culture. Ramshaw, "The Personalization of Postmodern Post-mortem
    Rituals," *Pastoral Psychology* 59, no. 2 (2010).

14 This need to memorialize the past, and particularly those who have
    died whether tragically or heroically (or both), is also a means of cop-
    ing with grief and loss. Erika Doss claims that the increasingly common

spontaneous memorials that appear at the sight of crime scenes or accidents—memorials in which flowers, stuffed animals, notes, and other personal tokens of affection gather—are a communal way of dealing with grief that is overwhelming or appears to have no end in sight. Doss refers to a "material culture of grief" by which she means that in a culture that has given up any theologically grounded hope, comfort must necessarily come from and be expressed by material goods. She suggests that the increase of such material displays of memorialization reflect what Mac-Intyre points to as the contemporary loss of telos. Doss, "Spontaneous Memorials and Contemporary Modes of Mourning in America," *Material Religion* 2, no. 3 (2006).

There are also those who argue that memorials are a way of pacifying the desire to honor important people and ideas in the past without actually paying heed to them. Cornel West makes just such a claim regarding the Martin Luther King Jr. Memorial in Washington, D.C., suggesting that King "weeps from his grave" at the replacement of action with symbolism. West, "Dr. King Weeps from His Grave," *New York Times*, August 26, 2011, http://www.nytimes.com/2011/08/26/opinion/martin-luther-king-jr-would-want-a-revolution-not-a-memorial.html.

15   In an NPR interview that aired on May 23, 2006, discussing the events of 9/11, Dave Isay, founder of StoryCorps, remarked, "There is no closure; the best we can hope for is to remember." His remark seems to reflect the predominant pathos of contemporary memorials.

16   Harold Bloom suggests that this sort of Gnosticism is, in fact, the new American religion—a development Bloom views favorably. Bloom, *The American Religion: The Emergence of the Post-Christian Nation* (New York: Simon & Schuster, 1993).

17   This sort of modern-day Gnosticism is illustrated in Alice Sebold, *The Lovely Bones* (Boston: Little, Brown, 2002), in which fourteen-year-old Susie Salmon is brutally raped, murdered, and dismembered. The novel is the story of Susie's disembodied soul watching her family attempt to come to terms with what has happened and occasionally interacting with those whom she has left behind. Such books on life after death provide modern-day images of a sort of reincarnation that denies the finality of death while offering a moralistic or psychologized explanation for continued life. The characters live on after death in order to learn some important lesson or to ease the pain of death's finality.

18   See, e.g., Irving S. Cooper, *Reincarnation, the Hope of the World* (Wheaton, Ill.: Theosophical, 1955); Mark Albrecht, *Reincarnation, a Christian Critique of a New Age Doctrine* (Downers Grove, Ill.: InterVarsity, 1987); and Geddes MacGregor, *Reincarnation as a Christian Hope* (Totowa, N.J.: Barnes & Noble, 1982).

206 ＊ Notes to pages 119–121

19   Though still quite prevalent, the myth of progress is not uncontested. See,
      e.g., John Leslie, *The End of the World: The Science and Ethics of Human Extinc-
      tion* (New York: Routledge, 1996), in which Leslie suggests the extinction
      of the human species—largely as a result of the "progress" made that
      results in war, disease, and damage to the environment—is likely in the
      relatively near future. Similarly, Christopher Lasch suggests that the con-
      temporary (nineteenth and twentieth century) notion of and drive toward
      progress cannot be sustained indefinitely. Lasch, *The True and Only Heaven:
      Progress and Its Critics* (New York: Norton, 1991).

20   For an example of the new atheists' focus on science, see Victor J.
      Stenger, *The New Atheism: Taking a Stand for Science and Reason* (Amherst,
      N.Y.: Prometheus, 2009). The very title implies not only a disjuncture
      between faith and reason but the placement of hope on science and rea-
      son alone. John F. Haught, however, argues that there is little, if any-
      thing, "new" in the writings of the new atheists. Rather, he claims that
      the wave of new atheists' books are rather shallow reincarnations of the
      intellectually more stimulating writings of Freud, Nietzsche, and Marx.
      Haught, *God and the New Atheism: A Critical Response to Dawkins, Harris, and
      Hitchens* (Louisville, Ky.: Westminster John Knox, 2008).

21   Despite the element of social Darwinism evident in sociohistorical con-
      ceptions of the myth of progress, the myth of progress as it is understood
      scientifically and as it is understood historically are not merely different
      but rather totally irreconcilable. The scientific myth of progress is largely
      based on evolutionary theory, the cosmological variety of which posits
      that the universe is continually expanding and will eventually reach a
      point where it will cease to be. This can perhaps be understood through
      the theory of entropy—the tendency of the universe to move from a state
      of order to disorder. The myth of progress as it applies to history pre-
      sumes movement toward a utopia, which could perhaps be restated as
      a historical movement from disorder to order. This reflects the general
      sense of confusion over what precisely constitutes progress.

22   For an engaging and insightful theological critique of the myth of prog-
      ress, see Lesslie Newbigin, *Signs amid the Rubble: The Purposes of God in
      Human History* (Grand Rapids: Eerdmans, 2003); and idem, *The Gospel in a
      Pluralist Society* (Grand Rapids: Eerdmans, 1989).

23   For an accessible overview of the Human Genome Project, see Victor K.
      McElheny, *Drawing the Map of Life: Inside the Human Genome Project* (New
      York: Basic, 2010).

24   Georg Wilhelm Friedrich Hegel, *Lectures on the Philosophy of World History*
      (New York: Cambridge University Press, 1975).

25   Francis Fukuyama, *The End of History and the Last Man* (New York: Free
      Press, 1992).

26   Think, e.g., of the popularity of dystopian novels such as George Orwell, *Nineteen Eighty-Four: A Novel* (New York: Plume, 2003); Ray Bradbury, *Fahrenheit 451* (New York: Simon & Schuster, 2003); Aldous Huxley, *Brave New World* (New York: HarperCollins, 1946); the more recent Lois Lowry, *The Giver* (New York: Houghton Mifflin, 1993); and Suzanne Collins' Hunger Games trilogy (New York: Scholastic, 2008–2010).

27   I suggest a theological account of hope as opposed to a theology of hope to maintain a distinction between this project and that of Jürgen Moltmann. Though any contemporary theological engagement with Christian hope is necessarily to a large extent a reflection of the significance of Moltmann and his *Theology of Hope*, I will not be engaging at length directly with Moltmann. For Moltmann, all Christian theology, including Christology, rightly flows from eschatology, and hope is the form this eschatology takes, making the distinction between hope and eschaton a bit blurry. Moltmann's theology of hope suggests that, in the end, eschatology is less about the end and more about hope. My understanding is that the end itself is of primary—in fact, ultimate—significance and that hope is the theological means, the virtue, by which we move toward that end. See Moltmann, *Theology of Hope: On the Ground and the Implications of a Christian Eschatology* (Minneapolis: Fortress, 1993).

28   The distinction between hope as ultimate and hope as penultimate is reflected in the tension between theologies of realized eschatology and those of inaugurated eschatology.

29   For more on the distinction between imagination and imaginary, see Garrett Green, *Imagining God: Theology and the Religious Imagination* (San Francisco: Harper & Row, 1989), chap. 4.

30   Stressing the importance of the imagination and the imaginative in speaking of hope is not to suggest that imagination is a panacea. In fact, imagination can be as much a source of harm as it can of good. The imagination can lead to hope as well as to despair. My contention is that hope requires the development of a particular sort of theological imagination and is not intended as a blanket approbation of the imaginative faculties.

31   Gotthold Lessing, in reference to what he perceives to be the chasm between the contingent truths of history and the claims of the Christian faith. "On the Proof of the Spirit and of Power," in *Lessing's Theological Writings* (Stanford, Calif.: Stanford University Press, 1956), 55.

32   Christian hope, grounded in the resurrection of Jesus, rules out the possibility of hope for anything less than the fulfillment of the promises of Jesus. This logically excludes the possibility of hope for anything contrary to the express will of God. One cannot rightly hope for the triumph of evil. Such cannot be hope, but is instead distorted desire.

33 As such, hope is necessarily connected with desire. As recognition of the distance between what is and what might be, hope is inextricably connected with desire. Desire is the reaching out for the good. Desire is the restlessness of which St. Augustine famously speaks (*Confessions* I,1). The desire we feel is an overflow of God's love in us, pulling us further into communion with God. Desire is productive; it produces a longing for God, a longing for relationship. That desire and hope are integrally connected to one another in the human experience of relationship with God highlights that distance that separates humanity from God. Rather than envisioning this distance as an absence, however, it is perhaps more helpful to see this distance as the space within which relationship exists. Insofar as distance is a necessary component of distinction, distance provides the alterity necessary for relationship. Because hope is the form that right relationship between the present and the future takes, hope works rightly to order desire. For more on desire as presence, see Daniel M. Bell, *Liberation Theology after the End of History: The Refusal to Cease Suffering* (New York: Routledge, 2001), 90.

Desire has, of course, often been denigrated in Christian theology and praxis. Insofar as this has been correct, it reflects the reality that desire is distorted by sin. Desire, however, is trainable. Mark A. Powell suggests that Matt 6:21, "Where your treasure is, there your heart will be also," is not merely an observation but a promise, a promise that we can train our hearts, our desires; we can actively participate in the right ordering of our desires. Powell, *Loving Jesus* (Minneapolis: Fortress, 2004), 137–45. On the trainability of desire, see also T. J. Gorringe, *The Education of Desire: Toward a Theology of the Senses* (Harrisburg, Pa.: Trinity International, 2002).

34 The concept that all time is rightly understood doxologically is an extension of John Howard Yoder's argument that history can only rightly be remembered as doxology. See Yoder, "To Serve Our God."

35 William F. Lynch, *Images of Hope: Imagination as Healer of the Hopeless* (Notre Dame, Ind.: University of Notre Dame Press, 1974), 37.

36 Garrett Green suggests an important distinction between "as if" and "as." "As if," he suggests, implies a sense of nonreality, a willingness to play make-believe akin to the story of "The Emperor's New Clothes," whereas "as" implies a reality that may or may not be apparent but is no less real as a result of its opaqueness. As I find this distinction logically compelling; it seems more correct to me to suggest that hope is the means by which the church lives as those waiting for the fullness of the kingdom. For more on this distinction, see Green, *Imagining God*, chap. 4.

37 That suffering may diminish hope does not suggest that suffering necessarily obliterates hope. Hope does not have to be destroyed in order

to be theologically problematic. To the extent that hope is disordered or distorted, the ability to envision redemption is likewise diminished.

38 Toni Morrison's novel *Beloved* offers a poignant illustration of the power of expectations of future suffering. Sethe, the main character, is a runaway slave who is pursued by four white men who intend to capture her and return her to slavery. When faced with the inescapability of her situation, in a desperate refusal to allow her child to be condemned to a future determined by the suffering of slavery, Sethe slits her baby's throat. Over this backdrop of the memory of profound suffering—both the violence of Sethe's own experience of slavery as well as her own desperately violent refusal to allow her child to be subjected to slavery—Sethe is befriended by another escaped slave, Paul D. Paul D likewise continues to suffer profoundly the effects of the memory of the violence against him as a slave and, in a moment of remarkable insight, tells Sethe, "[M]e and you, we got more yesterday than anybody. We need some kind of tomorrow." Morrison, *Beloved*, ed. Carl Plasa (New York: Columbia University Press, 1998), 322.

Sethe and Paul D are, in a sense, defined by their past suffering as slaves. However, that this is so is at least as much because of the lack of any promise that the future will be different from the past as it is because of the memory of slavery. In other words, that Sethe and Paul D have escaped slavery has not freed them from their suffering, because they have not yet found hope for a future in which they are, in fact, free. There is, as Paul D suggests, no way for yesterday to be redeemed in the absence of a promise of a tomorrow.

39 Rowan Williams, *Resurrection: Interpreting the Easter Gospel* (Cleveland, Ohio: Pilgrim, 2002), 23.

40 This is not to suggest that hope and desire are coterminous but rather to suggest that hope is ontologically prior to desire. Desire presumes hope; without hope, desire, as a reaching out for the good, is extinguished.

41 Brison, *Aftermath*, 96.

42 Even martyrdom, rightly understood, does not seek suffering for suffering's sake. Rather, martyrs accept, even embrace, suffering rather than reject God. As such, their suffering is the embracing of the positive good that is God. Were it possible to both embrace the positive good of God *and* avoid suffering the violence of martyrdom, this would, of course, be preferable.

43 An avoidance of suffering, as opposed to pursuit of a positive good, is precisely what Marie M. Fortune advocates: "I start from what may sound like a negative place: doing least harm. Why not 'doing most good' and 'making justice,' you may well ask? 'Doing most good' and 'making justice' are the vision of possibility for which we may strive in relationship.

But 'doing least harm' is probably what we are capable of. Doing least harm is a realistic and tangible goal to set for ourselves. I may not know what is the most good that I could do, and if I know, I may not be capable of it. But I probably have an idea about the harm that I could do and hopefully am capable of avoiding it." Fortune, *Love Does No Harm: Sexual Ethics for the Rest of Us* (New York: Continuum, 1995), 34.

　　Fortune's claim seems misguided on at least two counts. The presumption that avoiding doing harm is easier than doing good fails to take into account the human capacity for and propensity toward sin. The presumption that avoidance of a negative—as opposed to pursuit of a good—is the best we have to hope for overlooks the power of the Holy Spirit active in the world now. Fortune's claim that the avoidance of suffering is the best we have to hope for illustrates precisely the sort of loss of hope to which profound suffering can contribute.

44　Scarry, *Body in Pain*, 35.

45　In *Too Scared to Cry*, Lenore Terr describes the effects of profound trauma on children over an extended period of time. In 1976 a California school bus full of elementary school children was hijacked and the children were buried alive in a cargo hold in an abandoned rock quarry. The children escaped and none were seriously harmed physically. However, Terr, a child psychologist, interviewed the children and their families in the immediate aftermath and at regular intervals for the following two decades, and she notes that even years after the event itself the majority of the children continue to anticipate a short life. A number of them report making no plans for the future because *they do not expect to have a future*. A single event of profound suffering led to an expectation of a foreshortened future. Terr rightly suggests that this loss of expectation for the future is a direct result of an experience of overwhelming vulnerability such that the children were rendered incapable of imagining their vulnerability not being further exploited in the future. If such is the outcome of a single event—one in which there was no corresponding physical trauma—how much more so might this sense of a foreshortened future potentially be present in situations of prolonged, repeated, or physically harmful situations of suffering? Terr, *Too Scared to Cry: Psychic Trauma in Childhood* (New York: Basic Books, 1990).

46　Stephen Crites, "Storytime: Recollecting the Past and Projecting the Future," in *Narrative Psychology: The Storied Nature of Human Conduct*, ed. Theodore R. Sarbin (Santa Barbara: Praeger, 1986), 168.

47　James Baldwin claims "the most dangerous creation in any society is the man with nothing to lose." Insofar as this is true, it is true because someone with nothing to lose has no hope for anything better than what that person experiences as hopeless. This lack of hope may lead to the apathy of despair, but it may also result in rash and irrational behavior. See James Baldwin, *The Fire Next Time* (New York: Random House, 1993), 76.

48   In his book *A Dream of the Tattered Man*, Randolph Loney describes his experiences as a chaplain working with death row inmates, all of whom shared with him stories of profound personal suffering in the years leading up to the capital offense for which they are in prison. Though there is no simple calculus by which one might determine the reason for murder, lack of hope leading to the sense that there was nothing to lose is a common thread through many of the stories Loney shares. Loney, *A Dream of a Tattered Man: Stories from Georgia's Death Row* (Grand Rapids: Eerdmans, 2001).

49   Much of what follows is indebted to Jones, *Embodying Forgiveness.*

50   I am profoundly indebted to extended conversation with Greg Jones on the nature of forgiveness and its connection to memory.

51   "Our common experience in fact is the opposite—that the past, far from disappearing or lying down and being quiet, has an embarrassing and persistent way of returning and haunting us unless it has in fact been dealt with adequately. Unless we look the beast in the eye we find it has an uncanny habit of returning to hold us hostage." Desmond Tutu, *No Future without Forgiveness* (New York: Doubleday, 1999), 28.

52   "The point is that, if perpetrators were to be despaired of as monsters and demons, then we were thereby letting accountability go out the window because we were then declaring that they were not moral agents . . . it meant that we had abandoned all hope of their being able to change for the better . . . despite the awfulness of their deeds, [the perpetrators] remained children of God with the capacity to repent, to be able to change." Tutu, *No Future without Forgiveness*, 83. Recognizing the moral agency of the perpetrators of suffering includes the practice of holding them accountable for the behavior even, and perhaps especially when, such accountability becomes a matter of criminal law. Though revenge and forgiveness are clearly mutually exclusive, forgiveness does not necessarily entail a refusal to address the suffering through legal channels.

   Miroslav Volf, however, does see retributive justice as antithetical to forgiveness. He claims, "To forgive means, first, *not to press charges* against the wrongdoer." Additionally he suggests that "a person cannot forgive while at the same time *wanting* the state to punish the offender." Volf, *Free of Charge: Giving and Forgiving in a Culture Stripped of Grace* (Grand Rapids: Zondervan, 2005), 169, 171 (emphasis in original).

   Volf's claim seems problematic to me on a number of grounds. In addition to denying moral agency by refusing to hold the perpetrators of violence accountable for past actions, a refusal to consider legal recourse may well set the stage for future violence, and as such it fails to take seri-ously the call to protect not only other innocent persons but the perpetra-tor himself. Forgiveness does not negate agency, and neither judicial nor nonjudicial protective behavior precludes the possibility of forgiveness. In fact, insofar as forgiveness is the telling of a truthful story, protective behavior may—e.g., in situations of domestic violence—be a necessary precursor to, and condition of, forgiveness.

53 The danger of the complacency of those not directly involved is perhaps most famously noted by Martin Luther King Jr. in his "Letter from Bir-mingham Jail": "I must confess that over the last few years I have been gravely disappointed with the white moderate. I have almost reached the regrettable conclusion that the Negro's great stumbling block in the stride toward freedom is not the White Citizens Councillor or the Ku Klux Klanner but the white moderate who is more devoted to order than to justice; who prefers a negative peace which is the absence of tension to a positive peace which is the presence of justice."

54 Social psychologists have noted that the larger the crowd of onlookers, the less likely someone is to intervene on behalf of an innocent third party. They have labeled this phenomenon the "bystander effect." A recent hor-rendous example took place in 2009 when a fifteen-year-old girl was gang raped outside the gymnasium of Richmond High School in sub-urban San Francisco, California, over the course of several hours while dozens of students looked on. As news of the attack spread, the crowd of spectators grew, some onlookers using their cell phones to take pic-tures. Yet no attempt was made to stop the attack. For more on this, see Stephanie Chen, "Gang Rape Raises Questions about Bystanders' Role," CNN.com, October 30, 2009, http://www.cnn.com/2009/CRIME/10/28/california.gang.rape.bystander/.

55 E.g., the suffering of slavery, or of the Holocaust, or of social conditions that accept vulnerable persons. The forgiveness of such systems and powers is not acquiescence to injustice. In fact, forgiveness may include sociopolitical activity focused on the alleviation of the very injustice that creates the conditions for suffering.

56 E.g., Susan Brison, who was sexually assaulted in the midst of an early morning run, discusses at length her sense that, though the attack itself was not her fault, she was at least partially to blame insofar as she chose to run alone on a rural road, placing herself in a potentially vulnerable situation. Brison, *Aftermath*, 73–77.

57 Jones, *Embodying Forgiveness*, 149.

58 This, of course, is not to deny the very real possibility that one may genu-inely feel love toward those who have perpetrated great suffering. Rather, what I am claiming is that feelings are not reliable indices of love. Love is

something that can be willed and acted upon even in the absence of loving emotions. Thus, forgiveness can be a choice, in the form of concrete acts of love, grace, and charity, a choice through which the Holy Spirit may transform the heart.

59 For more on the concrete communal practices of forgiveness, see also L. Gregory Jones, "Crafting Communities of Forgiveness," *Interpretation* 54 (2000): 121–34.

60 In the aftermath of the Nickel Mines School shooting in which Charles Roberts shot ten young girls, killing five of them and seriously wounding the other five before killing himself, the Amish community immediately expressed its collective forgiveness of both Roberts and his family. "[T]he responsibility to forgive Charles Roberts was not assigned to the school children or even to their families but was embraced by the entire Amish community . . . the Amish would never place the responsibility to forgive an offense of this magnitude on the principal victims alone." Donald B. Kraybill, Steven M. Nolt, and David L. Weaver-Zercher, *Amish Grace: How Forgiveness Transcended Tragedy* (San Francisco: Jossey-Bass, 2010), 133.

This is neither intended to idealize the Amish nor to commend all that is integrally connected to their understanding of forgiveness. However, that forgiveness is woven into the very fabric of Amish communal life such that the community understands itself to have the responsibility to forgive on behalf of those who may not yet be able to do so, and perhaps more significantly that the individuals within the community rely on the community's willingness to do so, is a critical point.

Kraybill, Nolt, and Weaver-Zercher note that from the perspective of many outsiders the Amish forgiveness of Roberts appeared to be automatic, instantaneous. In a sense, they suggest, this is the case. However, this is the case only because of the habits of worship and discipleship by which the community has been and continues to be formed. What appears to be an automatic response is not incidental to an intentional way of life. The authors of *Amish Grace* demonstrate that what allows for forgiveness to spring up spontaneously is a practice that is carefully and painstakingly cultivated.

61 The problem of an individual offering forgiveness on behalf of a community, without the support of the community, is the poignant struggle of Simon Wiesenthal, *The Sunflower: On the Possibilities and Limits of Forgiveness* (New York: Schocken, 1997). Wiesenthal tells of being asked by a dying SS member for absolution for the officer's participation in the horrors of a concentration camp. Wiesenthal finds himself unable to respond and wonders later whether or not he ought to have forgiven the man.

62 Nor does the partial nature of forgiveness render it void. Whatever steps can be taken in the direction of forgiveness are steps worth taking. This may mean that acknowledging that there are times in which forgiveness means not wishing evil for another. Perhaps it means being able to pray for another's well-being. The point is, though the telos of forgiveness is reconciliation, forgiveness is not diminished by its incompleteness, because forgiveness is a reflection of, and movement toward, the eschatological redemption promised by Christ. As such, its fulfillment is contingent not upon human attempts to get it right but on the power of the Holy Spirit.

63 Tutu, *No Future without Forgiveness*, 271.

64 In her introduction to the second edition of her book, Pamela Cooper-White suggests that a third category—something beyond that of "victim" or even "survivor"—is needed, something that "makes room for entirely new possibilities that neither deny nor focus exclusively upon past injuries in the formation of who she is today." This is precisely what I am suggesting that "witness" might have the theological weight to do. Cooper-White, *Cry of Tamar*, 15.

65 John Milbank, *Being Reconciled: Ontology and Pardon*, Radical Orthodoxy Series (New York: Routledge, 2003), chap. 2.

66 I find the claim that spectator violence is qualitatively more violent than participatory violence to be unconvincing. However, the crucial point is that spectator violence is violence. It is the form that is different, not the degree.

67 Elie Wiesel, *Night* (New York: Farrar, Straus & Giroux, 1972), 63–65.

68 In her memoir *The Glass Castle*, Jeannette Walls offers a poignant example of the ways in which the scars of past suffering (whether physical or metaphysical) bear witness to the failure of suffering to prevail. Though not physically abused, Walls was neglected. As a young child she was routinely left alone to cook and care for herself. At the age of three, while preparing herself a hot dog, she scalded herself with boiling water, leaving a scar on her chest, about which she remained acutely self-conscious well into adulthood. She describes the first time her now husband saw the scar, "[H]e said it was interesting. He used the word 'textured.' He said 'smooth' was boring but 'textured' was interesting, and the scar meant that I was stronger than whatever it was that had tried to hurt me." Walls, *The Glass Castle: A Memoir* (New York: Scribner, 2005), 286.

69 Abraham Maslow, "A Theory of Human Motivation," *Psychological Review* 50, no. 4 (1943): 370–96.

70 Samuel Wells refers to this as "reincorporating the lost." Wells, speaking in largely eschatological terms, suggests that the end of a story is

recognized, at least in part, by the reweaving, into the thread of the narrative, previously discarded bits. Wells, *Improvisation*, chap. 10.

71 This is what the author of Genesis says in regard to Joseph's suffering at the hands of his brothers. What the brothers intended for harm, God intended for good. The Hebrew verb used is *chashav*, which means "intend" but carries with it the connotation of creativity or artistry. God's intention was *not* that Joseph suffer. God's intention was that even Joseph's suffering be creatively used within the larger narration of God's redemptive work.

72 This is *not* an instrumentalization of ecclesial practices. That forgiveness is a vocational practice does not mean that forgiveness can be practiced for the sake of receiving and crafting a vocation. Rather, the recognition that practices make evident redemption is a reminder that redemption is a reality that one has to be taught to see. The telos of the ecclesial practices is always right relationship with God. *That* the practices often aid us in right vision so that we can also see God is the result of God's grace, not the efficacy of our performance.

73 See 1 Cor 14.

74 Nicholas Wolterstorff offers an important cautionary note about how we interpret the acceptance and crafting of a vocation as an element of the redemption of the memory of suffering. Wolterstorff, writing of the loss of his young adult son, recognizes this vocation of those who have suffered to recognize the blessings they have both received and been enabled to give to others as a result of their unique experience of pain. However, in his recognition that his life has changed profoundly as a result of his suffering—in ways that have enabled him to be a blessing to others—he says, "[W]ithout a moment's hesitation I would exchange those changes for Eric back." I suspect this tension between embracing the redemption of the memory of past suffering while never embracing the suffering itself is a theologically necessary tension with which those who have suffered profoundly will struggle until Jesus' return. See Wolterstorff, *Lament for a Son*, 73.

BIBLIOGRAPHY

Aelred [Saint Aelred of Rievaulx]. *Spiritual Friendship*. Edited by Lawrence C. Braceland and Marsha L. Dutton. Cistercian Fathers Series 5. Collegeville, Minn.: Liturgical, 2010.

Albrecht, Mark. *Reincarnation, a Christian Critique of a New Age Doctrine*. Downers Grove, Ill.: InterVarsity, 1987.

American Psychiatric Association. *Diagnostic and Statistical Manual of Mental Disorders: DSM-III*. Washington, D.C.: American Psychiatric Association, 1987.

———. *Diagnostic and Statistical Manual of Mental Disorders: DSM-IV*. Washington, D.C.: American Psychiatric Association, 2000.

———. *Diagnostic and Statistical Manual of Mental Disorders: DSM-V*. Washington, D.C.: American Psychiatric Association, 2013.

Anderson, V. Elving. "A Genetic View of Human Nature." In *Whatever Happened to the Soul? Scientific and Theological Portraits of Human Nature*, edited by Nancey Murphy, Warren S. Brown, and H. Newton Malony, 49–72. Minneapolis: Fortress, 1998.

Arendt, Hannah. *On Violence*. Orlando, Fla.: Harcourt, 1969.

Aristotle. *Aristotle's Nicomachean Ethics*. Edited by Robert C. Bartlett and Susan D. Collins. Chicago: University of Chicago Press, 2011.

Augustine, Bishop of Hippo. *Augustine: Confessions.* Translated by R. S. Pine-Coffin. New York: Penguin, 1961.

———. *On Free Choice of the Will.* Translated by Thomas Williams. Indianapolis: Hackett, 1993.

Baldwin, James. *The Fire Next Time.* New York: Random House, 1993.

Barth, Karl. *Church Dogmatics* [Kirchliche Dogmatik]. Edited by Geoffrey W. Bromiley and Thomas F. Torrance. Edinburgh: T&T Clark, 1956–1975.

———. *The Epistle to the Romans.* Edited by Sir Edwyn Clement Hoskyns. London: Oxford University Press, 1933.

Bass, Diana Butler, and Joseph Stewart-Sicking, eds. *From Nomads to Pilgrims: Stories from Practicing Congregations.* Herndon, Va.: Alban Institute, 2006.

Bass, Dorothy C., ed. *Practicing Our Faith: A Way of Life for a Searching People.* San Francisco: Jossey-Bass, 1997.

Bass, Dorothy C., and Miroslav Volf, eds. *Practicing Theology: Beliefs and Practices in Christian Life.* Grand Rapids: Eerdmans, 2002.

Bass, Ellen, and Laura Davis, eds. *The Courage to Heal: A Guide for Women Survivors of Child Sexual Abuse.* New York: Harper Perennial, 1994.

Bauckham, Richard. *Hope against Hope: Christian Eschatology at the Turn of the Millennium.* Edited by Trevor A. Hart. Grand Rapids: Eerdmans, 1999.

———. "Reading Scripture as a Coherent Story." In *The Art of Reading Scripture,* edited by Ellen F. Davis and Richard B. Hays, 38–53. Grand Rapids: Eerdmans, 2003.

Bell, Daniel M. *Liberation Theology after the End of History: The Refusal to Cease Suffering.* New York: Routledge, 2001.

Black, M. C., K. C. Basile, M. J. Breiding, S. G. Smith, M. L. Walters, M. T. Merrick, J. Chen, and M. R. Stevens. *The National Intimate Partner and Sexual Violence Survey: 2010 Summary Report.* Atlanta: Centers for Disease Control and Prevention, 2011.

Bloom, Harold. *The American Religion: The Emergence of the Post-Christian Nation.* New York: Simon & Schuster, 1993.

Boff, Leonardo. *Jesus Christ Liberator: A Critical Christology for Our Time.* Maryknoll, N.Y.: Orbis, 1978.

Booth, Wayne C. *The Company We Keep: An Ethics of Fiction.* Berkeley: University of California Press, 1988.

Bowker, John. *Problems of Suffering in Religions of the World.* New York: Cambridge University Press, 1970.

Bradbury, Ray. *Fahrenheit 451.* New York: Simon & Schuster, 2003.

Brison, Susan J. *Aftermath: Violence and the Remaking of a Self.* Princeton, N.J.: Princeton University Press, 2002.

Brondos, David A. *Fortress Introduction to Salvation and the Cross.* Minneapolis: Fortress, 2007.

— — —. *Paul on the Cross: Reconstructing the Apostle's Story of Redemption.* Minneapolis: Fortress, 2006.

Brooks, Peter. *Reading for the Plot: Design and Intention in Narrative.* Cambridge, Mass.: Harvard University Press, 1984.

Brown, Brene. *Daring Greatly: How the Courage to Be Vulnerable Transforms the Way We Live, Love, Parent, and Lead.* New York: Gotham, 2012.

Brown, Joanne Carlson, and Carole R. Bohn, eds. *Christianity, Patriarchy, and Abuse: A Feminist Critique.* Cleveland, Ohio: Pilgrim, 1989.

Brueggemann, Walter. *A Commentary on Jeremiah: Exile and Homecoming.* Grand Rapids: Eerdmans, 1998.

— — —. *Isaiah 40–66.* Louisville, Ky.: Westminster John Knox, 1998.

— — —. "The Rhetoric of Hurt and Hope: Ethics Odd and Crucial." *Annual of the Society of Christian Ethics* (1989): 73–92.

Bultmann, Rudolf. *Existence and Faith: Shorter Writings of Rudolf Bultmann.* Translated by Schubert M. Ogden. New York: Meridian, 1960.

Burke, Peter J. *Identity Theory.* Edited by Jan E. Stets. New York: Oxford University Press, 2009.

Burns, Maree, and Helen Malson, eds. *Critical Feminist Approaches to Eating Dis/Orders.* New York: Routledge, 2009.

Burrell, David B. *Deconstructing Theodicy: Why Job Has Nothing to Say to the Puzzle of Suffering.* Grand Rapids: Brazos, 2008.

Campbell, Douglas Atchison. *The Deliverance of God: An Apocalyptic Rereading of Justification in Paul.* Grand Rapids: Eerdmans, 2009.

Carter, Rita. *Multiplicity: The New Science of Personality, Identity, and the Self.* New York: Little, Brown, 2008.

Caruth, Cathy. *Trauma: Explorations in Memory.* Baltimore: Johns Hopkins University Press, 1995.

— — —. *Unclaimed Experience: Trauma, Narrative, and History.* Baltimore: Johns Hopkins University Press, 1996.

Castelli, Elizabeth A. *Martyrdom and Memory: Early Christian Culture Making.* New York: Columbia University Press, 2004.

Cavanaugh, William T. *Torture and Eucharist: Theology, Politics, and the Body of Christ.* Malden, Mass.: Blackwell, 1998.

Charon, Rita. *Narrative Medicine: Honoring the Stories of Illness.* New York: Oxford University Press, 2006.

Coakley, Sarah. *God, Sexuality, and the Self: An Essay 'On the Trinity.'* Cambridge: Cambridge University Press, 2013.

— — —. *Powers and Submissions: Spirituality, Philosophy and Gender.* Challenges in Contemporary Theology. Malden, Mass.: Blackwell, 2002.

Coles, Robert. *The Call of Stories: Teaching and the Moral Imagination.* Boston: Houghton Mifflin, 1989.

Colijn, Brenda B. *Images of Salvation in the New Testament.* Downers Grove, Ill.: InterVarsity, 2010.

Collins, Suzanne. Hunger Game trilogy. New York: Scholastic, 2008–2010.

Connerton, Paul. *How Modernity Forgets.* Cambridge: Cambridge University Press, 2009.

— — —. *How Societies Remember.* Cambridge: Cambridge University Press, 1989.

— — —. *The Spirit of Mourning: History, Memory and the Body.* Cambridge: Cambridge University Press, 2011.

Cooper, Irving S. *Reincarnation, the Hope of the World.* Wheaton, Ill.: Theosophical, 1955.

Cooper-White, Pamela. *Braided Selves: Collected Essays on Multiplicty, God, and Persons.* Eugene, Ore.: Cascade Books, 2011.

— — —. *The Cry of Tamar: Violence against Women and the Church's Response.* 2nd ed. Minneapolis: Fortress, 2012.

Crites, Stephen. "The Narrative Quality of Experience." *Journal of the American Academy of Religion* 39 (1971): 291–311.

— — —. "Storytime: Recollecting the Past and Projecting the Future." In *Narrative Psychology: The Storied Nature of Human Conduct,* ed. Theodore R. Sarbin, 152–73. Santa Barbara: Praeger, 1986.

Culp, Kristine. *Vulnerability and Glory: A Theological Account.* Louisville, Ky.: Westminster John Knox, 2010.

Curtis, Andrew, Jacqueline Warren Mills, and Michael Leitner. "Katrina and Vulnerability: The Geography of Stress." *Journal of Health Care for the Poor and Underserved* 18, no. 3 (2007): 315–30.

Davis, Ellen F. *Getting Involved with God: Rediscovering the Old Testament.* Cambridge, Mass.: Cowley, 2001.

Dawkins, Richard. *The God Delusion.* New York: First Mariner, 2006.

— — —. *River out of Eden: A Darwinian View of Life.* New York: Basic, 1995.

De La Torre, Miguel. *Doing Christian Ethics from the Margins*. 2nd ed. Maryknoll, N.Y.: Orbis, 2014.

DeYoung, Rebecca Konyndyk. *Glittering Vices: A New Look at the Seven Deadly Sins and Their Remedies*. Grand Rapids: Brazos, 2009.

Dillard, Annie. *Teaching a Stone to Talk: Expeditions and Encounters*. New York: Harper & Row, 1982.

Dodd, C. H. *The Parables of the Kingdom*. New York: Scribner's Sons, 1961.

Dorfman, Ariel. *Death and the Maiden*. New York: Penguin, 1992.

Doss, Erika. "Spontaneous Memorials and Contemporary Modes of Mourning in America." *Material Religion* 2, no. 3 (2006): 294–318.

Dunfee, Susan Nelson. "The Sin of Hiding: A Feminist Critique of Reinhold Niebuhr's Account of the Sin of Pride." *Soundings: An Interdisciplinary Journal* 65, no. 3 (1982): 316–27.

Dunn, James D. G. *The Theology of Paul the Apostle*. Grand Rapids: Eerdmans, 1998.

Dykstra, Craig R. *Growing in the Life of Faith: Education and Christian Practices*. Louisville, Ky.: Westminster John Knox, 2005.

Edwards, Tilden. *Spiritual Friend*. New York: Paulist, 1980.

Eklund, Rebekah. "Lord, Teach Us How to Grieve: Jesus' Laments and Christian Hope." PhD. Diss., Duke Divinity School, 2012.

Erikson, Erik H. *Identity and the Life Cycle*. New York: Norton, 1980.

Erikson, Kai. "Notes on Trauma and Community." In *Trauma: Explorations in Memory*, edited by Cathy Caruth, 183–99. Baltimore: John Hopkins University Press, 1995.

Fagan, Sean. "Penitential Practices." In *The New Dictionary of Sacramental Worship*, 941–44. Collegeville, Minn.: Liturgical, 1990.

Fatula, Mary Ann. *The Triune God of Christian Faith*. Collegeville, Minn.: Liturgical, 1990.

Fink, Peter E., ed. *The New Dictionary of Sacramental Worship*. Collegeville, Minn.: Liturgical, 1990.

Ford, David. *The Shape of Living: Spiritual Directions for Modern Everday Life*. Grand Rapids: Baker, 1998.

Fortune, Marie M. *Love Does No Harm: Sexual Ethics for the Rest of Us*. New York: Continuum, 1995.

Fowl, Stephen E. *Engaging Scripture: A Model for Theological Interpretation*. Malden, Mass.: Blackwell, 1998.

———. *Philippians*. The Two Horizons New Testament Commentary. Grand Rapids: Eerdmans, 2005.

Freire, Paulo. *Pedagogy of the Oppressed*. Translated by Myra Bergman Ramos. 30th anniv. ed. New York: Continuum, 2000.

Fukuyama, Francis. *The End of History and the Last Man*. New York: Free Press, 1992.

Gadamer, Hans-Georg. *Truth and Method*. New York: Seabury, 1975.

Gaventa, Beverly Roberts, ed. *Apocalyptic Paul: Cosmos and Anthropos in Romans 5–8*. Waco, Tex.: Baylor University Press, 2013.

Gerhardt, Elizabeth. *The Cross and Gendercide: A Theological Response to Global Violence against Women and Girls*. Downers Grove, Ill.: Inter-Varsity, 2014.

Gilbert, Roberta M. *The Eight Concepts of Bowen Theory: A New Way of Thinking about the Individual and the Group*. Falls Church, Va.: Leading Systems, 2004.

Gladwell, Malcolm. *Outliers: The Story of Success*. New York: Little, Brown, 2008.

Goldstein, Valerie Saiving. "The Human Situation: A Feminine View." *Journal of Religion* 40, no. 2 (1960): 100–112.

Gorringe, T. J. *The Education of Desire: Toward a Theology of the Senses*. Harrisburg, Penn.: Trinity Press International, 2002.

Gottschall, Jonathan. *The Storytelling Animal: How Stories Make Us Human*. New York: Houghton Mifflin, 2012.

Green, Garrett. *Imagining God: Theology and the Religious Imagination*. San Francisco: Harper & Row, 1989.

Gutiérrez, Gustavo. *A Theology of Liberation: History, Politics, and Salvation*. London: SCM Press, 1998.

Haddon, Mark. *The Curious Incident of the Dog in the Night-Time*. New York: Doubleday, 2003.

Halbwachs, Maurice. *On Collective Memory*. Edited by Lewis A. Coser. Chicago: University of Chicago Press, 1992.

Hanisch, Carol. "The Personal Is Political." *Notes from the Second Year: Women's Liberation* (1970): 76–78.

Harak, G. Simon. "Child Abuse and Embodiment from a Thomistic Perspective." *Modern Theology* 11, no. 3 (1995): 315–40.

Hare, Douglas R. A. *Matthew*. Interpretation: A Bible Commentary for Teaching and Preaching. Louisville, Ky.: Westminster John Knox, 1993.

Hart, David Bentley. *The Doors of the Sea: Where Was God in the Tsunami?* Grand Rapids: Eerdmans, 2005.

Hauerwas, Stanley. *Character and the Christian Life: A Study in Theological Ethics*. San Antonio: Trinity University Press, 1975.

— — —. *Christian Existence Today: Essays on Church, World, and Living in Between*. Durham, N.C.: Labyrinth Press, 1988.

— — —. *The Hauerwas Reader*. Edited by John Berkman and Michael G. Cartwright. Durham, N.C.: Duke University Press, 2001.

— — —. *Matthew*. Brazos Theological Commentary on the Bible. Grand Rapids: Brazos, 2006.

— — —. *Naming the Silences: God, Medicine, and the Problem of Suffering*. Grand Rapids: Eerdmans, 1990.

— — —. *The Peaceable Kingdom: A Primer in Christian Ethics*. Notre Dame, Ind.: University of Notre Dame Press, 1983.

— — —. *Sanctify Them in the Truth: Holiness Exemplified*. Nashville: Abingdon, 1998.

— — —. *Suffering Presence: Theological Reflections on Medicine, the Mentally Handicapped, and the Church*. Notre Dame, Ind.: University of Notre Dame Press, 1986.

— — —. *Vision and Virtue: Essays in Christian Ethical Reflection*. Notre Dame, Ind.: University of Notre Dame Press, 1981.

Hauerwas, Stanley, and L. Gregory Jones, eds. *Why Narrative? Readings in Narrative Theology*. Eugene, Ore.: Wipf & Stock, 1997.

Hauerwas, Stanley, and Jean Vanier. *Living Gently in a Violent World: The Prophetic Witness of Weakness*. Downers Grove, Ill.: InterVarsity, 2008.

Hauerwas, Stanley, and William Willimon. *Resident Aliens: Life in the Christian Colony*. Nashville: Abingdon, 1989.

Haught, John F. *God and the New Atheism: A Critical Response to Dawkins, Harris, and Hitchens*. Louisville, Ky.: Westminster John Knox, 2008.

Heidegger, Martin. *Being and Time*. New York: Harper, 1962.

— — —. *The Concept of Time*. Athlone Contemporary European Thinkers. London: Athlone, 2011.

Hegel, Georg Wilhelm Friedrich. *Lectures on the Philosophy of World History*. New York: Cambridge University Press, 1975.

Herman, Judith Lewis. *Trauma and Recovery*. New York: Basic, 1997.

Hick, John. *Evil and the God of Love*. New York: Palgrave Macmillan, 2010.

Hinkle, Mary E. *Signs of Belonging: Luther's Marks of the Church and the Christian Life*. Minneapolis: Augsburg Fortress, 2003.

Hitchens, Christopher. *God Is Not Great: How Religion Poisons Everything.* New York: Hachette, 2007.

Hogg, Michael A., Deborah J. Terry, and Katherine M. White. "A Tale of Two Theories: A Critical Comparison of Identity Theory with Social Identity Theory." *Social Psychology Quarterly* 58, no. 4 (1995): 255–69.

Hogue, David. *Remembering the Future, Imagining the Past: Story, Ritual, and the Human Brain.* Cleveland, Ohio: Pilgrim, 2003.

Hume, David. *A Treatise of Human Nature.* 1739–1740.

Hume, David, Fate Norton, and Mary J. Norton, eds. *A Treatise of Human Nature.* Oxford Philosophical Texts. New York: Oxford University Press, 2000.

Hunsinger, George. *How to Read Karl Barth: The Shape of His Theology.* New York: Oxford University Press, 1991.

Huxley, Aldous. *Brave New World.* New York: HarperCollins, 1946.

Jeffrey, David Lyle. *Luke.* Brazos Theological Commentary on the Bible. Grand Rapids: Brazos, 2012.

Jenson, Matt. *The Gravity of Sin: Augustine, Luther and Barth on Homo incurvatus in se.* New York: T&T Clark, 2006.

Jenson, Robert W. *Systematic Theology.* 2 vols. New York: Oxford University Press, 1997–1999.

Jones, L. Gregory. "Behold, I Make All Things New." In *God and the Victim: Theological Reflections on Evil, Victimization, Justice, and Forgiveness,* edited by Michelle D. Shattuck, 63–74. Grand Rapids: Eerdmans, 1999.

———. "Crafting Communities of Forgiveness." *Interpretation* 54 (2000): 121–34.

———. *Embodying Forgiveness: A Theological Analysis.* Grand Rapids: Eerdmans, 1995.

Jones, L. Gregory, and Kevin R. Armstrong. *Resurrecting Excellence: Shaping Faithful Christian Ministry.* Pulpit & Pew. Grand Rapids: Eerdmans, 2006.

Jones, Serene. *Trauma and Grace: Theology in a Ruptured World.* Louisville, Ky.: Westminster John Knox, 2009.

Kalven, Jamie. *Working with Available Light: A Family's World after Violence.* New York: Norton, 1999.

Kant, Immanuel. *Critique of Pure Reason.* Translated by J. M. D. Meiklejohn. London: Henry G. Bohn, 1855.

Karen, Robert. *Becoming Attached: Unfolding the Mystery of the Infant-Mother Bond and Its Impact on Later Life.* New York: Warner, 1994.

Katongole, Emmanuel. *The Sacrifice of Africa: A Political Theology for Africa.* Grand Rapids: Eerdmans, 2011.

Kauffman, Jeffrey, ed. *The Shame of Death, Grief, and Trauma.* New York: Routledge, 2010.

Keck, David. *Forgetting Whose We Are: Alzheimer's Disease and the Love of God.* Nashville: Abingdon, 1996.

Keck, Leander. *Paul and His Letters.* Minneapolis: Fortress, 1988.

Kelsey, David H. *Imagining Redemption.* Louisville, Ky.: Westminster John Knox, 2005.

Kermode, Frank. *The Sense of an Ending: Studies in the Theory of Fiction with a New Epilogue.* New York: Oxford University Press, 2000.

Keshgegian, Flora A. *Redeeming Memories: A Theology of Healing and Transformation.* Nashville: Abingdon, 2000.

Kiess, John. "A Grammar of Touch: The Theo-political Significant of the Sacrament of Anointing During Northern Ireland's Troubles" (unpublished paper).

King, Martin Luther, Jr. "Letter from Birmingham Jail." April 16, 1963.

Kraybill, Donald B., Steven M. Nolt, and David L. Weaver-Zercher. *Amish Grace: How Forgiveness Transcended Tragedy.* San Francisco: Jossey-Bass, 2010.

Kübler-Ross, Elisabeth. *On Death and Dying.* New York: Macmillan, 1969.

Kushner, Harold S. *When Bad Things Happen to Good People.* New York: Schocken, 1981.

LaCugna, Catherine Mowry, ed. *Freeing Theology: The Essentials of Theology in Feminist Perspective.* San Francisco: HarperSanFrancisco, 1993.

Lasch, Christopher. *The True and Only Heaven: Progress and Its Critics.* New York: Norton, 1991.

Lawler, Steph. *Identity: Sociological Perspectives.* Malden, Mass.: Polity, 2008.

Lechte, John. *Key Contemporary Concepts: From Abjection to Zeno's Paradox.* London: SAGE, 2003.

Leman, Kevin. *The Birth Order Book: Why You Are the Way You Are.* Old Tappan, N.J.: F. H. Revell, 1985.

Leslie, John. *The End of the World: The Science and Ethics of Human Extinction.* New York: Routledge, 1996.

Lessing, Gotthold. *Lessing's Theological Writings*. Stanford, Calif.: Stanford University Press, 1956.

Lester, Andrew D. *Hope in Pastoral Care and Counseling*. Louisville, Ky.: Westminster John Knox, 1995.

Lewis, Michael. *Shame: The Exposed Self*. New York: Free Press, 1992.

Liguori Publications. *Catechism of the Catholic Church*. Liguori, Mo.: Liguori, 1994.

Lin, Brenda B., and Philip E. Morefield. "The Vulnerability Cube: A Mutli-dimensional Framework for Assessing Relative Vulnerability." *Environmental Management* 48, no. 3 (2011): 631–43.

Lindbeck, George. *The Nature of Doctrine*. Louisville, Ky.: Westminster John Knox, 1984.

Linden, David J. *The Accidental Mind*. Cambridge, Mass.: Belknap, 2007.

Lischer, Richard. "The Sermon on the Mount as Radical Pastoral Care." In *The Theological Interpretation of Scripture*, edited by Stephen Fowl, 294–306. Malden, Mass.: Blackwell, 1997.

Loney, Randolph. *A Dream of the Tattered man: Stories from Georgia's Death Row*. Grand Rapids: Eerdmans, 2001.

Loughlin, Gerard. *Telling God's Story: Bible, Church, and Narrative Theology*. New York: Cambridge University Press, 1996.

Lowry, Lois. *Gathering Blue*. New York: Houghton Mifflin, 2000.

— — —. *The Giver*. New York: Houghton Mifflin, 1993.

— — —. *Messenger*. New York: Houghton Mifflin, 2004.

— — —. *Son*. New York: Houghton Mifflin, 2012.

Luther, Martin. *Works of Martin Luther: With Introductions and Notes*. Vol. 25, *Lectures on Romans, Glosses and Schoilia* [*Luther Works*]. Edited by Jacob Preus. St. Louis, Mo.: Concordia, 1972.

Lynch, William F. *Images of Hope: Imagination as Healer of the Hopeless*. Notre Dame, Ind.: University of Notre Dame Press, 1974.

Lyotard, Jean-François. *The Postmodern Condition: A Report on Knowledge*. Theory and History of Literature 10. Minneapolis: University of Minnesota Press, 1984.

MacGregor, Geddes. *Reincarnation as a Christian Hope*. Totowa, N.J.: Barnes & Noble, 1982.

MacIntyre, Alasdair C. *After Virtue: A Study in Moral Theory*. Notre Dame, Ind.: University of Notre Dame Press, [1981] 2007.

— — —. *Dependent Rational Animals: Why Human Beings Need the Virtues*. The Paul Carus Lecture Series 20. Chicago: Open Court, 1999.

— — —. "What Is a Human Body?" In *The Tasks of Philosophy: Selected Essays.* Vol. 1. New York: Cambridge University Press, 2006.

Mackenzie, Catriona, Wendy Rogers, and Susan Dodds, eds. *Vulnerability: New Essays in Ethics and Feminist Philosophy.* New York: Oxford University Press, 2013.

Martel, Yann. *The Life of Pi.* New York: Harcourt, 2001.

Martyn, J. Louis. "The Apocalyptic Gospel in Galatians." *Interpretation* 54, no. 3 (2000): 245–66.

— — —. *Galatians.* New York: Doubleday, 1997.

— — —. *Theological Issues in the Letters of Paul.* Nashville: Abingdon, 1997.

Maslow, Abraham. "A Theory of Human Motivation." *Psychological Review* 50, no. 4 (1943): 370–96.

Mathewes-Green, Frederica. *At the Corner of East and Now: A Modern Life in Ancient Christian Orthodoxy.* New York: Jeremy P. Tarcher, 1999.

McElheny, Victor K. *Drawing the Map of Life: Inside the Human Genome Project.* New York: Basic, 2010.

Mehl-Madrona, Lewis. *Narrative Medicine: The Use of History and Story in the Healing Process.* Rochester, Vt.: Bear, 2007.

Milbank, John. *Being Reconciled: Ontology and Pardon.* Radical Orthodoxy Series. New York: Routledge, 2003.

— — —. *Theology and Social Theory: Beyond Secular Reason.* Malden, Mass.: Blackwell, 2006.

Moltmann, Jürgen. *The Coming of God: Christian Eschatology.* Minneapolis: Fortress, 1996.

— — —. *Theology of Hope: On the Ground and the Implications of a Christian Eschatology.* Minneapolis: Fortress, 1993.

Morrison, Toni. *Beloved.* Edited by Carl Plasa. New York: Columbia University Press, 1998.

— — —. *The Bluest Eye.* New York: Holt, Rinehart & Winston, 1970.

Murdoch, Iris. *The Sovereignty of Good.* New York: Routledge & Kegan Paul, 1970.

National Children's Alliance. *National Children's Alliance Statistical Fact Sheet.* 2010.

Nelson, Susan. "Facing Evil: Evil's Many Faces." *Interpretation* 57, no. 4 (2003): 398–413.

Newbigin, Lesslie. *The Gospel in a Pluralist Society.* Grand Rapids: Eerdmans, 1989.

— — —. *Signs amid the Rubble: The Purposes of God in Human History.* Edited by Geoffrey Wainwright. Grand Rapids: Eerdmans, 2003.

Niebuhr, Reinhold. *An Interpretation of Christian Ethics.* New York: Harper & Brothers, 1935.

———. *The Nature and Destiny of Man: A Christian Interpretation.* 2 vols. Louisville, Ky.: Westminster John Knox, 1996.

Oatley, Keith. *Such Stuff as Dreams: The Psychology of Fiction.* Malden, Mass.: Wiley-Blackwell, 2011.

Orwell, George. *Nineteen Eighty-Four: A Novel.* New York: Plume, 2003.

Outler, Albert C., and Richard P. Heitzenrater, eds. *John Wesley's Sermons: An Anthology.* Nashville: Abingdon, 1991.

Palmer, Parker J. *Let Your Life Speak: Listening for the Voice of Vocation.* San Francisco: Jossey-Bass, 2000.

Pannenberg, Wolfhart. *Metaphysics and the Idea of God.* Grand Rapids: Eerdmans, 2001.

Peters, Ted. *Anticipating Omega: Science, Faith, and Our Ultimate Future.* Göttingen: Vandenhoeck & Ruprecht, 2006.

Pineda-Madrid, Nancy. *Suffering and Salvation in Ciudad Juárez.* Minneapolis: Fortress, 2011.

Pinker, Steven. *The Better Angels of Our Nature: Why Violence Has Declined.* New York: Penguin, 2011.

Placher, William C. *Jesus the Savior: The Meaning of Jesus Christ for Christian Faith.* Louisville, Ky.: Westminster John Knox, 2001.

Plantinga, Alvin. *God, Freedom, and Evil.* Grand Rapids: Eerdmans, 1977.

Plantinga, Cornelius. *Not the Way It's Supposed to Be: A Breviary of Sin.* Grand Rapids: Eerdmans, 1995.

Polman, Bert. "The Role of Lament in American Musical Life: Concerto in Three Movements." *Calvin Theological Journal* 36 (2001): 91–102.

Powell, Mark Allan. *Loving Jesus.* Minneapolis: Fortress, 2004.

———. "Salvation in Luke–Acts." *Word & World* 12, no. 1 (1992): 5–10.

———. *What Do They Hear? Bridging the Gap Between Pulpit and Pew.* Nashville: Abingdon, 2007.

Quiller-Couch, Sir Arthur Thomas, ed. *The Oxford Book of English Verse, 1250–1918.* Oxford: Clarendon, 1961.

Raine, Nancy Venable. *After Silence: Rape and My Journey Back.* New York: Three Rivers, 1998.

Rambo, Shelly. *Spirit and Trauma: A Theology of Remaining.* Louisville, Ky.: Westminster John Knox, 2010.

Ramshaw, Elaine. "The Personalization of Postmodern Post-Mortem Rituals." *Pastoral Psychology* 59, no. 2 (2010): 171–78.

Ricoeur, Paul. *Figuring the Sacred: Religion, Narrative, and Imagination.* Minneapolis: Augsburg, 1995.

———. *Oneself as Another.* Chicago: University of Chicago Press, 1992.

———. *Time and Narrative.* 3 vols. Chicago: University of Chicago Press, 1984–1988.

Ritschl, Albrecht. *The Christian Doctrine of Justification and Reconciliation.* Edited by H. R. Mackintosh and A. B. Macaulay. Edinburgh: T&T Clark, 1902.

Root, Michael. "The Narrative Structure of Soteriology." In *Why Narrative? Readings in Narrative Theology,* edited by Stanley Hauerwas and L. Gregory Jones, 263–78. Eugene, Ore.: Wipf & Stock, 1997.

Rothschild, Babette. *Eight Keys to Safe Trauma Recovery: Take-Charge Strategies to Empower Your Healing.* New York: W. W. Norton, 2010.

Rowe, Christopher Kavin. *World Upside Down: Reading Acts in the Graeco-Roman Age.* New York: Oxford University Press, 2009.

Rowling, J. K. Harry Potter series. New York: Arthur A. Levine, 1999–2009.

Sartwell, Crispin. *End of Story: Toward an Annihilation of Language and History.* Albany: State University of New York Press, 2000.

Scarry, Elaine. *The Body in Pain: The Making and Unmaking of the World.* New York: Oxford University Press, 1985.

Schacter, Daniel L. *Searching for Memory: The Brain, the Mind, and the Past.* New York: Basic, 1996.

———. *The Seven Sins of Memory: How the Mind Forgets and Remembers.* Boston: Houghton Mifflin, 2001.

Schnackenburg, Rudolf. *Jesus in the Gospels: A Biblical Christology.* Louisvile, Ky.: Westminster John Knox, 1995.

Schwarz, Hans. *Eschatology.* Grand Rapids: Eerdmans, 2000.

Sebold, Alice. *The Lovely Bones.* Boston: Little, Brown, 2002.

———. *Lucky.* Boston: Back Bay, 2002.

Shattuck, Michelle D., ed. *God and the Victim: Theological Reflections on Evil, Victimization, Justice, and Forgiveness.* Grand Rapids: Eerdmans, 1999.

Shaw, David. "Apocalyptic and Covenant: Perspectives on Paul or Antinomies at War?" *Journal for the Study of the New Testament* 36, no. 2 (2013): 155–71.

Shengold, Leonard. *Soul Murder: The Effects of Childhood Abuse and Deprivation.* New York: Ballantine, 1989.

Sobrino, Jon. *Christology at the Crossroads: A Latin American Approach.* Maryknoll, N.Y.: Orbis, 1978.

— — —. *Jesus the Liberator: A Historical-Theological Reading of Jesus of Nazareth.* Maryknoll, N.Y.: Orbis, 1993.

Sölle, Dorothee. *Suffering.* Philadelphia: Fortress, 1975.

Steinmetz, David C. "Uncovering a Second Narrative: Detective Fiction and the Construction of Historical Method." In *The Art of Reading Scripture*, edited by Ellen F. Davis and Richard B. Hays, 54–65. Grand Rapids: Eerdmans, 2003.

Stenger, Victor J. *The New Atheism: Taking a Stand for Science and Reason.* Amherst, N.Y.: Prometheus, 2009.

Stewart, Robert, ed. *The Resurrection of Jesus: John Dominic Crossan and N. T. Wright in Dialogue.* Minneapolis: Fortress, 2005.

Stryker, S., and R. T. Serpe. "Commitment, Identity Salience, and Role Behavior: Theory and Research Example." In *Personality, Roles, and Social Behavior*, edited by W. Ickes and E. S. Knowles, 199–218. New York: Springer-Verlag, 1982.

Stubbs, David L. *Numbers.* Brazos Theological Commentary on the Bible. Grand Rapids: Brazos, 2009.

Suchocki, Marjorie Hewitt. *The Fall to Violence: Original Sin in Relational Theology.* New York: Continuum, 2004.

Surin, Kenneth. *Theology and the Problem of Evil.* Eugene, Ore.: Wipf & Stock, 1986.

Terr, Lenore. *Too Scared to Cry: Psychic Trauma in Childhood.* New York: Basic Books, 1990.

Tillich, Paul. *The Eternal Now.* New York: Scribner, 1963.

Traina, Cristina L. H. "Touch on Trial: Power and the Right to Physical Affection." *Journal of the Society of Christian Ethics* 25, no. 1 (2005): 3–34.

Tran, Jonathan. *The Vietnam War and Theologies of Memory: Time and Eternity in the Far Country.* Malden, Mass.: Wiley-Blackwell, 2010.

Trible, Phyllis. *Texts of Terror: Literary-Feminist Readings of Biblical Narratives.* Minneapolis: Fortress, 1984.

Tutu, Desmond. *No Future without Forgiveness.* New York: Doubleday, 1999.

Vanier, Jean. *The Scandal of Service: Jesus Washes Our Feet.* Arche Collection. New York: Continuum, 1998.

Verghese, Abraham. *Cutting for Stone.* New York: Alfred A. Knopf, 2009.

Volf, Miroslav. *The End of Memory: Remembering Rightly in a Violent World.* Grand Rapids: Eerdmans, 2006.

— — —. *Exclusion and Embrace: A Theological Exploration of Identity, Otherness, and Reconciliation.* Nashville: Abingdon, 1996.

— — —. *Free of Charge: Giving and Forgiving in a Culture Stripped of Grace.* Grand Rapids: Zondervan, 2005.

Wadell, Paul J. *Becoming Friends: Worship, Justice, and the Practice of Christian Friendship.* Grand Rapids: Brazos, 2002.

Wadell, Paul J., and Patricia Lamoureux. *The Christian Moral Life: Faithful Discipleship for a Global Society.* Maryknoll, N.Y.: Orbis, 2010.

— — —. *Friendship and the Moral Life.* Notre Dame, Ind.: University of Notre Dame Press, 1989.

Walls, Jeannette. *The Glass Castle: A Memoir.* New York: Scribner, 2005.

Warren, Andrea. *Surviving Hitler: A Boy in the Nazi Death Camps.* New York: HarperCollins, 2001.

Water, Mark Camp. *The New Encyclopedia of Christian Martyrs.* Grand Rapids: Baker, 2001.

Webber, Robert, and Rodney Clapp. *People of the Truth: The Power of the Worshiping Community in the Modern World.* San Francisco: Harper & Row, 1988.

Wells, Samuel. *Be Not Afraid: Facing Fear with Faith.* Grand Rapids: Brazos, 2011.

— — —. *God's Companions: Reimagining Christian Ethics.* Malden, Mass.: Blackwell, 2006.

— — —. *Improvisation: The Drama of Christian Ethics:* Grand Rapids: Brazos, 2004.

West, Cornel. "Dr. King Weeps from His Grave." *New York Times,* August 26, 2011. http://www.nytimes.com/2011/08/26/opinion/martin-luther-king-jr-would-want-a-revolution-not-a-memorial.html.

Westerholm, Stephen. *Perspectives Old and New on Paul: The "Lutheran" Paul and His Critics.* Grand Rapids: Eerdmans, 2004.

Wiesel, Elie. *Night.* New York: Straus & Giroux, 1972.

Wiesenthal, Simon. *The Sunflower: On the Possibilities and Limits of Forgiveness.* New York: Schocken, 1997.

Williams, Rowan. *On Christian Theology.* Malden, Mass.: Blackwell, 2000.

— — —. *Resurrection: Interpreting the Easter Gospel.* Cleveland, Ohio: Pilgrim, 2002.

— — —. *Wrestling with Angels: Conversations in Modern Theology.* Edited by Mike Higton. Grand Rapids: Eerdmans, 2007.

Willimon, Willam H. *Sinning like a Christian: A New Look at the Seven Deadly Sins.* Nashville: Abingdon, 2005.

Wilson, Timothy D. *Redirect: The Surprising New Science of Psychological Change.* New York: Penguin, 2011.

Wink, Walter. *Naming the Powers: The Language of Power in the New Testament.* Philadelphia: Fortress, 1984.

Wolterstorff, Nicholas. *Lament for a Son.* Grand Rapids: Eerdmans, 1987.

Wright, N. T. *Jesus and the Victory of God.* Minneapolis: Fortress, 1996.

— — —. *Paul in Fresh Perspective.* Minneapolis: Fortress, 2005.

— — —. *Surprised by Hope: Rethinking Heaven, the Resurrection, and the Mission of the Church.* New York: HarperCollins, 2008.

Yoder, John Howard. *The Original Revolution: Essays on Christian Pacifism.* Scottdale, Pa.: Herald, 2003.

— — —. *The Politics of Jesus: Vicit agnus noster.* 2nd ed. Grand Rapids: Eerdmans, 1994.

— — —. *The Royal Priesthood: Essays Ecclesiological and Ecumenical.* Scottdale, Pa.: Herald, 1998.

— — —. "To Serve Our God and to Rule the World." In *Royal Priesthood,* 128–40.

Zunshine, Lisa. *Why We Read Fiction: Theory of Mind and the Novel.* Columbus: Ohio State University Press, 2006.

SCRIPTURE INDEX

SUBJECT INDEX